'KWANIM PA

Oxford University Press, Walton Street, Oxford OX2 6DP

OXFORD LONDON GLASGOW
NEW YORK TORONTO MELBOURNE WELLINGTON
KUALA LUMPUR SINGAPORE JAKARTA HONG KONG TOKYO
DELHI BOMBAY CALCUTTA MADRAS KARACHI
NAIROBI DAR ES SALAAM CAPE TOWN

Published in the United States by Oxford University Press, New York

British Library Cataloguing in Publication Data

James, Wendy
    'Kwanim pa.
    1. Uduk (African people)
    I. Title
301.29'626'4   DT155.2.U/   79–40185
    ISBN 0–19–823194–6

Printed in Great Britain
by W & J Mackay Limited, Chatham

A Gurunya mother still 'sitting black' looks on, while Wa'bwosh cele-brates with red oil the transformation of her Gurunya into a real human being, one of the *'Kwanim pa*

'KWA

The mal
Uduk

*An Ethnograph
in the Sudan-Et*

WEND

CLARENDON

To my mother
and the memory of my father

PREFACE

This is the first full-length account of the Uduk people of the Sudan, who live uneasily between the northern and southern regions of the country, in the borderland close to the Ethiopian frontier. Although the book presents a good deal of new ethnographic material, it is not intended to be a comprehensive report on Uduk society and culture. It does not even properly reflect the content of my own notebooks, gathered during a five-year sojourn in the Sudan (of which nearly a year and a half were spent 'in the field') and a couple of later visits to Ethiopia (of which some eight months were spent in the west, working among peoples related to the Uduk). In particular, I have not attempted to present systematic information about religion, ritual, and healing among the Uduk, as I plan to publish this material separately.

The reader may therefore wonder why, in a book which plainly deals on the whole with mundane matters such as subsistence, kinship and settlement patterns, population history and migrations, I refer repeatedly to selected aspects of myth, symbol, and cult—and at length to the elaborate Gurunya ritual which is devoted to the saving of 'foundling' children. The answer is that I have tried to formulate and deal with a question which cuts across the conventional headings of descriptive ethnography. Throughout my field research, I was forcibly struck by the importance of the past among the Uduk, and in this book I have tried to explore the nature of the link between past and present in their society. There are in the first place externally demonstrable links between the historical record of devastation and the main features of Uduk communities today. But there are also inner connections between the past experience of the people, their digested memory of that experience, and the way in which they represent themselves, the 'kwanim pa, as still a 'foundling people' who have survived the repeated destruction of their former world, and are putting together a new. My conviction, which I defend in this book, is that this self-image is the key to understanding present-day Uduk economic, political, and kinship institutions and behaviour. Of particular interest, I believe to lay readers as well as to professional social anthropologists, is the way in which the Uduk have apparently reconstructed their society along matrilineal lines in response to historical pressures. In developing this presentation, I have had to introduce some aspects of religious and imaginative thought in anticipation of further accounts which will provide a fuller picture. But I hope that the present book, in dwelling on the significance of the past in the making of the present, will prove a secure foundation for future Uduk studies.

ACKNOWLEDGEMENTS

My field-work in the Southern Blue Nile Province of the Sudan
was of an exploratory nature, since there are few ethnographic
sources on this region. It was carried out from the University of
Khartoum, where I held a Lectureship in Social Anthropology
from 1964–9. The University supported my work by giving me
two terms' leave in 1966, by generous funds from the Ford
Foundation grant allocated to the Faculty of Economics and
Social Studies, and also through the provision of a Land Rover
for most of my trips. On several occasions I took individual
students from the University with me to the field, for training
purposes; I would like to acknowledge, in particular, the assistance of Abd-al Ghaffar Muhammad Ahmad, now teaching in
Khartoum University.

My most direct debt is to my principal research assistant,
Shadrach Peyko Dhunya, from Chali, whose patient and loyal
help made it possible for me to start learning the Uduk language
and to become established in the field. His assistance with the
collection, transcription and translation of tape-recorded
material, both in the field and in Khartoum, was invaluable.
Others who helped me very greatly in the field include William
Danga, William Dhupa, Philip Suga, Stephen Missa, and Joshua
Abdalla. Among my most staunch friends and sympathetic
informants were Tente, Ha'da, Bukko, Nyethko, Algo, Losko,
Ngau, Umpa, Saba, Rapka, Maya, and Sheikh Puna Marinyje.

I am grateful for the hospitality of Pastor Paul Angwo and
the Church community at Chali, who enabled me to make an
entry into local society; and for the help and hospitality of a
series of Government officials in Kurmuk and Damazin. I thank
the Anthropology Board of the Ministry of the Interior for
sanctioning my research, in particular Sayed Mohamed Ibrahim Ahmed, who as Government Archivist arranged for me to
consult some of the historical records relating to the southern
Funj region.

Within the University of Khartoum, I am indebted to Sayed
Omer Mohamed Osman, then Dean of the Faculty of Economics and Social Studies, for supporting my research throughout;
and to the Faculty Research Committee. I received a great deal

of encouragement and good advice during the period of field-work from my colleagues in the Department of Anthropology and Sociology, and from other friends both in Khartoum and Oxford.

I managed to acquire a good working knowledge of the Uduk language, with the help of materials produced by the former station of the Sudan Interior Mission at Chali, and most of my later enquiries were carried out directly in Uduk.

Within the Uduk territory, I was based on the village of Waka'cesh in northern Pam'Be (see Figure 3), and came to know the Beni Mayu–Pam'Be area quite well. Several short trips were made to the Bellila area, on the Khor Ahmar. In 1966 I made a brief visit to Belatoma and Yabus Bridge, and visited some Komo villages; in 1967 I spent two weeks in Belatoma, and in 1969 a further two weeks, one of which was spent travelling to Jebel Bisho and the Ganza country.

My seven trips to the southern Funj totalled about seventeen months, and the period actually living in Uduk country, over fifteen months. The trips were as follows (dates in and out of Khartoum): Sept. 1965 (one week in Roseires); 13 Dec. 1965–5 Mar. 1966; 9 Apr.–29 Sept. 1966; 3 Apr.–27 May 1967; 1 Dec. 1967–4 Jan. 1968; 8 Apr.–20 July 1968; 15 Apr.–12 June 1969. Intensive field work therefore extended intermittently over a total of three and a half years. Work on texts and archives was continued in the intervening periods.

From 1969 to 1971 I held a Leverhulme Research Fellowship at St. Hugh's College, Oxford; this period was of immense value in enabling me to draw together my field material. A D.Phil. thesis and various papers were completed which form much of the basis of this book, and which contain documentation and detail it was not possible to include here. A subsequent year spent partly in Denmark, at the University of Aarhus, and partly in Norway, at the University of Bergen, enabled me to benefit from the fresh and stimulating criticism of Scandinavian colleagues and students.

Since first embarking on field-work among the Uduk, I had hoped to extend my knowledge of the Koman peoples as a whole by visiting western Ethiopia. This became possible through an SSRC Research Project grant and a term of sabbatical leave from Oxford, and as a Visiting Scholar of the

University in Addis Ababa I carried out research in Ethiopia, particularly among the Komo and the Gumuz, during the periods June 1974–Jan. 1975, and June–Sept. 1975. In this work I was greatly helped by members of the Evangelical Church Mekane Yesus, in particular Pastor Øyvind Eide and Pastor Jan Ulveseth of the Norske Misjonsselskap. The project could not be completed in 1976 because of the unhappy security situation in Ethiopia, but the stimulus of gathering comparative material helped me to revise and clarify the argument of the present book. The comparative information on the Komo, Gumuz, and other Koman peoples included in the book is mainly derived from my own work in Ethiopia.

Grateful acknowledgement is made to the editors of *Sudan Notes and Records* and the *Scientific American* for the use of material which has appeared in articles in those journals; and to Peter Jackson, who painstakingly worked over the text of the book and compiled the index.

The late Sir Edward Evans-Pritchard, as my supervisor through most of the years of my apprenticeship in social anthropology, kept a kindly and encouraging eye on my work; his own first field trip was to Dar Funj, and I have found myself tracing many of the paths he pioneered. In matters touching on the Sudan and its history, I am especially indebted to Ian Cunnison, who examined my thesis and carefully worked over an earlier draft of this book; and to Talal Asad and Andrew Baring, who have shared their knowledge and enthusiasms with me. Peter Lienhardt has immensely deepened my sensitivity to the world of Islam and the Arabic language, and to the wider context of my own work. I have been sustained throughout by the friendship and patience of Godfrey Lienhardt, who by positive encouragement did not allow me to be satisfied with my original doctoral thesis on the Uduk; and above all I am indebted to my parents who gave me support and understanding at all the most difficult times. To Douglas Johnson, my dear husband, I owe that final burst of energy and confidence which enabled me to complete this book.

Wendy James, Oxford,
September 1978

CONTENTS

LIST OF PLATES

FIGURES

NOTE ON TEXTS

The texts used in this book are selected from many hours of tape-recorded material, collected throughout the periods of field-work, and later transcribed and translated. A small portable machine was used, at first as an amusement, for recording and playing back songs and music, so that the people would get used to it. Later, it was occasionally used in relatively formal interviews, but on the whole simply switched on when general conversation took an interesting turn. Eventually informants became quite accustomed to it.

The more significant passages of recorded material were later transcribed, mostly by Shadrach Peyko Dhunya, with whom I worked both in the field and in intervening periods in Khartoum. The translation was largely his responsibility in the early stages, but later became largely my own, supplemented by occasional consultation with him.

The system of orthography employed is that worked out by the Sudan Interior Mission at Chali. An apostrophe indicates implosion or explosion in the consonant it precedes; underlining indicates aspiration; and the oblique stroke represents a glottal stop. Tones are not marked. Further details are given in Appendix 1, which also includes sample vernacular texts.

PROLOGUE

One of the best-known stories among the Uduk is of the origin of marriage, or rather the discovery of sex. The tale is received with gales of laughter and cries by an Uduk audience, and is told with particular relish by the older women. The scene is from very early times. Women are living in a village community, cultivating sorghum (the present-day staple grain) and are quite ignorant of men, who live out in the bush as wild creatures. One day a woman out in the woodland sees what she takes to be a bird—a *gurunya/* (a glossy blue-black starling), perching in a fig tree and pecking at the fruit. She calls it. It is not in fact a *gurunya/* or any other bird, but the first discovered man. Here is the old lady Emed's version of the story, which I have borrowed to introduce my account of the making of the Uduk people (for reasons which will become progressively clearer):

'"Gurunya, throw me a fig!"[1]

'He dropped one down. She said, "Oh, it's delicious. Another one, please. You bird, shake them all down."

'He dropped another down. She ate it, and exclaimed, "How very sweet it is!"

'She sat eating figs, and after a while Man climbed down, the story goes, he climbed down and sat on the ground. Maybe something was swinging underneath . . . She asked, "What is that? What is that little thing hanging like that there?"

'And Man said, "This little thing is called *yisayis, yisayis.*" He said, "And do you have something too?"

'She replied, "It's called *kukgor, kukgor.*[2] Will you try, shall we do something? Will you come and place yours in mine, here? We will come together, here."

'Man grew strong. He clasped Woman, and they mated. He penetrated, *ra'b.* Huh! She cried, "Aaaii! What is this hurting me so?" He did it again, and she cried, "Aaaii!"

'And then at last they were finished, satisfied maybe. She bound him up straight away in leafy branches, carried him to her hut and

---

[1] This cry recalls the opening line of a song sung for special 'Gurunya' children, who pass through rites which are designed to save them from the death which has their older siblings. The song is quoted in Chapter 7.

[2] A sing-song pronunciation of the normal words for the sex organs (*yis*, penis, and *kuk*, vagina).

they mated again. The branches were taken in the hut. The bundle of branches taken in the hut was very long, enormous. And they did it again. Again they had sex in the hut.[3]

'And the others [the other women] called, "Oh, you—why are you crying like that?" She replied, "I am burnt by the fire."[4] She cried, "Aaaaii!" And another called, "With fire? What are you doing with it?"

'"Why do you do it?"

'Another woman got in at last, and found them: "Oho! And is that the fire?" She replied, "Yes."

'"Goodness! Where did you get this great thing like that from? What is it? What is it? What is it?"

'She was seizing it like this—"Oho! You are by yourself! Where are the others you have left behind?"

'He replied, "There are plenty of men over there—I left them back there!"

'My goodness, the bodies were crowding in, a great crowd was pressing at the door there. They shouted, "You girls! Leave us space! Oh! We are running to see this new thing! What is it that he's got, what is it?"

'His body became very weak, because the people were all climbing on him. They were fighting over the penis like that, and Man became very weak; meanwhile the rest were thrusting their bodies about excitedly in the air, for lack of a man . . . They turned upon him, crying, "Try me too, please, aaaii! Try me too, aaaii! Try me too, aaaii!" But Man was quite powerless, it is said. He was tired out, but still they went on pressing him like that. Now his fellows were gathered in a distant place, very far from there. He said, "I have left lots of men over there."[5]

'They rushed off at last, in a turmoil, searching for the men. The first Man cried out loudly, for he was exhausted. He waddled, staggering about, they say. His hips were bruised all over, bruised very badly. He went on and found that the others had taken all the girls, and he was left without. He remained without any, and in the end he had to make do with a very old woman, they say. . . .

'Now it happened thus because long ago people appeared from

[3] In these two paragraphs there is an implied progression from mating as a purely animal act to human, and social, sexuality; the verb *ha'k*, usually used of animals, is here translated 'mated', in contrast to the verb *mash*, used exclusively of human beings 'having sex'. The latter is used often in the sense of 'marry', as in the final paragraph of this text.

[4] *O'd* is the normal word for fire. The expression used here is *o'd cep*, which I understand to mean specifically 'fire of the penis'.

[5] It was explained later that all these men were found in the fig-tree.

under the '*thika͟th* grass. That is how the penis—called *dalle* by you men—first appeared.[6] And you gathered yourselves together, and you grew grain by yourselves. It is said that you grew *biriny*. We women are the ones who grew sorghum, they say, long ago. You just grew *biriny*.[7]

'But at last you married: and all people then came to grow sorghum. At last they grew sorghum. The men finally grew sorghum. You men began to grow sorghum: but we women were the owners of sorghum in the beginning. You just had *biriny*, they say.'

[6] A version of the tale which suggests that people appeared from a clump of '*thika͟th* grass ('*sika͟th* in the southern dialect) is given in Chapter 4. This seems to be better known among the southern Uduk, and to be reminiscent of a Murle tale (see Lewis, 1972, p. 20). I could not find any certainty on this matter among my northern informants. I believe that *dalle* may be an obsolete word.

[7] *Biriny* is a variety of wild grass, with tiny edible seeds. In times of famine people may be reduced to eating *biriny*.

I

AN ETHNOGRAPHIC REMNANT

*A few of us were saved, and
that is why we are here today.*

Between the heartlands of the Sudanese Nile valley and the
Ethiopian highlands live a series of relatively ancient and relatively unknown dark-skinned peoples. They are ancient in the
culture-history sense, for they belong on the whole to the 'Old
Sudanese' type of general material culture and their forebears
occupied the region probably long before the expansion of the
Nilotic-, Arabic-, and Galla-speaking peoples who have undoubtedly exerted pressure on them in recent centuries. The
main contributions to the ethnography of the region have come
from V. L. Grottanelli, who coined the useful term 'pre-Nilotes'
for the peoples of the border as a whole.[1] They share a similar
subsistence way of life, based today on hoe cultivation of sorghum and maize, hunting and fishing, and the rearing of a few
domestic animals. Hunting was probably far more important in
the past than it is today.

Linguistically, the border region is riddled with divisions and
sub-divisions; the patchwork pattern, with languages belonging
to several families, suggests that the region may have provided
a refuge for groups of people from elsewhere repeatedly over the
centuries, as indeed it has been a political refuge in recent
history, particularly for nothern Sudanese immigrants during
the nineteenth century. But the predominant language group
of the border, usually termed Koman (following Greenberg's
classification),[2] shows every sign of having very ancient roots in
this region. It is a highly distinctive group of languages, and

---

[1] Professor V. L. Grottanelli's researches in western Ethiopia were carried out
during the 1930s, and although a major investigation was planned for the border
region, it was unfortunately cut short by the Second World War. Professor
Grottanelli visited the southern Mao again briefly a few years ago, and reported on
his findings in an article 'The Vanishing Pre-Nilotes Revisited'. Details of his major
writings on the region are included in the bibliography.

[2] J. H. Greenberg, 1963.

appears to have diverged from the rest of the Nilo-Saharan family at a very early date. The present distribution of Koman languages, of which Uduk is the best documented, is sketched in Figure 1. These tongues are almost certainly the last remaining representatives of related languages once spoken more widely, which have been encroached upon by others, including younger members of the great Nilo-Saharan family. In both a general cultural sense and a strictly linguistic sense, then, the border peoples represent a remarkable fragmentary survival of an ancient cultural tradition.

It is ironic that the border peoples are relatively unknown in the ethnographic literature, for they lie between two of the great historic areas of inner Africa: more is known about the civilizations and history of the central Nile valley and the Ethiopian plateau than about most parts of the continent. On the Nile, the succession of kingdoms from Meroe, through the medieval Christian Nubian states and the Funj kingdom of Sennar, and in the highlands the development of modern Ethiopia from the times of ancient Axum can be traced in the archaeological and written records. Something is known of the relations between these two centres of state power, the expeditions which have been mounted by each against the other and the network of trading links which have connected them. In the records which tell of the long neighbourly strife of the Sudanese lowlands and the Ethiopian highlands, references to the border peoples are not absent; and nor are they absent from the oral traditions of the modern Sudanese and Ethiopian people. There are plenty of such references; but they tell us little. There are passing mentions of raids on the 'Shangalla' in the chronicles of the Ethiopian kings, and there are brief notes in the files of the Anglo-Egyptian Sudan administration on the sparse settlements and shy character of the border peoples; but in such records these peoples are briefly glimpsed from the outside. A few sympathetic accounts of them have been based on interviews with slaves encountered at the courts of princes, as was Henry Salt's early nineteenth-century description of Shangalla life, as remembered by Ethiopian slaves (see his *A Voyage to Abyssinia*, 1814). From the standpoint of those powerful societies which create states and write history, the fringe people of the Ethiopian plateau have played a historical role as a source of

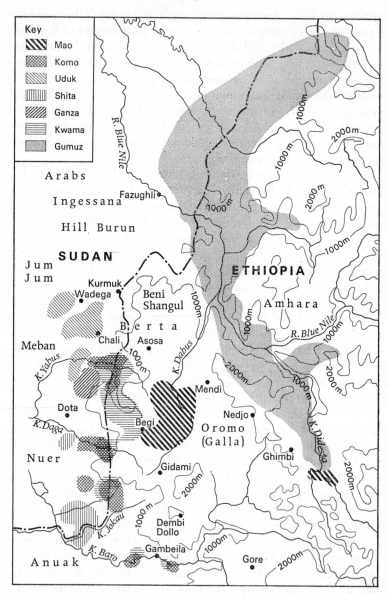

1. The Koman-speaking peoples

slaves and clients, cheap labour, and army recruits, but little else. Their languages and cultures were valued as cheaply as their persons in the pre-modern nations of the Sudan and Ethiopia.

Academic investigations have refined and filled out our sketchy picture of the border regions. But from the early nineteenth century, when detailed descriptions and surveys of the area began to appear, to the present, there have been only two main lines of enquiry. The first has been that of identifying and classifying ethnic groups and languages, as a task in itself; this dominated the enquiries of Hartmann and Lejean in the last century, for example; and of E. E. Evans-Pritchard, Margaret Bryan, and Ernesta Cerulli in the present century.[3] A recent example of fresh investigations oriented towards the classification as such of the border languages is that of the American linguist, M. L. Bender.[4] The second main line of academic enquiry, which can be traced back at least to the late eighteenth-century writings of James Bruce, has been into the connections between one or another of the border peoples and the great known civilizations of the Sudan and Ethiopia. The connections sought have been of all kinds—racial, linguistic, and historical. One of the most prominent of these concerns has been the frustrating search for the 'origins' of the Funj nobility of the kingdom of Sennar; many have combed the evidence for links between this supposedly distinct people and the tribal groups of the Ethiopian foothills. But in the absence of a fuller record of the present life and oral traditions of the border peoples themselves, further speculation on ethnographic connections and the refinement of ethnic classifications is not likely to be fruitful.[5]

There is a gulf between the very language in which the academic ethnography of the border is discussed and the living languages of the people themselves; 'the Gumuz' do not call themselves Gumuz, 'the Koma' do not call themselves Koma, 'the Ingessana' do not call themselves Ingessana, and 'the Uduk'

---

[3] References may be found in the bibliography.

[4] See particularly M. L. Bender's *The Ethiopian Nilo-Saharans*, 1975; Bender and Fleming's work suggests that Ganza may be very close to Mao, and that Mao should not properly be considered a member of the Koman family at all, but of the Omotic grouping of languages based in south-western Ethiopia (See Bender *et. al.*, 1976, Part I, Ch. 2). Bender's work on Gumuz also throws doubt on its close relation to Koman; see for example Bender, 1976.

[5] I have discussed this question in my essay 'The Funj Mystique: approaches to a problem of Sudan history' (James, 1977).

do not call themselves Uduk. Examples of this inconsistency between what is described by the outsider and what is observed from within can be harvested on all sides; one reason for the confusion is that local languages are rarely familiar to investigators, and no ethnographer of the Koman peoples has yet worked through the medium of one of the Koman languages. Those who compile general accounts are therefore muddled by the proliferation of outsiders' terms for the border peoples; Burun, Gumuz, and Hamaj are derogatory Sudanese names, the latter sometimes associated with the Anaj of Sudanese antiquity; Shangalla is an Amharic term merely meaning, according to one highland Ethiopian friend of mine, 'one who is black and one who is sold'; the Amharic Bareya, literally meaning slave, has become an ethnic label accepted by academics; and the western Galla or Oromo use 'Mao' in a patronizing accent and with little regard for linguistic or ethnic precision when referring to several 'pre-Nilotic' minority populations who have largely become their clients. Academic classification of the ethnographic type must continually run up against the historical and political realities of such relations between communities, which themselves often redefine 'ethnic' usage.

The separation and subdivision of the border peoples according to language or other external criteria is bound to distort in another sense their sociology. For none of these tiny communities is monolingual. For example, Uduk as a mother tongue is spoken by only about 10,000 people, living in three separate valleys, as Figure 2 shows. If none of these people could speak anything else, they would indeed be a sociological fragment as they are a remnant on the ethnographic map. But almost all Uduk, including women and many children, speak something of another language or two, and many individuals are fully bilingual or multilingual. Nearly all adults speak some Arabic, through contact not with the towns or the educational system of the Sudan, but with the nomad Arabs of the Rufā'a el Hoj, and more recently with groups of nomadic Fulani ('Fellata'). The Uduk as individuals are in frequent contact and interaction with a variety of neighbouring settled peoples, and it is not difficult to find Uduk who can speak Meban, Jum Jum, Hill Burun (of the various dialects of Jebels Mufwa, Surkum, Kurmuk, etc.), Berta, Ganza, or the tongues most closely

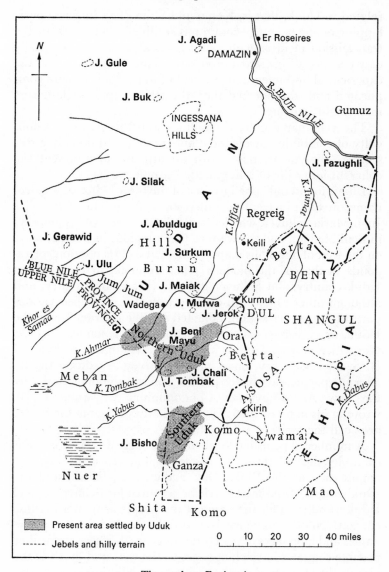

2. The southern Funj region

related to Uduk, that is, Komo and Shita. This intricate overlapping of one language community with another has made the
transmission of ideas, cults, and fashions at least superficially
easy between the different groups. It suggests moreover that the
experiential and imaginative world of individuals is more complicated and sophisticated than the ethnographic or language
map might indicate.

The very name *Uduk* exemplifies well this particular difficulty of combining academic ethnography, traditionally a dis-
secting, analytic exercise, with an attempt to represent the
coherent inner life of a fragmented people.

I have found only one instance of the term Uduk, as a place-
name, in the nineteenth-century sources: the Dutch traveller
Juan Maria Schuver, who left a detailed account of his journeys
in Beni Shangul and the western Galla regions in 1881–2, notes
on the west of one of his maps a Jebel Uduk.[6] Its position corresponds to that of the modern Jebel Tombak, in the heart of
Uduk country. But Schuver did not visit Uduk country, and
although other nineteenth-century travellers described various
parts of the border region, none left specific information on the
Uduk, or even referred to any people by this name. The first
visit which yielded detailed information was that of Kaimakam
G. S. Nickerson Bey, on a military survey expedition shortly
after the pacification in 1904 of the Sudan-Ethiopian border by
the new Anglo-Egyptian Condominium Government. He
wrote in his notes of 1906: 'The northerly villages of the Burun
area call themselves "Uddug" . . .'[7]

A number of plausible local cognates suggest themselves. For
example, the Nilotic usage *duk* for a hill, especially in place
names such as the Dinka Duk Fadiet, Duk Faiwil, and the
'Duk' Ridge. 'Duk' might well be a source for Schuver's Jebel
Uduk—and even for the name of the people as it later became
current. Nilotic influence is certainly marked in the place-
names and languages of the border in general. There are further
possible cognates in the languages to the west and north of the
Uduk (little known but classified as Nilotic); these may

[6] The term appears as 'G. Uduk (*unbewohnt*)', in the approximate position of J.
Tombak (or J. Be as it is known to the Uduk), on the map accompanying the
account of Schuver's travels in Petermann's Mitteilungen (1883).

[7] This note appears in Nickerson's report entitled 'Dar Fung and Burun
Country' (for details see bibliography). The term is also written 'Uddung'.

even be linked with the Dinka *duk*. The Meban call the Uduk *Ocon* and the Jum Jum call them *Odhun*. Nickerson's *Uddug* might easily be a mishearing of the Jum Jum *Odhun*. To the south, the term *Ojang* occurs more than once as an ethnic label; it is used for example of the Majangir, described by Stauder.[8] I do not feel qualified to judge the likely connections between these dominantly Nilotic local terms and the name *Uduk*; what is clear is that no one locally uses the name *Uduk* and I have not heard it used as a topographical name.

A further possibility, linking the name with the Arabic language, is of more than taxonomic interest. It was first put to me by an educated man, a northern Sudanese merchant and politician who had spent most of his life in Kurmuk. He considered that a possible derivation of Uduk might be the colloquial Arabic عتق (which would be transcribed *'atog*), itself derived from معتوق (*ma'tūg*), meaning a freed slave. Another Sudanese friend has since told me that *ya'ātig* may be said of a slave who was set free because of his master's recovery from an illness, or even because his master has committed a religious offence, such as breaking the observances of Ramadan. I discussed this question with Peter Lienhardt, who told me that in the Arabian Gulf, in addition to its literal sense of 'freed slave', عتوق (*'attuq*) or عتيق (*'atiq*) can be used of any person who has been spared by God, through being saved from illness and death. It may also be used of a child, born to his mother after she has lost one or two other children. As I explain in the course of this book, the image of such a child is frequently used by the Uduk of themselves and their history. Whether the parallel is fortuitous or not, I cannot say; but even if the Arabic derivation of Uduk suggested to me in Kurmuk is not etymologically sound, it is greatly interesting as a hypothesis formulated by a man of local knowledge. For it does match in political and moral terms the self-image of the Uduk people. They are, and they know themselves to be, both freed slaves in the literal sense, in part, and also a people spared by God from the very real possibility of historical extinction.

The Uduk are known by a further variety of terms to their neighbours. They are *Currara*, or *Korara*, to the Arabic-speakers of the Ahmar valley, and *Cai* (along with other border peoples

[8] J. Stauder (1971).

such as the Hill Burun, Meban and Komo) to the Nuer and
Shilluk. They are called *Kamus* by the Komo and Ganza of the
Bisho area, and the Ganza also call them *Tam*. The 'Pur' of the
Daga, whom I assume to be Shita, are said to call the Uduk
Je Barka. But in spite of this variety of available terms, and in
spite of the absence of the word 'Uduk' in any local language,
as far as I can discover, it became a standard ethnic name during
the colonial period. It seems first to have acquired an English-
language currency and a stamp of authority through the
enquiries of J. D. P. Chataway of the Sudan Political Service
in the 1920s;[9] the term was taken up by the administration and
by Seligman, and confirmed by Evans-Pritchard after his brief
investigations just south of Wadega in 1927.[10] It gained wide
currency through the work of a station of the Sudan Interior
Mission at Chali, initiated in 1938, interrupted by the war but
taken up in earnest afterwards, until 1964 when in accordance
with general Government policy the mission was virtually
closed.[11] If I had carried out my own research during the 1950s,
I would have spoken of 'the Uduk' with some confidence—and
so might they.

But my enquiries were undertaken more than a decade after
the independence of the Sudan, some years after Arabic had
replaced English as the language of local administration, and a
few years after the withdrawal of the missionary presence at
Chali. I had read of 'the Uduk' in a few scattered sources, and
was therefore surprised when I began work in the region to find
that no one used this term, although it was politely acknowledged
when I brought it up, both by officials and by villagers. 'Uduk?
Yes, that's what they call us.' But both administrators and
administered pronounced the word with uncertainty, as though
it belonged to a foreign world of discourse; which I believe it
does. It belongs to the discourse of colonial administration and
missionary endeavour, and more significantly perhaps now to
academic linguists and other scholars. But although the label
Uduk as an ethnic designation is an invention of the colonial
period, it does refer in existing literature to a distinct language

[9] Chataway's MS notes of 1927, though numbering only some 8 pages, seem to
have been the first substantial record of the name, the people and the language.
[10] See Seligman, 1932, and Evans-Prichard, 1932, pp. 31–4.
[11] The establishment, and something of the work of this mission station, is
described in Forsberg, 1958.

and a more or less distinguishable population, for which there is no obvious alternative name, and with reservations I shall therefore use it.

Within the Koman group, in terms of external classificatory criteria, there are three peoples speaking languages which are distinct, but closely related to each other and to Uduk. These three have often been bracketed together in the literature as Koma, or Coma; regional differences have been noted, however, and are summarised in Cerulli's 1956 survey of sources on the 'Koma'.[12] Field enquiries carried out by M. L. Bender, and more recently by myself, have now clarified the situation: under the traditional label Koma (a Sudanese Arabic term) are mutually unintelligible languages most conveniently referred to as Komo, Shita, and Kwama (all self-designations). In general culture, the appearance of dress, huts, fields etc., all these people closely resemble the Uduk. So do the Ganza, living immediately to the south of the Uduk, although their language is quite different, and possibly close to Mao. The other members of the Koman group, according to Greenberg, are the Mao of Ethiopia (Grottanelli's northern Mao), whose language has strong affinities with the Omotic family of south-western Ethiopia, according to Bender and Fleming, and may not be primarily 'Koman'; Gumuz, spoken by a large population in the Blue Nile valley on both sides of the border, which is by no means very close to Uduk; and the now virtually extinct language of Jebel Gule in the Sudan. Thus the Uduk–Komo–Shita–Kwama cluster forms the nucleus of the Koman family.

How do the Uduk speak of themselves? The northern Uduk call themselves *'kwanim pa*, though the southern Uduk do not use this in an ethnic sense (preferring *Ḵamus*). In literal terms this expression means roughly 'people of the homeland'. Used by the northern Uduk as an ethnic term, *'kwanim pa* may be contrasted with terms used for surrounding peoples: the Aru (Komo), the Gwama (Kwama), the Gwami or Gwami Nonu (Ganza), the Gwami or Bunyan Gwami (Berta),[13] the Wadke

[12] See Cerulli, 1956, and Corfield, 1938, *passim*.

[13] This double application of the term Gwami for two quite contrasting peoples, the Berta and the Ganza, is easier to explain if we assume, with Bender and Fleming (see Bender *et al.*, 1976) that Ganza is closely related to Mao, and that the Ganza people are relatively recent arrivals from the east. It is possible that the Uduk used the term Gwami of all those living in the Ethiopian escarpment and hills to the

(Jum Jum), the Gwara (Meban), and the Mufu and other 'Hill
Burun' peoples, each called by their particular hill. Further
away from home are the Tabe (Ingessana), and the fierce
Dhamkin (Nuer, Dinka, and Shilluk) and Gale (Galla). There
are then the light-skinned peoples, the Bunyan or Buncyan
(primarily northern Sudanese Arabs, though any clothes-
wearing person may be included), the Arab or Arab Bwasho
(the nomad Arabs, literally Arabs of the bush) and the Turuk
(white people, or officials of any colour). In one respect,
'kwanim pa in its ethnic sense is not an exact equivalent of Uduk.
Although people will often say that those who speak *'twam pa*,
or Uduk (the language of the homeland) are the real *'kwanim pa*,
people also insist that there is a community called Pur living on
the Daga river, downstream from the Aru (Komo), who are
'kwanim pa, although they speak a different language which the
Uduk do not understand. They are supposed formerly to have
been one with the Uduk, and to have been left behind in a
former north-westerly migration. The evidence I have points
strongly to these Pur being speakers of the Shita language.

But the matter of translation goes further than this. Beyond
its simple ethnic sense, *'kwanim pa* has historical, political, and
moral implications for the northern Uduk which are quite
excluded by its simple translation as 'Uduk'. In its singular
form, *wathim pa*, or 'Uduk person' it can mean a person in the
sense of a moral person, a human being as distinct from animal
or spirit, a person of responsibility and trust as against a feared
stranger. *Miim pa* or 'customs of the home' can mean Uduk
practice as distinct from Meban or Ingessana practice; but it
can also mean decent and civilized behaviour. The imagery of
the home and the homeland runs powerfully through these
expressions. And yet, ironically and suggestively, although the
notion of the home, *pa*, is so vital for the Uduk, the word *pa*
itself is a Nilotic loan word and not Koman at all. There are
perhaps a couple of dozen such Nilotic loan words used by the

east of them. This usage might well be derived from the self-designation of the
Berta (which I understand from Alessandro Triulzi to be *ga-mili*, or literally
'children of the black men'. With the fresh encounters resulting from Uduk
movement northwards and perhaps a westerly movement of the Berta and Ganza
(formerly closer to the Mao), Uduk speakers might have then found it necessary to
distinguish between various kinds of Gwami—the arabized Berta becoming Bunyan
Gwami, and the Ganza, Gwami Nonu.

Uduk, which may have entered the language through contact with the Meban or possibly with the Dinka or Nuer at an earlier stage of history. But no Nilotic loan word is used as frequently and with such import as *pa*. Even in their self-designation, the northern Uduk embrace elements drawn from a foreign tradition and language. No doubt, in settling their present area, they had to establish their position and their claims *vis-à-vis* Nilotic neighbours, the Meban as much as any other group.

The Uduk live in small but closely scattered hamlets in woodland bordering the main river-courses of their country. Each hamlet carves out a settlement site for itself in the bush and woodland, clears the grass from the centre, leaving an open space, and clears it behind each hut to keep away the damp, the frogs, and the snakes. The huts face roughly inward, with their 'backs' to the bushland and their doors opening onto the rest of the community. Each hut is built for a woman, the wife, sister, or mother of a man of the hamlet. Each woman makes a hearth inside her hut for the domestic fire, and sweeps clean the space outside her hut for people to gather and talk in the evening, and to sleep around an open-air fire in the warmer nights of the dry season. The open ground in the centre of the hamlet, preferably with one or two good shade trees, is a place for meeting, ceremonies, entertaining guests, and in the evening for dancing. One or two animal sheds for pigs and goats, on the model of dwelling-huts, may dot the hamlet, and there may be a thorn enclosure for cattle just beyond the huts. High square platform-shelters are built here and there in the hamlet, to keep meat away from the dogs, to spread out grain for beer-making, or to provide shade from the hot sun. This little settlement is the *pa*, the home or hamlet, as opposed to the encircling bushland, the *bwasho*. A settled area, together with its fields, as opposed to a virgin stretch of woodland, is usually termed *bampa*, and the whole of the area settled by the Uduk is called *bampaŋ 'kwanim pa*. The sense of hearth and home is very strong; people treasure the relative safety of their present fields and settlements, and do not relish travel or long periods away from home. In the past, they have known what it is to have the homeland destroyed, and even today, no little hamlet is built to last permanently, or even for very many years. Huts are built roughly and are not expected to last for more than four or five years; quite often a hamlet will be abandoned, and a new one built, after only three years. There is a continual shifting of hamlet sites, new clearings are always being made in the woodland both for building and for new fields, and the old sites are left to revert to wild vegetation. The home has continually to be rebuilt, many times over in the lifetime of an individual; and the historical memory of losing the homeland in time of war and having to resettle and rebuild it from scratch in times of peace closely touches the everyday lives of the people. Their society in the past has been built up in the face of insecurity, and the people of the homeland, the *'kwanim pa*, are those who have struggled to clear the woodland and settle down together, perhaps after having lived in insecurity, even perhaps literally as refugees in the wild bushland and hills, without home or fellows. A *wathim pa* is one who has participated in this process of creating and recreating the settlement and the homeland. He is distinct from a refugee in the bush, who is not a socially identifiable person but a *çiŋkina/*, a waif or lost thing, who to survive would have to be brought into the village and made into a member of the community, a *wathim pa*. Things of the bush (*tom bwasho*, a phrase primarily applied to wild animals) and things of the village (*tom pa*), are engaged in an historic struggle; bringing in wild and lost people and making them into a part of the moral community of the homeland is basic to the people's understanding of who they are and how their society has come to be what it is.

The Uduk hamlet today is thought of as a matrilineal unit. Those living in it are ideally related through women—they are members of the same named matriline, or what we may call birth-group. The home is very much the preserve of women; unmarried youths or men temporarily without wives do not even live in a proper dwelling, but in groups in the bush, or in some deserted and tumbledown hut. The building of an individual home, or a hamlet, and the establishment of the settled community, are very strongly associated with the presence of women, and the settled community endures by virtue of the matrilineal connections between its members— whether male or female, they are connected across the generations through mothers, sisters, and daughters within the wider birth-group. This is thought of as a 'naturally' based community, for all are physically of the same blood, passed on in the matriline, from mother to children. The assimilation of lost persons of the bush to a settled community is thus a question of their being brought in to an enduring community identified with a particular line of mothers and daughters, an image which recurs in myth and ritual as well as in oral history and genealogy.

The most recent period of upheaval and disturbance which can be remembered in any circumstantial detail is that of the turn of the present century. Since 1904, however, there has been relative peace and prosperity in Udukland. 'Women have given birth and the country has been filled up.' But the fundamental political and moral realities of earlier history were not forgotten in the colonial interlude. By the late 1950s, the civil war in the Sudan which had broken out in 1955 meant a return of uncertainty, apprehension, and sometimes real insecurity to the small communities bordering the southern provinces. This uncertainty and political suspicion hampered the development of the marginal regions during the long years of the civil war. The war was mercifully halted by the Addis Ababa agreement of 1972, and peace has returned. But the Uduk and the communities to their south suffered considerably from the long years of disturbance.[14] On the southern borders of the Blue Nile Province there was little protection and no administration. There were incursions of Nuer into the Jebel Bisho area in 1964–5. The Ganza and Uduk of the Jebel Bisho area fled north to the Yabus valley, abandoning their homes and fields, and they were only beginning to return in 1969. Large numbers of Ganza and Komo to the south moved into Ethiopia. There were repeated accounts and rumours in circulation during the 1960s of skirmishes and incidents from the nearby Upper Nile Province, and fears at all levels from time to time of surprise

[14] The southern Komo villages of the Gerre valley (the upper Jokau) in Ethiopia have suffered multiple disturbances in recent years, as a result of the civil war in the Sudan. They originally lived around Jebel Gemi, and sought refuge in the Sudan earlier in the century, because of Galla raiding. In the 1960s they appear to have returned to build their homes in Ethiopia because of the fighting and police and military reinforcements on the Sudan side of the border. The Sudanese security forces ordered that these runaways should be rounded up and brought back to the Sudan, and this was carried out in 1969 or thereabouts. Several villages were burned, but a few escaped and reported the matter to the Ethiopian authorities. High-level negotiations resulted in the release of most of those involved after a couple of months. These people then rebuilt their villages, and secured Ethiopian protection to some extent.

attacks by the rebel forces. Once the rumour of an imminent rebel incursion led to the temporary flight of whole Uduk hamlets in the Tombak valley into the bush; and once my own sleep was disturbed by bangs in the night and alarmed shouting. The reaction was of real panic, until—pretty quickly—it was discovered that some boys had been roasting a couple of bad eggs! The authorities were continually on their guard, and I believe equally sensitive to rumour. Small defence works had been constructed at Chali by the military forces. But the Uduk, who had been forbidden from 1956 to carry fire-arms because of suspected rebel sympathies, were on particularly uneasy terms with the authorities by the late 1960s, after the closing of the mission station. They were in the unhappy position of fearing the southern rebels, whom they assumed all to be from the Nilotic peoples, especially the Nuer, their ancient foes, and yet they were themselves an object of suspicion in the eyes of the local northern Sudanese merchants, officials, and armed forces.

Fieldwork was not always easy in these circumstances. But the atmosphere of insecurity and the fragility of the peace made it easier for me to understand the records and memories of the last century, and the way in which whole populations could abandon their homes and possessions, become broken up through flight, and reconstitute their community life elsewhere. It was not possible to mistake the grim importance of loyalty to kin, trust in friends, and sharing of resources in these circumstances, nor the strength and emotional compulsion of images drawn from such historical experience.

The 'pre-Nilotes' as a whole are an ancient cultural survival; the Koman languages are a fragmentary record of early African linguistic history; and of the Koman-speaking peoples, the Uduk are one of the groups most broken up and disturbed by recent history, at least as far as the evidence of the last century or so goes. For the outsider, the Uduk are certainly little more than an ethnographic remnant, and perhaps only of interest to those cataloguing the shrinking number of the world's languages and cultures. They know themselves to be something of a remnant; they look upon the situation sometimes with frank acceptance, sometimes with resentful passion, and sometimes with humour. The realization of their historical position as a weak and politically unsuccessful people colours their thinking and action in many fields; this common past experience, and the shared knowledge derived from it, is one of the main social facts of Uduk life. It is impossible today to distinguish the ancient elements of Uduk culture from the modifications they have undergone in the course of historical events, so completely does the knowledge and imagery of past events pervade the thought and valuations of the present. Of course, a tenuous relation between the memory of past events and the motive of present action often exists in human communities; but today it is a primary fact of Uduk society. These people have experienced some of the grossest indignities and sufferings known to mankind, and they know it. Their present society is in part a response. They have developed an egalitarian and defensive ethic and a way of preserving some sense of worth in their predicament, a way of seeing themselves nevertheless as whole men and women, as *'kwanim pa.*

It is the first aim of this study to describe something of the historical knowledge of the northern Uduk, and to discover the significance of this historical knowledge in the lives the people lead today—from their everyday working activities to the intimacy of their marriage and family relations. Their past is not, in any of these matters, a mere appendage to their ethnography, but a central point of reference for their living society, from which their moral thought and symbolic representations commonly take bearings. This study shows how concepts crucial to social and political organization, such as their notions of persons and things, of work and exchange, of women and natural kinship, of friendship, protection and alliance, are firmly rooted in the Uduk people's understanding of their own past. Successive chapters explore the economic, kinship, and political spheres of Uduk society in the light of these central notions. An account then follows of a series of rites, the Gurunya rites, designed to save vulnerable children from death, which show remarkable parallels with the history of the people as a whole. Historical themes are consciously used in the elaboration of these rites, which can even be seen as a dramatic play upon Uduk historical self-knowledge, a collective 'work of art' nourished by roots in a particular past.

The second aim of the present study is to indicate what we know or can guess from *external* evidence about the Uduk past.

Evidence of this kind, drawn both from the historical record and from comparative ethnography, is presented mainly in the second and final chapters. On the basis of this evidence, the hypothesis is developed that the northern Uduk, the *'kwanim pa*, have constructed a 'new society' of their own, distinguished particularly by its matrilineal bias. This appears to have followed their repeated scattering and decimation, their separation from the other Koman peoples, including the southern Uduk, and their enforced contact with more powerful and wealthy peoples to the north over the last century and a half or so. This interpretation of the genesis of the modern society of the northern Uduk can be placed side by side with their own oral tradition of how they have survived the past. It strikingly confirms the truths contained in their own tradition, truths not always embodied in literal statements, but often in the symbolic form of myth and rite. This is illustrated vividly by the symbolic representations which cluster around the cult of Gurunya children. But beyond confirming the validity of Uduk self-knowledge, the juxtaposition of 'our' knowledge with theirs obliges us to sympathize with the moral directives they base upon their past experience, and which guide their lives today. The Uduk are not as foreign as they might appear. Given comparable experience in recent times of devastation, enslavement, and loss, would we not adopt a similar negative attitude to commerce, a similar positive one to the traceable ties of kinship, perhaps especially the surest one which is through one's mother, and so forth? On this level, the exotic can be brought close to home.

LANDSCAPE, SETTLEMENT, AND LAND-USE

The belt in which Uduk settlements are now found corresponds closely to the administrative division of the *omodiya* (the area administered by one *omda*) as it existed in the 1960s. It stretches some fifty miles narrowly north and south, parallel with the Ethiopian escarpment and the international boundary, as the sketch-map shows in Figure 3. There are some isolated low hills, outliers of the plateau, but they are partly submerged by a plain of sedimentary rocks extending into the region from the open expanses of the Upper Nile basin. The Khors Ahmar,

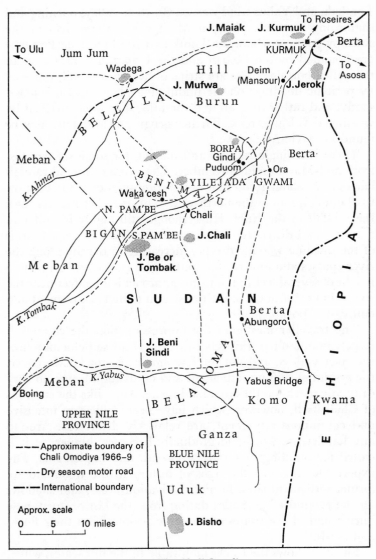

3. The Chali Omodiya

Tombak, and Yabus wind westwards, their valleys opening and shallowing into this plain, until they lose themselves in the swampy country where the Uduk and the Blue Nile Province are bounded by the Meban and the Upper Nile Province. In the valley bottoms there are strips of heavy, silty soil, renewed by periodic flooding; on the undulating plain the soil is loose, sandy, and rather dry; around the hills, it is often enriched by weathered volcanic rock. Further geographical details may be found in Davies, 1960.

There is a single rainy season lasting for some six months, from mid-May to mid-November. The average annual rainfall varies from about 1,000 mm in the south-east of Uduk country to about 800 mm in the north-west. This is rather heavier than the rainfall in the Nuba Hills, though still highly irregular in quantity and distribution from year to year. The vegetation is of the savanna woodland type, increasing in density along the river courses and towards the south. The grass cover grows to a height of several feet in the rains, approaching ten feet near the rivers, but is burnt off in the dry season to make movement and cultivation possible.

The traveller may gain the impression that the country is largely uninhabited; this is because the Uduk settlements follow the river valleys, and not the few motorable roads. Moreover, the system of shifting settlement and cultivation leaves no very dramatic marks on the woodland scene. Areas like the environs of Chali itself, however, which have been subject to intensive and continuous settlement, are relatively deforested. Around any hamlet the woodland gradually becomes thinner, as it is culled for building materials, firewood, and implements. The expert eye can read the signs of history in the woodland: of former settlement sites, former cultivation areas, and shadows on the ground of stockades dating from the last century, now burnt; and of the routes of nomadic peoples with their flocks and herds.[15]

Figure 3 shows the tracks motorable in the dry season which pass through the area connecting Kurmuk, Wadega, and the market villages of the border with Boing, in the Upper Nile

[15] An account of the oldest-established of the nomadic peoples utilizing this region, and their interaction with the settled peoples, may be found in Abd-al Ghaffar Muhammed Ahmad's book on the Rufā'a el Hoi (1974).

Province. These roads are officially closed for five months of the year during the rainy season, making Kurmuk a relatively isolated town, but it does not rain continuously and vehicles can occasionally get through from Roseires and Damazin. During the rains, Chali is normally dependent on donkey or mule transport.

Very few of the local Uduk people possess donkeys, and nearly everyone travels on foot. In the settled belts, there is a dense network of footpaths, connecting hamlets with their waterpoints and fields, and with each other. Long journeys, from one valley to another, or to distant Meban or Berta villages, are usually made in the dry season through open woodland. Quite a number of Uduk men have been to Kurmuk on foot or as lorry passengers, but very few of the women have been. Only those people in search of wage employment or education have been beyond Kurmuk, and they are very few. The relatively remote Uduk communities south of the Yabus have little contact with their northern neighbours, or with the town of Kurmuk.

There are a number of huts in the countryside visited by petty merchants from time to time, who buy grain and sesame from the Uduk, and sell them minor items, but Chali is the only substantial centre. It had in the late 1960s two shops, very poorly stocked in the rains, a Police station, a dispensary with one medical assistant, a recently opened elementary school, a Government midwife, and the remains of the former flourishing Christian community still living around the old mission station and just keeping things going.

I have mentioned that the Uduk population, in the late 1960s, was in the region of 10,000. Appendix 2 gives the basis for this figure—a count of huts and an estimate of slightly over four people, on average, living in each hut. Of the total, some 7,000 were living in the Ahmar and Tombak valleys, comprising what I term the 'northern Uduk', and some 3,000, the 'southern Uduk', were living in the Yabus valley and in the neighbour-hood of Jebel Bisho. On the basis of my estimate, there has been a small increase since the first and only accessible Census of the Sudan in 1955/6, when the population of the Chali Omodiya was 8,300. The Uduk birth-rate is undoubtedly high, as my genealogies suggest (Appendix 3 gives a sample). But as the genealogies also suggest, and as the sad experience of the Uduk repeatedly confirms, infant mortality is also very high. I would guess that almost half the children born die before they reach five years of age. The basic diet of porridge and sauce must often leave children short of protein and vitamin-rich foods, and they are certainly susceptible to all kinds of disease, infestation, and infection. Malaria and kalazar are only two of the worst problems. No study of the society, culture, and imaginative life of the Uduk can ignore the basic fact that illness and death are a distressing but central part of their regular experience.

Uduk hamlets today tend to be small and impermanent, splitting, re-combining, and shifting site every few years. In Waka'cesh in the Tombak valley, where I was based during most of my field-work, the hamlets were abandoned and rebuilt every three or four years—previous sites were remembered back to about 1940 (dateable because of the memory of the Italian threat from Ethiopia). It is difficult to be sure of general reasons for such frequent movement. Contingent explanations are however abundant, usually including the dilapidated state of the huts, or white ants, or the presence of snakes; the need to move nearer the river for carrying water, or on the contrary, away from the river to be near the fields. Often part of a hamlet will move elsewhere after a quarrel. The fundamental reasons for this degree of mobility lie in the lack of long-term commitments and the flexibility of personal ties in Uduk society, particularly in the marriage relation; a man builds a house for his wife, but does not expect his wife to stay with him for the rest of his life, and so he builds a much less substantial hut than Meban or Berta wives would get. The generally spare and shaggy construction of Uduk huts necessarily means that they must be rebuilt fairly often; but the multiple, varied, and casual social ties within and between hamlets, with people coming and going all the time, mean that rough and ready huts are only common sense. It seems to me likely that the tendency to rebuild a hamlet every three or four years may be correlated with the fluctuation in the produce of the fields from year to year; at a rough guess, there would be a reasonably good harvest and a distinct surplus perhaps once every three or four years, and in the others a barely adequate yield for subsistence. When the grain yield is average or low, extra projects such as hut-building or big ceremonial occasions are postponed. It may be that when a good year comes round, people feel it is time to move; for once, they have enough grain to brew beer for the neighbours to help in building, roofing, and plastering new huts and they might as well take advantage of it. In a good year there is a general intensification of the work effort as well as the social round, and a whole string of hamlets may decide to move site and rebuild. New fields may also be cleared and planted. On the other hand, in a poor year people conserve what grain supplies they have for eking out their own existence until better times come round, and make do with their present huts and fields.

In former times, and probably until well into the present century, the pattern of hamlets was not so scattered. Settlements tended, for reasons of security, to be grouped together in the vicinity of one or other of the various hills. Some of these nucleated settlements appear to have been stockaded, if we may believe oral tradition. With conditions of greater general security, these larger communities have become fragmented and the component birth-groups have now spread out into dispersed hamlets. But in the neighbourhood of each hill, hamlets are still identified as the people of Chali, or the people of Beni Mayu, or the people of 'Be (Jebel Tombak). These and the other main 'territorial clusters' are marked on the sketch map in Figure 3, and Chapter 6 includes a discussion of their historical and enduring political significance.

Figure 4 displays in detail the present-day pattern of settlement in the Ahmar and Tombak valleys. The territorial settlement clusters are still partially identifiable, although the hamlets have tended to spread out evenly along the river-courses. The hamlets are restricted to within a couple of miles of the river beds, because there are no other water sources. Water is carried by women, in gourds on their heads. Only the Yabus is a perennial stream, and in the other valleys the women get dry-season water from holes dug in the sandy bed of the river-courses. In particularly dry years the water may sink below the level at which it can be reached by this method, and people in those stretches of the Ahmar or Tombak valleys which are affected have to abandon their hamlets and build temporary camps either upstream or downstream at the nearest place where water is still accessible. For example, in March 1968

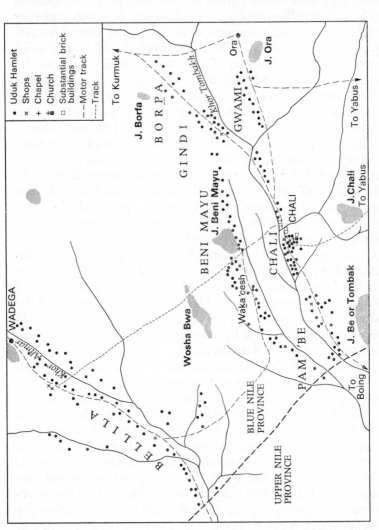

4. Northern Uduk settlements, 1968

several hamlets to the west of Waḵa'cesh had to move; some came upstream and built camps near the Waḵa'cesh water-point, and others moved downstream near to the Meban border. They remained in these temporary homes for several weeks, until the river flowed after the beginning of the rains.

The sketch-map shows however that hamlets are not built on the very banks of rivers, or even very close to them. This is partly because of the direct danger of floods and partly because of the indirect disadvantage of building too close to the maize fields in the river-meadows. The pigs and goats, for example, can cause great destruction in the fields. Another reason why the hamlets are some distance from the river is that the sorghum fields usually lie towards the hills; if the settlements are too far from the fields, it creates extra work both for men, in walking to and fro to cultivate, and for women, who sometimes provide the men working in the fields with food and water and have to transport the crops home on their heads. There is therefore a tension between the need to be near the water source, and the need to be near the sorghum fields; and a compromise position is usually fixed on, mid-way between. This position is also con-venient because it gives ready access to the resources of the woodland, especially building materials and firewood.

At harvest time (December–January) a good deal of vigilance is needed in the sorghum fields. This is partly because of the danger that birds will consume most of the crop, and partly because at this time of year the nomadic flocks and herds are moving south through the area, and wandering animals may cause havoc to the crops. One or two people, sometimes young boys, therefore move to the fields and mount a continuous guard. If the harvest is a good one, and if the hamlet is a long way from the fields (say, at least a mile), then the whole hamlet may move and build a temporary harvest camp, *paŋkalu*, near the fields. They will transport equipment such as grinding-stones and cooking-pots, and bring the chickens and goats; but they leave the pigs behind (because of the danger to the crops). The biggest chore is bringing the water all the way from the river to the harvest camp. This movement does not take place every year, nor is it undertaken by every hamlet, and therefore does not qualify for the description 'transhumance'.

Outside the hamlet, there are three main categories of land:

bunto, the open fields cleared for sorghum in dry, light woodland; *bangap̱*, the riverain meadows where maize is the staple;
and the *bwasho* or open wild bush and woodland. Odd fields,
especially for sesame, may be cleared anywhere in the bush,
though the sites of old settlements (*madu/*) are often used for
their richer soil.

There is a clear rationale behind the distribution of *bunto* and
bangap̱ (see Figure 5). The meadowlands are cultivated because
the soil is richer than anywhere else, and, being heavy, particularly suitable for maize. But the *bunto* are located as far away
from the river as possible. This is because the woodland cover
becomes thinner away from the river, and consequently there
are fewer birds. Birds are one of the greatest hazards in the
cultivation of sorghum, here as elsewhere in the Sudan. Any
crops grown close to the hamlets, or small plots of vegetables
such as okra grown near one's hut, have to be protected by a
substantial thorn stockade from domestic animals.

In the *bangap̱* meadows, some of the land is cultivated year
after year, without any apparent decline in fertility. Occasional
floods add silt to the soil, and the relatively rich vegetation
provides humus. Even here, there are however open stretches
and the land is not completely under cultivation. In the more
open woodland, on sandy soils, where the *bunto* are cleared,
there is no regular enrichment of the soil. When a field has been
cultivated for four or five years, the quality of the crop deterior-
ates, and the owner abandons it and clears a new field from
open woodland. There is no systematic return to previously
abandoned fields, though this may sometimes occur. Like the
meadow lands, the woodland area is by no means being used to
capacity, even under the system of shifting cultivation. There
are vast stretches of potentially cultivable woodland which are
simply too far away from water supplies to be utilized. If
pressure on land were to build up, then more and more areas
could be cultivated at the cost of extra effort in walking to and
fro, and transporting water and crops. The provision of waterpoints, such as deep wells or *hafirs* (reservoirs) in the stretches of
dry woodland would of course transform the whole position.
As yet, however, the existing opportunities for settlement and
cultivation are not exhausted, and access to land is not a
primary problem in the area.

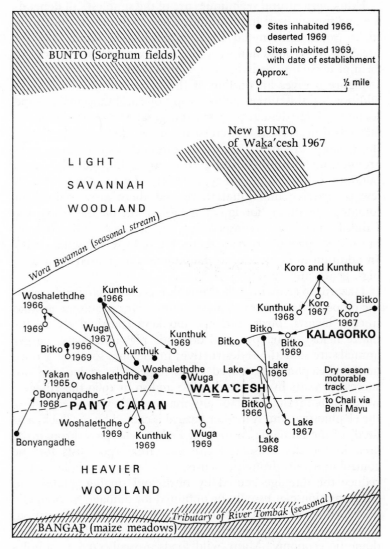

5. Hamlets of Waka'cesh and neighbourhood

Uduk agricultural techniques are of the simplest, all depend-ing on unspecialized hand labour. Their tools consist of digging sticks (some with metal tips), broad-bladed hand hoes for breaking the ground and weeding, and axes for felling trees. No form of terracing, or irrigation, is practised.

Figure 6 gives an outline of the agricultural calendar. In addition to the three staple crops of sorghum, maize, and sesame, which demand by far the greater proportion of the farmer's time, some minor crops are grown: for example, two or three kinds of beans, a few cotton bushes (for home use), ground-nuts, squashes, okra, tobacco, chilli, gourds, sweet potatoes. In the Yabus valley, a variety of yam is cultivated. A few progressive individuals here and there grow onions, or tomatoes, or other 'foreign' vegetables, but on the whole the Uduk farmer is very conservative, remarking 'We like onions, but it's not our job to grow them. We're busy enough as it is!' In addition to cultivation, some animals are reared: chickens, pigs, goats, and cattle.

Hazards to crops include drought, especially dangerous when the crops are immature; flooding of the river meadows, ground insects, locusts, birds, rodents, monkeys (particularly in the maize fields), antelopes, and domestic pigs and goats. Larger animals are sometimes destructive: in the area south of Yabus, herds of elephant destroyed crops, especially maize, for two successive years in 1967 and 1968; and so in 1969 the villagers were not bothering to plant any maize, as they were expecting the elephants again. A further hazard is caused by the flocks and herds of the nomadic Arabs and Fellata who pass through the area in the dry season. There are ritual specialists for the control of floods, drought, locusts, and elephants; vigilance can reduce the damage caused by birds and smaller game; and compensation can usually be obtained for damage by nomadic flocks, either by a settlement on the spot or through litigation.

The wild bush and woodland is a vital resource for the Uduk domestic economy. Many wild foods are collected to supple-ment the diet, especially in the rains. They include leafy and root vegetables, bark substances for making sticky stew, woods used for making ash to flavour stew, and many fruits and mushrooms. Starchy roots, of at least a dozen varieties, form an important reserve to fall back on when grain supplies are

Month	Weather	Uduk season	Sorghum	Maize	Sesame
mid-April	Hot, increasing humidity	MONYJOCO/	Plant		Plant
		–		Plant	
May	Early rains	–	Plant	Plant	Plant
		–		Weed	
June		–		Weed	
	Rains	–		Weed	
		–			Weed
July		–		Weed	
	Rivers flow	MONDIT	Weed		
				Harvest	
August		–			
			Weed		
		–		Harvest	
September		–			
	Decreasing rains	MOYURUN			
October		–			Harvest
		–			Harvest
November	Occasional storms	MOŊ'KUCU/			
			Harvest		
		–			
December	Dry	–			
January	Rivers dry	–	Harvest		
		–			
		MOYURANTE			
February		–			
		–			
March		–			
		–			
April (to middle of month)		–			

6. The agricultural calendar (main crops)

Note The seasons are reckoned as follows:

Monyjoco/: begins when the first light covering of grass appears, after the first rains. It is time to plant maize.

Mondit: the opening of the 'heavy' season. Begins when the first green maize is harvested, for eating 'on the cob'. The grass by this time is several feet high.

Moyurun: The short period in which sesame is harvested; sometimes defined as the time when the *nyaran cul* ('girl stars', Seven Sisters) appear.

Moŋ'kucu/ The sorghum ripens and is harvested.

Moyurante Begins when the sorghum harvest is complete.

running low in a poor year. Wild honey is collected; and fishing
is important in the later rainy season, when the rivers are
beginning to subside. Hunting was formerly of more significance
than it is today; the Uduk say that the increasing numbers of
nomads, usually armed, have driven away the game. The hunt
is however still of imaginative importance, and it is very likely
that hunting and gathering formerly played a vital part in Uduk
life. The woodland is also the source of many medicines, from
roots and bark; and of building materials (woods and grasses,
bark fibres), firewood, and materials for a wide variety of
domestic objects, such as forked branches for stools and head
rests, drinking straws for beer, and formerly seeds and ostrich-
egg shells for beadwork, etc. Mineral resources are also utilized:
a variety of rocks are used for making grinding-stones, every
woman's basic implement for making flour, extracting sesame
oil, grinding spices and coffee, and pounding vegetables—the
large flat lower stone, the female, is usually made from a coarse
granitic rock which can be chipped repeatedly to roughen the
surface as it wears down, and the smaller oval hand-stone, the
male, from a smooth basaltic rock. Clays are extracted for
pottery (though the Uduk say the best clays are not found in
their country), made by the women using the coil method and
fired on an open fire; and iron-rich soils for manufacturing 'red
ochre' used as a cosmetic, mixed with sesame oil.

As the plates in this volume show, the everyday dress and
personal adornment of the Uduk is very simple. Men used to go
naked but now wear shorts, occasionally with a vest or shirt or
even the knee-length Sudanese *jibba*. They usually retain their
beads, however, often as necklets or armlets. They usually wear
a pair of sandals—often home-made from leather. A man
regularly carries his six- or seven-foot bow with arrows, some
spears and throwing sticks and perhaps his fire-drill, when he
traverses the bushland and forest. When visiting another hamlet, he props his weapons up against a tree on the edge of the
clearing before approaching his friend's home. Diviners, when
actually practising their art, wear a goat-skin loin-cloth and the
complicated paraphernalia of the calling; and men of the cult
of *arum* (spirit) wear a cloth *jibba*, or even the long *jelabiya* for
ceremonial purposes, if they have one. Women wear a twisted
cotton belt and strings of beads around the waist, and small

front aprons. The outer apron used to be of threaded ostrich-eggshell beads, but is now of cotton with a beaded edge. Beads used to be mainly made from seeds and fruits, but now are mostly bought. A woman sometimes winds a long skirt around her waist, of soft leather or cloth, but only very rarely does she cover her bright necklaces with a blouse or wrap. Both girls and young men are proud to display the decorative emblems made by scarring on their cheeks, shoulders, arms or almost anywhere else, often symmetrically on the right and left-hand sides of the body. A characteristic emblem, without an explicit meaning as far as I could tell, is a cross within a circle (incidentally found also among the Gumuz). Both sexes, when children, have their two lower front teeth removed; although there is no formal initiation, this is a part of becoming grown-up.

The small scale of Uduk endeavours is reflected in the scattered pattern of tiny fields and hamlets. From this delicately-etched, hand-made landscape we can see at once that the people produce by their own labour for their own subsistence; there is little evidence of fields devoted to single crops, produced for the cash market, for one crop is interplanted with another— the gourd vines are entangled with the maize and peanuts, a few okra plants may be sprouting inside the walls of an old hut, and beans and a few precious cotton bushes hide in the tall fields of sorghum. Weeding these fields, the main task of the Uduk, is a skilled job—and a task which could only be done by hand. The landscape itself shows no sign of capital investment, of special-ization or of the expansion of neighbour against neighbour. There are matching sets of intricately made and irregularly-bounded fields for every little hamlet, and the way in which the pattern shifts subtly this way and that with the years, suggests individual mobility, a freedom to come and go, to plant in one place or in another at will, as well as a rock-steady, enduring tradition of subsistence living.

EVENTS, MEMORIES, AND MYTHS

For the period before the middle of the last century, the main source of information on the former homelands and life of the Uduk has to be oral tradition. Combined with some scraps of tradition from other peoples and some circumstantial evidence of language distribution, this gives a clear indication that the Uduk formerly lived considerably to the south of their present position, and have gradually moved northwards in response to pressure from the Nilotes and the western Galla. The mountain of Bisho, and the Yabus valley, were probably settled quite early from further south. At what date the valleys of the more northerly Ahmar and Tombak were settled by Uduk speakers it is impossible to say; but at a guess it might have been between the late eighteenth and mid-nineteenth century. The Ahmar may have been settled later than this, in the course of the disturbances of the later nineteenth century. There are three dialects of the Uduk language, corresponding to these three main settlement areas. Those of the Ahmar and Tombak valleys are very close, consisting mainly of a difference in 'accent', but the Yabus dialect is substantially different, in many items of vocabulary and usage as well as in accent, though there is no real problem of mutual understanding.

There is general agreement among the Uduk people that they have arrived from further south. As already mentioned, they even claim kinship with a group of people they call Pur, who have been left behind in the Daga valley, while the rest of 'the Uduk' have moved northwards. The traditions are rather general in the northerly valleys of the Ahmar and Tombak, but become more specific to the south. Among the Uduk of the Yabus valley, and Jebel Bisho, it is stated precisely that the people came from a place called Kolop, said to be known to the Nuer as Pa Kur, and now in Nuer country. Near Jebel Bisho, I was told that Kolop was about two days' journey away, and my informant pointed in a south-westerly direction. He said that the Uduk lived there first, but were chased out eventually by the Nuer, whom they often fought, and sometimes defeated.[1] I assume that 'Kolop' was in the Daga valley, downstream from the present Komo and Shita villages. 'The Uduk' moved north-wards away from the Nuer, and were then attacked by the Galla. They retreated for safety to the flat table-top of Jebel Bisho, where I have seen fragments of Uduk-style pottery and grinding stones, indicating former habitation. All this is said to have happened before the attacks of the Bunyan, that is the slave-raids of the later nineteenth century.

Specific birth-group histories often trace a southerly origin. For example, northern representatives of the traditionally central and most numerous of the Uduk birth-groups, the Lake (pronounced as a disyllable), point to Jebel Bisho itself as their immediate origin. The mountain is of course far to the south, from their point of view, and many have never been there. But Sheikh Puna Marinyje, of the Yabus valley, has explained to me that the Lake, although they settled at Jebel Bisho, previously lived on the Daga river even further south (which I have not visited). He claimed that there are still members of the Lake people living in the Daga valley, known locally as Buldit, to the Nuer as Cai Buldit and to the Kurmuk police as Haŋ'kash. 'Buldiit', a place-name on the Daga, was applied by Corfield to one of the dialects of the 'Ciita' (Shita) language. And 'Haŋ'kash' is one of the names by which the Shita are known, according to Shita I have met in Ethiopia.[2] I have also been told by a Berta-speaking man at Yabus Bridge that the Uduk originally came from the Haŋ'kash people on the Daga river. All this points to clear connections between the Uduk and the Daga valley, and their references to the 'Pur', their relatives left in that valley, are almost certainly to some of those we now classify on linguistic criteria as Shita. A tradition noted by Corfield even names a former Uduk settlement close to the Daga: 'The Koma of the Daga valley say that the village of Dota which is now deserted was once inhabited by the Kebeirka who were raided by the

---

[1] Evans-Pritchard, 1940, refers to Nuer encounters with the 'Burun' (see p. 133). The account as a whole presents a picture of the Nuer expanding to the east. Kolop is mentioned in a 'mythical' sense below, on p. 114.

[2] See Corfield's article on the Koma (1938). I was told in Ethiopia by Komo that Haŋ'kash is a common exclamation of the Shita people, and means 'there is isn't any'.

Berta'. Dota is marked on the official maps, and on Figure 1; and the Komo of the Daga still call the Uduk 'Kebeirka'.[3]

Some of the northerly Uduk birth-groups can point to specific sites marking their later journey northward from the Yabus, and individual histories give the same general picture of a northerly movement. In one of the few records of early enquiries among the Uduk, Chataway gives the story of an old man, whom he judged to be about ninety years old in 1926.[4]

The original home of the tribe was five days beyond Arwa (beyond Galla country). In his grandfather's time they were badly treated by the Abyssinians, who used to steal their children for slaves, so they moved to Arwa (5 days away—15 days journey from Chali). They were no better off there so they moved in a few years to Berzem (in the south of the Kurmuk district). There my informant was born. When he was about seven his father took his family to Chali (Jaali on the map). He remembers being very frightened as the Nuers were raiding the country at that time. . . .
Since then they have been raided from all around for slaves.[5]

Several old men have told me of their having left the Yabus area because of insecurity from Nuer and Meban, even during the present century. The tendency to move north was probably a pattern established several generations earlier.

There is further evidence of the northward movement of the Uduk in some of the northern clan names; for example, *Bersaŋ* refers to Jebel Berzem, well to the south of the Yabus, and *Kwamas* is almost certainly derived from the term used by the Ganza and Komo for the southern Uduk—Ḵamus—and these clans have a tradition of southern origin.

There is no contradiction between accepting both Chataway's informant's story of having come from 'Abyssinia', and my informants' stories of coming from the Daga. The Sonka-Daga valley was in any case under Galla control, at least at the time of Schuver's visit in 1881/2 and through the period of Jote Tullu. 'Galla country' might well have referred to areas in the

---

[3] Corfield, op. cit., p. 129; cf. the term Je Barka which I use above, p. 12.
[4] These enquiries were made in the neighbourhood of Chali, the modern centre of Uduk country, in the Tombak valley. See Chataway (1927, p. 5; reference in Evans-Pritchard, 1932, p. 32).
[5] If we take seriously the dates indicated, this would be evidence of Nuer raiding near the Yabus in the 1840s. Douglas Johnson tells me that this is very likely.

present borderland, below Gidami, in the valley of the Sonka-Daga or in the region of Jebel Gemi and the Garre-Jokau plain. 'Arwa' may be a form of the modern Uduk term Aru for the Komo, suggesting that the Uduk once lived to the south of the Komo, where the Shita, with whom the Uduk have close cultural affinity, mainly live today.

There seems therefore to have been a sustained movement of the Uduk people northwards; the central Lake birth-group still has specific links with the Daga valley and with Shita. The population of course did not move as one body; the pattern was probably a trickle of individuals and small groups. The present population may represent an amalgam of refugees from various sources, particularly from other Koman peoples under pressure from the Nuer and the highland Ethiopians. This interpretation is made more likely by the internal structure of birth-groups, particularly the Lake. Although the Lake constitute about a third of the Uduk population, it is sometimes said that not all are 'real Lake'—almost with the suggestion that they are not all 'real *'kwanim pa'*. A good proportion of them are said to have been 'brought in' by the Lake, 'looked after' by them, and in one story I heard even 'bought' by the Lake, and now 'just call themselves Lake' without really being so. Most other named birth-groups have a shorter traditional history than the Lake; and the Lake are the only birth-group to appear in stories of the 'mythical' kind, linking them with the beginnings of history and humanity. This birth-group, and its traditionally accepted southerly origin, gives some shape to the early history of the Uduk and provides some continuity from their beginnings, in close touch with the other Koman peoples, down to the present, which finds the northern Uduk especially rather separated from their fellows.

DISTURBANCES OF THE LATE NINETEENTH CENTURY

The Uduk and their neighbours were on the fringes of the major upheavals of the Sudan and Ethiopia in the nineteenth century.[6] The establishment of the Turco-Egyptian regime, the eastward

[6] See James, 1968; and Triulzi's account of disturbance on the Ethiopian side of the border (1975).

expansion of Mahdism and its clashes with Ethiopia, the unifica-
tion of the western Galla country, the expansion of Menelik's
Ethiopia, and the establishment of the Anglo-Egyptian Condominium in the Sudan in 1898, all were experienced in these
remote regions, sometimes directly. Uduk tradition records for
example the appearance of Baggara and later 'Turuk' raiders
from the north and north-west, probably during the 1870s or
1880s.

The major impact of the nineteenth century on the Uduk
came not from the main political developments of the Sudan or
Ethiopia, however, but from local developments in the border
region following the early Egyptian expeditions up the Blue
Nile. The lure of gold, combined with the political difficulties
which led many from the northern Sudan to seek a southerly
refuge, attracted a long stream of immigrants from the north to
the border hills, from 1821 onwards. Many of these Arabic-
speaking immigrants settled down, married locally (usually
Berta women) and built up a position of wealth and power
through employing the local Berta population in the production
of alluvial gold, and controlling trade with Ethiopia. A series of
small empires arose, under dominant merchant families who
claimed connection, through intermarriage, with the older 'Funj'
aristocracies of the border hills. These chiefdoms were sufficiently strong by the 1880s to resist control both from the
Mahdist state in the Sudan, and from Menelik's Ethiopia. They
were able to exploit their intermediate position between the two
countries, in spite of attempts by both sides to secure their
allegiance. Political strength was built up partly through the
export of gold to Ethiopia for fire-arms; and these arms were
used increasingly for slave-raiding expeditions, particularly
among the border peoples to the west of Beni Shangul, Dul, and
Asosa.

Conditions were bad at this time in the Blue Nile valley for
the Gumuz people, many of whom fled upstream as far as the
Didessa river as a result of raiding from the Sudan side; and
farther south, the extended raiding of the western Galla led to
the flight of the Komo from their traditional home on Jebel
Gemi. But in the central 'Burun' belt, conditions were perhaps
worst. By the middle of the 1890s the Uduk country, and probably much of the Jum Jum and Hill Burun country too, was

virtually depopulated. Among the Uduk, those who were not captured or had not surrendered to the border rulers had fled to take refuge in the remoter hills to the south or at Government posts to the north-west. From official Sudan Intelligence reports, and from local oral tradition, a picture can be pieced together of the impact of the raiding. Two main chiefdoms were raiding Uduk country: Dul and Asosa. Dul was under Mohammed Wad Mahmud until he was detained by the Abyssinians in 1900, when his brother Ibrahim Wad Mahmud took over, later making his headquarters at Jebel Jerok. Asosa was a bigger and probably stronger chiefdom, at first under Khogali Hassan until he was detained in 1898, and then under his deputy, Hamid Hassan whose headquarters were at Kirin. Khogali was known as Kujul to the Uduk, and was regarded as the arch-enemy; one hears of Kujul this, Kujul that quite frequently, though often when they speak of him they do not mean him personally, but simply one of his men. All the sheikhs were regarded as being allies of Kujul, and the Berta people were regarded as being solid in their support of the sheikhs.

The effects of the raiding period on the distribution of the Uduk were briefly as follows. A large number were captured and sold in Asosa, where it is said there are still Uduk today; others were sold to the northern Sudan (in 1966 I heard of, though failed to find, an old woman in Wad Medani who ran a little shop and spoke Uduk); others were captured, and settled as agricultural 'serfs' in village communities near to Jerok (at Gwarayo) and Kirin (at Bade).[7] These captive communities were swelled by large numbers of people who came to surrender

[7] In the notes of Chataway, the following brief account appears, which corresponds in part to what I was told some fifty years later. The 'tribute' paid in the mid-nineteenth century was almost certainly in the form of slaves (see Chataway, 1927, p. 1). Triulzi (1975, p. 63) notes a Mahdist post at Surkum from 1885.

'When they came no one was living on the Yabus or Tombakk (so they say) . . . Before the Mahdia no one came to the Tombakk Uduks. Their first experience of superior civilization being when the Mahadists raided them for slaves. Later they were roped in by Wad Mahmud to cultivate his lands, being allowed to return to their villages in the dry season with sufficient aish [sorghum] to keep them alive. The Uduks on the Khor Ahmar (Kurara) however are said (by Idris Ragab [sheikh of Gule]) to have been under Gule during the "Turkia". This however probably means they were raided for slaves and plundered by the Meks of Gule. They seem to have paid tribute to the Rufaa tribe at the begining [*sic*] of the Mahadia, but later were taken off in a body to Jerok by Wad Mahmud there to work on his cultivation.'

of their own accord, since conditions were so bad in the country-side. The communities were mainly composed of men, since women were sold as slaves and concubines, and they not only supplied grain for their overlords but also served in battle. However, not all the Uduk population lost its freedom in this way; a large number from the Tombak and Ahmar valleys managed to flee to Ulu, some 45–50 miles to the north-west, where there was a sheikh subject to Gule. And in the extreme south, in the Yabus valley and hills to the south, in spite of heavy attack, the people were able to defend themselves to some extent through utilizing the stronghold of Jebel Bisho. The three river valleys where the Uduk had been living were quite emptied; and only after several years, in 1904, did Sudan Government action and a decisive military patrol to Jerok make it possible for the Uduk to return to their homes. Their existence, as a distinct people, had indeed been in the balance.

CONDITIONS IN THE 'BURUN' COUNTRY, EARLY TWENTIETH CENTURY

There are a few documents from the early years of this century which give, directly or indirectly, some useful information on conditions in the 'Burun' area. The first field report on Burun country was submitted by Major Gwynn, who was undertaking the task of international boundary delimitation, after a journey from Kirin to Fashoda on the White Nile down the Yabus River, in early 1902.[8] This was, of course, before the battle of Jerok in 1904, and during the period when the northern Uduk were at Ulu, Gwarayo and Bade, and the southern Uduk had retreated away from the Yabus, towards the hills, on the south side of the river. Major Gwynn reports that for 43 miles down the Yabus from Kirin, a stretch which is now partly settled by Uduk, the country was deserted, but game was very abundant. For the next 60 miles of the journey, game gave way to a large population of 'Buruns'. This population we can say was certainly Meban. The absence of settlement on the upper reaches of the Yabus is consistent with Uduk oral tradition which tells of the flight of their people into the local hills.

The Inspector of Slavery from Roseires led a patrol from

[8] See Gwynn, 1903.

Surkum through Wadega and Funka to the White Nile in March and April 1904, shortly after the battle of Jerok. His comments on the Jum Jum near Wadega were probably just as relevant to the people in Uduk country:

On my first visit here on January 20th with Smith Bey these people were rather shy, but this time they came down bringing eggs, merisa, and honey, and were delighted at the capture of Ibrahim Mahmud, by whom they have been terribly harassed. In fact, although there are about 40 men, there are only six or seven women. There is also hardly a sheep or goat left . . .[9]

Shortage of women, and of children, appears to have been general in the region at this time; in Funka, the same writer tells us there were sixty men and four women.

In early 1906 Kaimakam G. S. Nickerson Bey led a patrol through the Burun region, and submitted a report in May 1906 on 'Dar Fung and Burun country'.[10] This unpublished report contains valuable comments concerning local sheikhs of the time, as well as notes on peoples, communications, and so on. It seems as though the central Uduk area was still only sparsely settled. Nickerson mentions, for instance, tobacco being grown in the Tabi Hills (Ingessana) and in large quantities on the Khor Yabus; but he does not mention any on the Khor Tombak, although the name of this Khor ('Tobacco River') is known to him. This suggests that the Khor was not yet fully resettled and under cultivation. He notes a large number of repatriated slaves living on the Yabus; these are probably mainly Meban, but may include some Uduk. He visited the village now known as Chali (Jalei in his report), the modern focus of Uduk country, as well as Beni Mayu and other places undoubtedly inhabited by Uduk people. Nickerson defines the boundaries of the Burun 'and their sub-tribes' as being a line from Jebel Ulu to Jebel Kurmuk; Jebel Kurmuk to Jebel Barfa and then due south to the Khor Yabus; along this Khor, including both banks and round to Ulu again. The area defined includes most of the present country of the Hill Burun, Jum Jum, Uduk, and Meban. Nickerson also heard reports of more Burun living two days' march to the south of the Yabus but did not investigate as he had no camels and the

[9] S.I.R. 120, July 1904, p. 4.
[10] Nickerson, 1906; MS in Central Archives, Khartoum.

country was waterless. Nickerson realized he was dealing with several different groups, for he writes of 'sub-tribes', and notes the existence of the Uduk, probably for the first time in the official record, describing the 'Uddug' as a branch of the Burun. However, he considers, 'All the Buruns as far south as and including the left bank of the Yabus are one unit. There are no geographical divisions and if they were divided between Sennar and Upper White Nile Province the line would be quite arbitrary and would be very troublesome to administer' (the provincial boundary was in fact later drawn through the region). Nickerson mentions that 'On the plain between Khor Tombak and Khor Yabus there are small villages of 10 to 20 men dotted about five miles apart.' The size of each village was roughly the same as it is today, but today they are scattered more thickly. Nickerson notes that the Burun sheikhs have little power, and mentions a certain Faragalla as being the biggest sheikh of the region; he was himself a freed slave, and apparently lived near Jebel Tombak. Of the Burun in general, Nickerson tells us:

The family is the unit more than the tribe, many villages consist entirely of blood relatives, and in the bigger villages families live together. Each village has a sheikh, his power depends entirely on himself, and his strength and intelligence. There is no Sheikh who really rules a large District, some . . . have much influence but merely because everyone can see they are cleverer than the others and stronger and not because of a sort of recognised kingship . . .

They are very communistic in their habits and leave their dura in the forest, their pipes, spears etc. lying about . . .

As far as I saw the individual has great freedom, no one hesitated to express his opinion in public.

Their women are free to marry whom they will . . .

Owing to raids by Ibrahim Mahmud and the Gallas the men outnumber the women . . .

Villages are small at present. People say that the villages used to be large but during the raids they lived in the forest in twos and threes and many people were captured.

The lack of political organization and of powerful sheikhs is hardly surprising in view of the previous disturbances. Nickerson's comments confirm again the excess of men over women, and the point will be discussed below. This, and the point about living in the forest, have become key themes in oral tradition too.

The people living to the south of the Yabus, even including those south of the Daga, were also known as 'Burun' in the early days. The following observations, assembled in 1927 from reports of an earlier date,[11] concern these people (probably Komo and Ganza) but the conditions described were almost certainly common throughout the region in the early part of the century:

Starting from the North, there are two small villages on the Yabus and ten villages on the Khor Daga. Among these villages are an ever increasing number of refugees from Abyssinia, mostly runaway slaves. Quite a number come from Sheikh Khogali . . .

Among the Barun the number of men greatly exceeds that of the women, owing to the fact that when raided by the Abyssinians (who attack at dawn) the women were easier to catch than the men, who invariably fled into the forest without attempting to offer the slightest resistance. The shortage of women is responsible for such disputes as there are, and it is no unusual thing to find a woman who has been allowed to live with three husbands. So long as a man's wife bears him three or four children he does not seem to worry much if she goes off with someone else . . .

The villages of the Barun are completely separate units. In the past when after raiding one village the Abyssinians used to take guides from it for their attack on the next village, bitter ill feeling arose between villages; this ill-feeling is not likely to disappear during the lifetime of the present generation. It is, therefore, improbable that any attempt to group villages under paramount chiefs would meet with any measure of success. The chiefs as a whole are of little consequence . . .

Dr Pirrie, who was the earliest scholarly traveller to Burun country, in 1907, and who died of illness contracted there, left the following notes on the condition of the people:

Except the northerly part of the tribe, the Buruns are sheikhless. They have not recovered from the effects of the raiding. There is not a head of cattle in the whole country, and their goats and sheep are of the poorest. They have few women, they are overrun with syphilis, and they offer poor resistance to disease. I passed through two epidemics of smallpox, which more than decimated them . . . The Buruns are addicted to merissa. There is a system of merissa meetings

---

[11] From 'Reports on Eastern Frontier District, U.N. Province', 1927; neither authors nor dates are given for the sources used in this report. Central Records Office, Khartoum, Dakhlia I, 112/17/102.

in neighbouring villages, by means of which each man attends about three in a week. Fighting is common at these orgies, the poisoned arrow being the usual implement employed. I consider that the lack of women has largely to do with their addiction to drink, facilitated by the superabundance of their grain.[12]

The general picture which emerges for the whole of the 'Burun' of the southern Funj region in the early twentieth century is one of tiny scattered villages, short of women and children and containing many refugees and ex-slaves. Against this, Nickerson's note that repatriated Burun slaves on the Yabus 'act as "missionaries of Government" ' is no surprise.

The wretched conditions of poverty and a shortage of population, especially of women, must have persisted for at least a generation; that is, until the late 1920s. The early observers who visited the Uduk, Pirrie, and Chataway, saw them in this state; and Evans-Pritchard who did not visit Uduk country proper during his survey of the region in 1926 because of sickness, but did travel a few miles south of Wadega writes of the Uduk: 'From what I saw of them they seemed to be a miserable remnant . . .'[13]

After the establishment of peace in the border regions after 1904, there were no more major upheavals for the Uduk. The dealing in slaves, especially across the Ethiopian border, did continue (and of course slavery was not outlawed in Ethiopia until the nineteen-thirties). Because of continued reports of slave dealing in which Sudanese were involved, a special inquiry was held at Kosti in 1927, with A. J. Arkell in charge, into the situation.[14] Scores of cases, going back to the early days of the Condominium administration, were investigated. The Kosti inquiry ended most of the slave-dealing activities on the Sudan side of the border, although isolated incidents continued. During the Second World War there was a good deal of military activity along the Sudan-Ethiopian border, and the work of the Sudan Interior Mission started at Chali in 1938 was interrupted. Older people among the Uduk remember the war—the 'Italian

---

[12] Dr Pirrie's notes are quoted in Waterston, 1908, esp. p. 328.

[13] Evans-Pritchard, MS version of 1932 article; Central Records Office, Dakhlia I, 112/17/102.

[14] Arkell, 1928. Notes of the cases investigated are now in the library of S.O.A.S.

aggression'—and describe troops, armoured vehicles and trenches. East African troops of the King's African Rifles were active in the Kurmuk area, and I have met one or two Uduk men called Jambo—the Swahili greeting, and a name dating from this period. But the Uduk were not directly affected by the military situation.

It was shortly after the war, in 1953, that the Uduk and 'Koma' areas were transferred from the Upper Nile Province, in which they were remotely administered from Renk on the White Nile, to the Blue Nile Province, for the greater convenience of administration from Kurmuk. The consequent southern extension of the Province was something of an anomaly; the Uduk area had been developed along the same lines as the southern rather than the northern Sudan, and the mission presence, for example, was already well established before the transfer to the Blue Nile Province. Mission activity had never been allowed in comparable parts of the Blue Nile Province, for example in the Ingessana Hills. At the time of the transfer, it was debated whether the Uduk (and the 'Koma') should have separate administrative boundaries and hierarchies of their own, forming separate *omodiyas* as tribal units, or whether they should be administered from Ora, a Berta/Arabic-speaking merchant village, where northern Sudanese sheikhs from immigrant families would be responsible for them. The decision was made to give them separate *omodiyas*, each under an *omda* and several sheikhs, and thus theoretical parity of status with their former oppressors within the Kurmuk district. This protection and administrative development of a relatively unsophisticated people was in line with the general 'indirect rule' policy of the Sudan government of the day. A few government-appointed chiefs had been created among the Uduk previously (more than one having been appointed as a result of his knowledge of Arabic and official procedures acquired through long years in prison). But by 1966 the Omda of the Uduk, living at Chali, was responsible for sixteen subordinate sheikhs selected from the population—by now about 10,000—of the three valleys where the Uduk were settled. Uduk interests could now in theory be represented in a wider political framework: some appointed and some elected members were sent to the district council in Kurmuk, and a number of Uduk even participated in national elections in the 1960s. With local government reorganization in 1970, a new system of wholly elected councils was inaugurated.

As I have already suggested, the civil war which followed the independence of the Sudan in 1956 led to economic and political stagnation in the whole Kurmuk area; among the Uduk, in particular, mission activity was virtually closed down by 1964, and little replaced the educational and medical services which the mission had provided. I understand that new development has been initiated locally since peace in the South was achieved by agreement in 1972. But during the war, although there was no major rebel or military activity in the Kurmuk district, some of the old apprehensions of insecurity returned, perhaps particularly among the Uduk people.

UDUK MEMORIES AND TRADITIONS

The events of the turn of the century, from the Uduk point of view, centre upon themselves. After having survived the earlier pressures of the Nuer and the Galla, of which there is today little detailed recollection, they see themselves in their new homeland as the chief victims of the ruthless 'Bunyan', led by 'Kujul' (Khogali Hassan), 'Hamid', and 'Burhen' (Ibrahim Mahmud), who attacked them and some of their neighbours viciously and repeatedly, until they had to surrender or flee from their homeland; and it was only when some of their own people led by the now famous figure of Abu Magoud from the Tombak valley went to call in the Turuk to help, that the Bunyan were defeated, peace restored, and the people could return to their home area. The Bunyan raiding has become a standardized legend, known to everyone through story and song. The period has become a standard reference point in discussing the history of individual people and birth-groups. In collecting genealogies, for example, I found that informants could never give me names of their forebears more than three generations back from the present adult generation. When trying to pursue genealogies further back than this, or trying to find brothers and sisters of people named in that generation, I would often be told that everyone was fighting the Bunyan in those days and lost touch with their relatives; or that so-and-so had brothers and sisters, but they were all killed or taken away by the Bunyan, and are now lost and forgotten. The loss of women at this time, which was greater than the loss of men, was a crucial cause of discontinuity, as Uduk trace their genealogies through women—and have done so as far back as they themselves can remember. The reduction and scattering of the female population at the turn of the century helps to account for the foreshortened genealogies and patchy pattern of birth-groups today. Present genealogies, in fact, begin about the time of the period of destruction, and I have been able to pursue none further back. Shallow genealogies may perhaps be expected in a dispersed matrilineal society; but their foreshortening coincides with that of birth-group histories, on the whole, and general historical memories. The origin of many small birth-groups is attributed to this period, when lost girls, *çiŋkina/*, were rescued from the bush, and some small birth-groups bear the names of places to which people fled at the time of disturbance (for example, Jerok, Ulu). Uduk tradition thus represents the upheaval as a major break in the continuity of their own society, attributing many features of the present to that period and its consequences. The historical imagination of the people is centred upon this destructive period and their own narrow survival. And of course in a longer perspective it was not the first crisis of this kind that they have experienced: their images of history are proving no doubt quite durable, as the crises to which they refer succeed one another.

The imaginative focus of traditions as they describe the destruction of the homeland, now some three or four generations ago, is upon the way in which *just a few* managed to escape the dangers of loss of home and fields, of living in the wild and 'running about in the bush like antelopes'.[15] The bases of home life were lost—people were rained on at night, had to eat wild roots, had no fire, lost their friends and kinsfolk. Many died, or were captured, and some children were abandoned in flight. But in the end a few managed to find refuge and eventually

---

[15] The image of people being reduced to the condition of *antelopes* recurs in the historical texts and elsewhere in this book, and requires a brief comment here although I hope to discuss it in detail elsewhere. There is a tradition that people evolved physically from the hoofed creatures in the very early days, and that there is therefore still a basic kinship between humankind and the hoofed animals, both wild and domestic. To be like the antelopes therefore suggests a reversion to a pre-civilized, even pre-human, condition.

return home; after the wreckage a few could begin community
life anew, and thus the people as a whole 'managed to remain
alive'. These themes recur in informants' accounts of this period
of disaster, and knit their memories into a cohesive tradition.

Ngau, a middle-aged and quietly thoughtful bachelor of
Waka'cesh in the Tombak valley, often talked of the past, and
sang old songs. His account of the disturbances, from which I
first quote, is not first-hand, but reflects common knowledge and
general feeling on the question today.[16] Those factual details
which can be checked against official records of these events
(for example, Ibrahim's escape and recapture) are quite accurate. The emphasis throughout is on the destruction of settled
village life, and the necessity to live in the bush on wild foods and
so forth.

Ngau: The people who used to fight us lived over there [pointing
east], Kujul [Khogali Hassan] led them, and his wife called
Amna. They raided people until they were captured by the
Turuk. Then they disappeared.

As Wad Ragab[17] came from there [pointing north], he
seized clothes and tore them in pieces—*puw*!—saying, you are
wearing the clothes of my father. For Wad Ragab has a
mother from the Turuk.[18]

People fled, all of them. Kujul attacked all the people, and
scattered them completely. Burhen [Ibrahim Mahmud] then
took the place of Kujul. People fled, all over the whole homeland. The disturbances went as far as Meban country there.
People were running about over there. It was Kujul's aim to
kill all the people just by himself alone, together with Burhen.
The whole population of Pam'Be was attacked by Kujul, and
all chased over there.

W.J.: Where is place they ran to?

Ngau: People fled and lived in the middle of the forest, right there
[pointing]. Don't you know those big cooking stones still lying
in the red soil land there? Those stones were just for cooking
wild roots because people were on the run and used to sleep
with the heavy rain falling on them like that.

---

[16] In this text, paragraphs 6 and 7 came first in the original, but have been
placed later in order to put the story more or less in chronological order (the
speaker was prompted from time to time).

[17] This refers to Sheikh Idris Wad Ragab of Gule, who according to this account
actively aided the Government forces, tearing clothes off the supporters of Ibrahim.

[18] This represents a claim to kinship between Sheikh Idris and the Turuk.

The people of Bellila [the Ahmar valley] fled too. The people of this area also went as far as Ulu.[19] The people of Pam'Be fled to Ulu. The people of Chali also ran, it is said, to Bade. The people of Gindi went to their own village at Bade. The people of Beni Mayu divided up; some took the way to Ulu and others split off and went to Bade, all of them. The Borfa people went to Bade also. The Belatoma [Yabus] people too, they ran about in their own area. They ran about in their home area.

Abu Magoud went from Ulu because the people were being chased by Burhen. Abu Magoud took the road to the English Turuk there. He went and gathered together all the people of Wad Ragab's place, all of them. Then he came and found the Uduk people at the home of Bade,[20] near Ulu. Then he went, and they defeated Burhen there at Jerok. Burhen was coming from an attack on the Meban people. Burhen was raiding the Meban people over there, and he came with his band of followers and went up the mountain. He went up the mountain with a small band of followers.

Then there came a certain Turuk called Mis-Mis.[21] Mis-Mis was of the English people from over there.

And since then, people have lived in their home areas. They give birth to children and have filled the country now. Abu Magoud led the people home.[22]

Then Burhen ran away. He ran on, and on, as far as a great country of which there are many over there. Mis-Mis followed him, went and captured him there. He followed him and captured him; he came tied up to the great tail of a horse. He was dragged at the back of a big horse, an enormous one. He was brought back, dragged, dragged, came and was made

[19] Ngau is referring to his own village, Waka'cesh in Pam'Be. All the other localities mentioned in this paragraph from which people fled are in Uduk country.

[20] At Ulu, there was a certain Sheikh Bade; his village should not be confused with Bade near Kirin. 'Bade' is a common name in the Funj region.

[21] In his recently published memoirs, Sir James Robertson mentions a policeman with whom he went crocodile-shooting upstream from Roseires, during his service at Roseires in 1930–3. This policeman was called Mismeith. It seems extremely likely that this name is a mispronunciation of 'Smith' or 'Mr Smith'. The most probable original is Kaimakam N. M. Smyth, V.C., who was stationed at Roseires from September 1898, for several years, though another candidate is Kaimakam G. de H. Smith, who accompanied Gorringe's patrol to Jebel Kurmuk in 1904. Robertson's policeman might well have been an escaped or freed slave from the early period of occupation, and therefore named after an English officer; and the Uduk Mis-Mis is almost certainly the same name. (See Robertson, 1974, p. 59).

[22] This paragraph is a reflective aside.

to thresh grain, a pile of grain as high as the top of that roof.
He, together with that big fellow Yukur—Basha—the two of
them threshed the grain together. A great pile of grain like
that roof—all of it. Burhen was tied by the other behind a
horse. That was Burhen.

Ah! How many years did people stay away? It was Abu
Magoud who led people back and prepared people to settle
down at home. People then stayed at home; for they had
moved from here to fill up the Ulu area, full, full, full. People
had many years there, they say. They had many tens of years!
They stayed and cultivated things, including *kala* grain [a
sorghum]. People came home because Burhen was defeated by
the Turuk.

And that is the story.

My second text is also a generalized account of the disturbances, in the sense that it was given by a middle-aged man,
Thuga of Kalagorko, also in the central Uduk area, who was
not an eyewitness to the events. His account, therefore, can also
be regarded as distilling the essential character of the period, as
seen by the succeeding generation of people.

Thuga: In the past, people did not live a settled life at home. People
were chased by the Bunyan. They were chased by Burhen
and killed, killed, killed . . . People were just running about.
People were just running in the bush like antelopes, on and
on, on and on like that, running about in the bush. Meals
were never eaten at all. People were eating wild things in the
forest. They only had wild roots which they dug up to eat.

And after many years, people were frightened, and they
went to Burhen and surrendered to him at his home in Jerok.
Then he cared for people there. But those people who
remained behind, he came from his place there and attacked
them again. Some people fled to Ulu. Then others went to
Burhen; and when Burhen saw that there were no longer any
Uduk people in the villages, he stopped his business of killing,
and he looked after people in his country, Jerok, in peace.
People spent years and years and they cultivated there.

After that the Turuk came from over there [pointing
north]. The Turuk came from there, came, came . . . One
Turuk came and found Burhen. He dressed in a ragged
garment and went to Burhen, and said to Burhen, 'Oh, my
children are hungry. I want to buy some grain, to take to my
children to help them. I am very poor'. And Burhen gave him

grain. And the Turuk deceived him, and said, 'I heard a rumour that the Turuk will come for you and kill you'. Then he abused the Turuk. Burhen himself abused the Turuk and said '. . . [a coarse Arabic expression]. Let him come. I will seize him with my hands and he will pound the coffee for me. How strong is he?'

W.J.:   What was the name of the Turuk?

Thuga: The Turuk was called Mis-Mis, Mis-Mis. He came, then returned with the grain, and went and waited three days. Then he arrived with a group and found that Wad Mahmud had gone from Gwarayo to make war there in Meban country. He waited for him there in Gwarayo for a long time. Then he [Ibrahim] came home from Meban country and found that Mis-Mis was already in his village at Jerok waiting for him. He was informed by others as they were coming. Burhen began to blow the bugles[23] from there up to his home. The Turuk were just watching him, gazing at him as he played the bugle. He came and climbed the mountain to his house. Then he slept.

In the morning the following day, the Turuk got up and fought, fought, fought . . . throughout the next night. Burhen ran away from the other into the mountains over there, to the place called Koshol, a mountain in Ethiopia. Burhen escaped in the night, right away. In the mountains there, there was no more shooting, *pew, pew, pew* . . . no sounds of the guns, all was quiet.

And he, the Turuk, followed him. They were following his footprints, *tukh, tukh, tukh, tukh, tukh* . . . right to Ethiopia in the mountains, where they found some Ethiopians. They asked the Ethiopians, and said 'Tell us about Burhen. Burhen escaped and he fled here. Where is he? He is around here; we followed his footprints.'

Some Ethiopians said they didn't know. The Turuk said to them, 'Are you unwilling? If you deny him and hide him from us, all of you will be destroyed completely.'

One Ethiopian said, 'No, I have seen the man over there in that mountain. You go over to that mountain'.

They went, and went, and found him. They found Burhen and caught him, *'ce'b*. Some Turuk were about to cut his throat. But others said, 'No, don't slaughter him. His name is very famous. Let us take him away. Let us take him home.'

---

[23] I am not sure what instruments were used; the Uduk word in the original means reed pipes.

Then they seized Burhen and they came and stayed for some time, stayed and stayed. They looked after all the people there [presumably at Gwarayo, near Jerok]. And as he [Mis-Mis] was going away, he told the Uduk: 'Arise, arise, get up and go back to your homeland.'

Then all the people came from there to their homes here. Those from Ulu came back too, and everyone met here in the homeland.

Mis-Mis caught Burhen and took him away down there [pointing north] and they killed him there. And then people lived in peace at last, because of the Turuk. People lived quietly from then, up to the present time. There was no running about. The Turuk looked after people very firmly. People could settle down in their homeland.

Thuga's parents themselves had been in Gwarayo, but he himself was still a babe in arms at the time. His account tallies in many respects with the official story; but the incident of the Turuk leader Mis-Mis dressing as a beggar in order to spy on Ibrahim does not appear in the official records. The incident is strongly reminiscent in manner of Uduk folk-tales, which often centre on a wily character such as the fox outwitting the strong but stupid characters such as the hyena and elephant. It is possible that the Government patrol of 1904 did send a spy to find out what the situation was at Jerok before they attacked it, but it is hardly likely that Smith, or any British officer would take on this job himself. The whole campaign of the Government is centred in Uduk eyes on the figure of Mis-Mis; and however much truth the spy story may have, it reflects Uduk admiration of the clever, wily nature of the Turuk leader.

The account is also valuable in that it indicates that the Uduk community at Gwarayo, near Jerok, was composed largely of people who had surrendered, and who were working for Ibrahim Mahmud by growing grain. It was obviously preferable to grow grain in peace than to be slaughtered in the bush; and it seems that the news of the peaceful havens of Gwarayo and Bade, where there was a similar community in Hamid's country near his residence at Kirin, reached many fugitives in the bush.

The next account I am going to quote is by a man who remembered the period in question personally. He is Rusa of

Beni Mayu, and if we believe his statement that he married at Bade, near Kirin, where he went with others to surrender to Hamid Hassan, the deputy of Khogali Hassan, he must have been at least 75–80 years old in 1966 when my friend William Danga and I talked with him. The community at Bade apparently started with a nucleus of captured men, who were required to grow grain and sometimes serve as soldiers for Sheikh Hamid. Since it was relatively safe to join this 'serf' community, many people went to surrender to Hamid when life in the free villages became intolerable. It also appears that certain individuals were actually leading groups of Uduk to Sheikh Hamid; one might guess that he and Ibrahim Mahmud had a network of paid collaborators who would collect up people for voluntary surrender. Bade and Gwarayo appear to have been communities of the same type, cultivating and fighting for Hamid and Ibrahim respectively. Ulu on the other hand seems to have been a free community of refugees.

Rusa: The people of those mountains chased us up to Bade. That Kubur[24]—you can forget him. These are the ones who finished off the people[25]—by killing them with guns, *dip*, *dip*. Kubur did not come to kill people with guns; he just frightened people. But these others finished off the people with guns, including our mothers. Heh. Our mothers were finished off by the people from over there. Did Kubur take anyone away there?[26] The people who finished our mothers are from there [pointing east]. Some of them would have lived until now. Were they taken when they were old? No—they were all girls. Kubur went empty-handed: but these are the ones who finished the people in the heart [lit. 'stomach'] of the mountains there.

William Danga: Did you run away from your house?

Rusa: Agi! Were people not running from death? People were running from death. If people had stayed in their huts, would they be alive? Would they not have killed all the people? Heh. People ran away, and that is why you see people alive now. Because they fled. If we had stayed in one place, they would have finished everyone. People were running like ante-

[24] Kubur, or Kubri, appears to have attacked the Uduk some time before the main raids of the border chiefdoms. He is supposed to have taken the people's cattle, and may have been an Ansar leader.

[25] i.e. Kujul, Ibrahim and Hamid.

[26] The form of the question implies that he did not.

lopes. Heh. We ran in the bush, and we threw little children
down in the bush. Young babies, small like this [indicating].
They cried, the cry of *çiŋkina/* in the bush,[27] while their
mothers ran away.

W.D.: What did you eat in the bush?

Rusa: We were running from the Bunyan. What could we eat?
People were hungry. All the food was left at home.

W.D.: How many days did you stay in the bush?

Rusa: How many days? People were running. They cut *'ba'th* wood
for shelter, until the rain fell and quenched people's fires.
People were seized with the cold. Heh . . . We were just
dodging about in the bush, in the bush like that. While some
men went off to look out for them. 'Here they are coming!'
Then we would pull away the women and dodge this way,
dodge that way . . . We just went to their country there . . .
That is why people are alive today. If people had remained
around their homes, they would not be alive today. Would he
not have finished people? People just went there, in spite of
the danger of death.[28] Yes. They seized people. Then people
built houses there. Then he took all the people, and went and
fought the Meban. This was when we had already settled
down. He collected a lot of Uduk to take there, to fight the
Meban. At this time people were planting dura. We produced
a lot of grain. He led people to fight in Meban country,
leaving the women behind. It was the Bunyan who led everybody there . . .

Rusa went on to explain that there was a large area for cultivation at Bade, and that people had to pour their grain into a
big grain store at the village of Hamid, nearby. They were not
disturbed by raids in Bade. He reflected again on the period of
the raiding, saying that Hamid used to go down the Yabus river
to Meban country, and that Kujul and the fellow from Gwarayo
(Ibrahim) would go through Chali, down the Khor Tombak to
Meban country, where they would all meet up.

'Hamid fought people as far as Ulu, when the Uduk were still at home.
People were running about, and when he came back [from Ulu] he
caught some people on the way and took them home. As he was
coming from there, he seized people; this was before people went to

---

[27] *Çiŋkina/* are homeless, lost people without kin, or slaves, or bereaved people; a
detailed account follows below.

[28] Rusa is referring to Bade, in Bunyan country; and the pronoun 'he' in this
paragraph refers to Hamid Hassan.

him there [to Bade]. Heh. Later, people surrendered to him. That is why people are alive today . . . If people hadn't got up and gone [to him], would they be alive? We should all be destroyed. This young Gwarayo fellow was the one killing people with guns. Killed some people, *dup, dup*. Yes! Those people there, were they not shot with guns? Co Dhanyka's brother was killed, in the place where we grow maize. He went and died on the other side of the river . . .

'Many of my sisters were taken. Taken by the people of the mountains. Not a single man was taken [i.e. from Rusa's family], just the women. Not a single man. Only the women were captured by them.'

The last point about the capturing of women rather than men tallies with the reports discussed above; I have already indicated its particular significance for the Uduk as they trace their genealogical connections through women. I will quote one last paragraph from Rusa, concerning an incident when apparently the raiders came off worse than their quarry, which gives a good general picture of the raiding period:

'We were once attacked at Jebel Borfa, while people were sitting together in one place, as we are now sitting, on a muddy day. Then mules came, *thu'b, thu'b, thu'b*. People thought the wind was blowing, because the mules were going *tukutukutukutuku* . . . People said, "What's making that noise?"—while the Bunyan surrounded everyone. People were just escaping like antelopes—*buw, buw, buw*.[29] My father's people resisted the Bunyan and shot some with arrows—*dam, dam, dam*. They escaped; they were not killed that time . . . The Bunyan were the ones who were killed, because our people didn't separate brother from brother.'

Rusa also gave an account of the arrival of Idris Wad Ragab (of Gule) and the Turuk, to fight Ibrahim at Jerok, after which everyone could go home in safety.

Another old man, Jahalla (also of Beni Mayu), told the story of his experiences when he was a boy and was forcibly taken to Bunyan country to work for Kujul. It is not clear exactly where he was taken, but it may have been Asosa. I do not have a verbatim record of this material; notes were made with the help of Shadrach Peyko Dhunya, in April 1967. Jahalla then was probably over 75 years old. After giving us some information on

[29] The analogy here is with a large-scale hunt, in which men will surround an area of forest and gradually close in; the animals attempt to leap out of the circle, the ideophone *buw*! expressing their bounding movement.

the period before the severe raids he tells us that people were then raided by Kujul and Ibrahim. They were again 'running about in the bush like antelopes'. Many escaped, to Ulu, Bade, Mufu (Jebel Mufwa), and some went to a place beyond the mountains, the home of Mahmud. People in Belatoma (the southern Uduk) remained at home.

Jahalla himself, a small boy at this time, the size at which children carry babies, was caught by a man with a gun. He was beaten and taken to join others in a thorn stockade, at a place called the Fig Tree of Binna (near Beni Mayu). The people there included Meban, and women and girls. There were three Uduk women. Jahalla made a hole in the enclosure and got out. He got his little brother out too by pulling him on a rope. They ran away to their village, farther downstream. Many people were killed by Kujul and Ibrahim.

Many people were so frightened that they went by themselves to Kujul's place, to surrender. Jahalla was among those who went to Kujul's place, together with his small brother. They were kept there. People built houses. It was a very big village, including some Meban. The Meban were taken to Ethiopia. The people worked for Kujul for many years, carrying wood, cultivating grain which was poured into grain stores for Kujul. Jahalla himself didn't work—he was too young. They stayed there until the Turuk came.

Suddenly the Turuk appeared, from Gule, to help people because they were being killed and taken as slaves, said Jahalla. The Turuk told people to go to the old places where they used to live. They fought with Ibrahim, who ran to Kujul. After the fight, people went home. Jahalla came back to Beni Mayu. After the Turuk victory there was no more trouble.

I have a number of other eyewitnesses' as well as second-hand accounts of the period of the raids; but in character they are very similar to those already quoted. I will quote from only one more account, which is of especial interest since it concerns events in Belatoma, the southern Uduk area, in the valley of the Yabus river and the mountains to the south. Informants were generally agreed that the southern Uduk did not vacate their homeland, as the northern Uduk did. The following story, told by Losko who grew up in the Belatoma region, and who was 80–5 years old when we talked with him in 1967, explains why:

'Yes, we fought with the Bunyan . . . Ay, Ooooh! That great gathering in Jebel Bisho[30]—that big mountain is where people gathered, while I was there in the Bisho region. It was because of Kujul. Huh. They surrounded the mountain by making a thorn fence. From the top of the mountain people were jumping down like gazelles, from right up there: *puur-thuku'b! puur-thuk'b!*[31]—in order to stay alive; and that place we call today the home of the Bisho people.

'The Bisho people were all dealt with by the Bunyan. They all fled up the mountain, everyone. They ambushed the path. Their elbows were tired from throwing spears, as they sat by the entrance [to the thorn enclosure]; meanwhile, others were rolling rocks down. The rocks killed the Bunyan, *nuru'd.*[32] Others were struck by spears, *pup, pup.* The dead were lying all around, all over the place. Some killed by rocks and toothed spears were piled up on top of each other like this [indicating a great pile] on the path. Because the path was like this [i.e. very narrow and enclosed]. People were lying in wait and spearing them, *pup, pup.* Up comes another—he's hit, *pup.*'

'And then the spears they were carrying were all used up, finished.

'Up in the mountain, they were chewing the bark of the baobab, in Bisho mountain there. The baobab bark was chewed, until it was finished up by the people, because they were prevented from going to get water. People were prevented from getting water. They had climbed up the mountain, and they were thirsty, so they were chopping off the baobab bark for water. How wretched they were to have to chop baobab bark for water . . .

'Then the Bunyan came up the mountain. People went into the caves. I myself was in a cave. The caves were full up to the entrance. The mountain was full of people.

'The ones in the caves survived; others were captured—everyone was captured from the mountain, everyone. Those of the caves remained in the caves while others opened a way through [the thorn stockade below] and were all scattered, scattered.

'And I was there. Huh. It was when I had grown up.

'Water was carried like this, over the shoulder on each side.[33]

---

[30] See the sketch-map in Figure 2. The whole of the southern Uduk region is known as the Bisho region to the Uduk, and as Belatoma to Arabic speakers.

[31] This suggests the bounding movement of gazelles, their hoofs punctuating the leaps downhill.

[32] An ideophone suggesting the crushing roll of heavy rocks.

[33] The beseiged people had to risk fetching water from below by night. Women normally fetch water, of course, but at this time it was so dangerous that men had to go. The water was carried in skin bags, one suspended at each end of a stick carried horizontally across the shoulders.

Brought, brought at night until the cock-crow. *Gala, gala, gala, gala*[34]
—water was brought by men as well. The Bunyan would shout
"Stop!" . . .

'The mountain was completely surrounded. Was this a place
where people could remain alive and call themselves the people of
Bisho? This was not a place where people could survive.

'Those who did survive married girls and they gave birth to children: and these are the people of Bisho.

'Our people were very thoroughly dealt with by the Bunyan.'

Losko gave much more information of value, particularly in
relation to the way in which at least one group of Uduk from
Beni Mayu allied themselves with the hated Bunyan to kill their
own people; and the way in which the Uduk birth-groups, being
broken up and scattered during the disturbances, formed blood
alliances with each other, which persist to this day.

I will conclude with a last quotation from Losko. He had
been describing the disturbances in the central Uduk area:
'Everyone fled, everyone, completely. This land was empty.
Who could stay behind and cultivate? People were running for
their lives. And those who did, are the ones who survived and
returned to marry and build up their villages. That is why you
see villages around you now.'

A few songs survive from the raiding period, and although
people are unable to explain all the references they contain,
enough is remembered for them to carry still a conscious
memory. The call upon Mis Mis to redeem the country clearly
places the following song. The Bunyan with a bent back is
possibly Sheikh Hamid of Kirin; and Belwara is a village near
Kurmuk. I give the lines of which the song is made up; the
singer plays freely upon the lines, combining and recombining
them in his own style. The dialect is that of Bellila, the Ahmar
valley:

> *Hila mornye ma Uja wa*[35]
> *Gu coma Atheya ya wan pa*
> *Ciki kola Ahmed, i Yakuree*
> *Bunycana kemu/ bese/ be ti komakomee*
> *Bunycan ga Belwara*
> *Dhan tapa ti yukka Yakuree*

---

[34] The sound of a line of people quietly slipping along with water skins.

[35] *Wa* here, with some other line endings in *ee, aa* are for rhythmic purposes only
in the context of the song.

Deka, buthi mi ya wana tha[36] *ma*
Butha Mis Misi wan pa
Dhal doru wa ikam 'kon tan jinyciye/

See the castrated goat of Uja
Go with the father of Atheya, go and redeem the country
Listen to the words of Ahmed, you people of Yakur
They speak of a Bunyan, with a bent back
A Bunyan of Belwara
The great leader is called Yakur
Deka, take the goat and change it for a camel
Take [it] for Mis Mis to redeem the country
We let him be beaten in front of his brothers

This song was taught by his grandfather to Joshua Abdalla, who sang it for me; and he sang many more, of which I quote only one, which dates also from the late nineteenth century, according to tradition and internal evidence:

Aa mudha bunycan e gu yol shun, 'kode yee
Jenthuga roçi /e taki shey 'ka me'd waa[37]
Ba sona so 'kup ka Meen Meen pi yi'de/ Pentup
Pa/ kwala kum 'pesh 'kun 'koni cem uma
Mmiga mii ya dotee
Up bunycan wol ko ki thus

I was tricked by foreigners and taken to be sold, in truth!
Jenthuga, stand firm! You with the toothed spear in your
 hand
Let us run towards Meen Meen, and drink water at Pentup
The shoes were stolen by those among you from the central
 hills
I will go and enquire
The Bunyan women wept copiously

MYTH AND IMAGES OF HISTORY

It is against the background experience of this particular historical period of the late nineteenth century that the 'myths' of the Uduk may be understood as presenting, and to some extent transforming, the problems of human survival. They are

---

[36] *Tha* is an 'old word' for the camel, no longer used in ordinary speech.

[37] Jenthuga was a leader of the people; but I could not discover details about him.

not myths of origin, or the foundations of the present secure social order, as so many myths of tribal peoples are supposed to be; nor are they primarily unconsciously structured speculation on matters of logical and abstract import. They carry a conscious set of meanings which are rooted in the idea of survival; they do not claim to explain the ultimate origins of the world or mankind, any more than the people themselves regard their present society as the final production of civilization. Yet myths of the earliest times embody important truths for the Uduk. I frequently heard references to myths in the course of discussion of other matters, sometimes of a historical kind but sometimes of a purely personal nature such as the death of a relative. Reflection on present-day woes, and sickness and death in particular, often prompts allusion to myth; and songs and folktales draw upon myth for their allusive imagery. I came upon many 'myths' in this indirect way, by pursuing allusions which I did not at first understand in another context. It was difficult on the other hand to elicit 'myths' as such, and it is not possible to regard them as a distinct category of oral literature. Together with 'folk tales' and personal anecdotal stories, accounts of what happened in the earliest times are termed *gwololop*, or 'story'; historical accounts are termed *gwoŋ gana*, 'true words', and this is sometimes applied to 'myths' as well. But the stories I have called 'myths', essentially by analogy with other societies where such texts form a coherent corpus, are distinguished by the fact that they are regarded as being very old, and authentic in the sense that these stories were known to earlier generations, and have been passed on, at least partially. They embody truth also in the sense that they represent the creation of society out of a state of fragmentation and chaos which the Uduk consider to have experienced themselves directly, in the disastrous periods of their own history. The same images dominate the mythical emergence of Uduk society as dominate the representation of its loss during the upheavals of the late nineteenth century: people were originally without fire, half the population lived on wild things in the bush and ran about like antelopes, there was no kinship between people, and so forth. In the very emergence of Uduk society they left some of their number behind, and others did not survive at all.

A story I have heard in outline several times, though never in clear circumstantial detail, is of the making of the landscape itself. In contrast to the myths of the Nilotic peoples, which often refer to rivers, and the crossing of rivers in the course of the migrations of the people, Uduk myths refer to hills and mountains. Among the northern Uduk it is often said that the hills came from the lower western country, and moved eastwards to their present position. The tiny rocky mounds which mark the plain are the droppings left behind by the hills in their journey. There is a story of Jebel Chali having once lived closer to Jebel Beni Mayu, but Jebel Chali was chased away, out of the village and across the valley, because of its adultery. In the region to the south of the Yabus, I have heard that the mountains came from the north. Jebel Bisho came from the region of Kurmuk, and all the other hills around it are its children. Sometimes Uduk say that the people came together with the mountains, each little community with its own mountain; and at other times the mountains are spoken of as though they were established long before the people came. There is a story I have heard once or twice of the people arriving in their present homeland after travelling on a long journey from the west, in little groups, a journey on which some perished and were left behind. All known people were on this journey, the Berta travelling ahead of the Uduk, and consequently reaching their hilly home further to the east. The Meban were to the rear of the Uduk, and so are now settled in the lower country to the west. Bukko, an old man of Beni Mayu who had a better store of such tales than anyone else I met, pondered on the possibility that the Turuk were also on this journey; they were probably in the lead, he thought, and showed others the way. If this myth has any historical reference, it is to a period antedating the movement of the Uduk northward from the Daga valley, which is in any case a migration much more precisely described and only just beyond personal memory. The lack of circumstantial detail in the story of people moving eastwards from the lower country towards the mountains does not matter; for the insistent indication, at least among the northern Uduk, of an ancient westerly home may be an older and profoundly significant memory of retreat from the expansion of the Nilotic peoples—the eastward push of the Anuak, Nuer, Meban, northern Dinka and the Niloticization of the Hill Burun peoples must have left a deep impression on the historical memory of all the border peoples, particularly the Koman peoples, who almost certainly were among those comprising the autochthonous and possibly hill-based population of areas to the east of the White Nile before the Nilotic expansion. Their association with the hills, and the 'red soil', is now very strong, in contrast to the association of the Meban, for example, with the swamp and the 'black soil'.

The image of the *çiŋkina/*, so often opposed to that of the *'kwanim pa*, the people of the moral community, must be considered further, before going on to examine more 'myth'. Linked by antithesis to the concept of the *wathim pa*, the Uduk person established in his own homeland, it is one of those connecting ideas which recur by analogy in different contexts of Uduk thought and make it possible to perceive the way they have put together the fragments of their experience into an understandable whole.

A *çiŋkina/* is sometimes said to be *to*, a thing or an animal, rather than a human being, *wathim pa*. The word may mean a waif, a foundling, a lost child rather in the manner of the 'babes in the wood' or the lost children of the European forests, without home or kin and without much hope of solitary survival. The primary reference is to lost persons of history and legend, wandering in the bush without clothes or food. Those who are in a position to offer help to a waif of this kind have an obligation to do so. The action of taking in and protecting a waif in this way is termed *buthi me'd*, to take charge of, literally to hold in the hand. There used to be a series of special ceremonies for adopting a *çiŋkina/*, which involved among other things presenting the girl waif with a cotton belt, *mantom*, of the type all women wear. I once referred to myself as a *çiŋkina/*, being a stranger on my own and being looked after in Waka'cesh, but I was laughed and shouted down; who had given me a *mantom* to wear? And who had given me things to eat? I was obviously not in need of such patronage! But in Uduk history, many small birth-groups trace their descent, through women, from girl waifs protected and reared in this way. A waif is often married by a man from the protecting birth-group, but no permanent relation of clientage remains. The link between the descendants of such a girl waif and her protectors, termed *abas*, a blood-link, is one of mutual aid and reciprocal defence. Through acquiring affines and kin, and entering relations of mutual support, the former *çiŋkina/* and her descendants are absorbed into the community as *'kwanim pa*. In memories of the disturbances at the turn of the century, when many people were literally lost, cut off from their kin and fleeing in the bush, the Uduk are insistently represented as reduced once more to *çiŋkina/* of the forest.

In the following account, William Danga explains how households which could afford to maintain refugees in a time of trouble used to hang a special black ant, *'cume*, at their doorway as a sign; and it might be worn later by the *çiŋkina/* around her neck. Danga, a young man of some education who nevertheless had a deep interest in Uduk tradition, remembered playing with a *'cume* ant hung at his mother's doorway when he was a child. The ant is quite large; it has the appearance of a beetle, with a hard shell, and I am told that it lives for a long time without eating or drinking. Its suitability as a sign is clear—it can survive long periods of hardship. 'The *'cume* ant is tied by people at the doorway here. Tied at the doorway as a thing of *çiŋkina/*. As a *çiŋkina/*. People tie it round the neck. The Gurunya people, haven't you seen, have a string tied round the neck? They are kept as *çiŋkina/*.'

Danga is here referring to the women's cult, known by the name Gurunya, designed to save children who might otherwise die; the Gurunya children are themselves *çiŋkina/* and given special care. I describe the cult in a later chapter. Danga continued:

'Then one day a man will come running up, or perhaps a woman, or a little girl, just a child, will come running up. Running wild. "That is a *çiŋkina/*!", they say. The *'kwanim pa* call her, "Ay! A little *çiŋkina/*, oh!" That's what people say. "A little foundling, oh!"

'People catch her and bring her to keep at home, to keep as a foundling in the village. They civilize her [*nyoŋ*, to treat, prepare, groom, put right]. They prepare clothes for her . . . She has no clothes. No clothes at all. She goes quite naked; so they spin cotton, and twist a cotton belt for her, and dress her in it. They dress her in the cotton belt, and then in clothes. They keep her at home, because she ran in from the bush there, like . . . She is a *çiŋkina/* through having run in from the bush there; she has no relatives. She is poor, they say; she has no people [of her own]; that is why she is called a *ciŋkina/*. Her people are nowhere; she ran from the bush out there, and they see she has no control over her behaviour [*ta pus*]. And they put her right, give her clothes to wear, thread a few beads for her to dress herself up, and she stays in the village, eats food, and grows up.

'That is how it is, for people who are protected [*budhu me'd*]. She grows up through eating food there, until she is a beautiful girl, and then somebody will marry her . . . You will marry her.

'She and her children will stay there and become *abas* with those people, from being looked after and protected [*budhu me'd*].'

Danga explained further about the ant: 'Yes, it is to say "welcome", come in. To tell the *ciŋkina/* to come in: this house is very good. If a *ciŋkina/* comes, we will look after her properly, by keeping her here. We will be very happy to take her in and keep her. It was often done by people of old, to call *ciŋkina/* to come in.'

It is pessimistically thought that if it were not for the generosity of a few fortunate communities in saving kinless starving people from the bush in times of trouble, the Uduk people would have died out by now. Nobody, however, likes to be reminded of his own specific origins as a *ciŋkina/*, or to point out others who have this background.

Details of the ways in which particular birth-groups were saved in history are given in a later chapter. This is certainly the most direct and primary use of the concept of the *ciŋkina/*. But there are many other common usages. Those who are lost to the community through being captured by slave-raiders, or surrendering to them; or who have become clients of outsiders, are *ciŋkina/*, and remain so. Those who today leave the Uduk region and enter wage-labour elsewhere, are referred to sometimes as *ciŋkina/*; they are not seen as independent, but as tied to the source of their wages, whereas if they return and once again enter the network of reciprocal working relations of their own village, they regain a relative freedom, as people, within the home community. Even though poorer perhaps in material terms, they have the security of kin and friendship links, built up through the history of their own people, and are not anonymous *ciŋkina/*.

Death and sickness remind the Uduk of their weakness and impotence as *ciŋkina/* in relation to the powers of spirit. At funerals, especially of young children, the cry '*Ciŋkina/*! we are *çiŋkina/*', is heard through the wailing; and those who are bereaved, who 'sit black' for a period after the death in mourning, are *çiŋkina/*, through the loss of their kin.

Of animals in general, dogs in particular are *çiŋkina/*; dogs are dependent on man for their nourishment and life, and are worthless, and helpless, on their own. What they know, they have been taught by men, and men give them names and individuality. If a man on his own is killed in a hunt, he is called a dog, for 'Where are his fellows?' A dog on his own does not naturally form associations with others, in the Uduk view; the community of dogs is created quite deliberately by man, through protection, feeding, and training. The parallel with the bringing in of *çiŋkina/* to form a community is very interesting. The dogs of a hamlet are trained to act together as a team, and not to fight among themselves, by the careful sharing out of food between them all. Nobody feeds his dog on its own. If you have some spare food, you call all the dogs of the hamlet, and throw a chunk of food to each dog in turn, as they sit around in a semi-circle, eager but restrained. Through sharing food in this disciplined way, the dogs will learn not to snatch from each other, and to co-operate in the hunt. The moral is consciously pointed; a community of people, too, can be forged from unconnected individuals through the bonds of sharing, just as the *çiŋkina/* of history is transformed into a kinsman and neighbour. A *çiŋkina/* is not a client, a slave, a waif in any permanent sense; he does not have a fixed status, but is always potentially a full member of the community again, and potentially a person of worth and dignity.

If on the other hand, social life is not kept in being, if householders neglect their neighbours and parents their children, people may regress or return to the state of *çiŋkina/*. There is a story to this effect, of a brother and sister who were maltreated by their father's wife, when their own mother had died; they eventually went off to the bush, where the father found them like *çiŋkina/*, and they refused to come home. They grew tails and became monkeys. The monkeys you see today are descended from them. Bukko, the elderly but sprightly man of Beni Mayu with a lively knowledge of tradition, gave me this version:

Bukko: There were two children, one was a little girl, and the other was a boy. The other was a boy. It was as if I married a certain woman, and the children were left as orphans [*dhipa*, i.e. motherless]. They were kept by the father as orphans with a woman he had newly married, later on, because that mother had died. But that woman continually deceived [*cesh*] the children.

William Danga: By serving food on stones [i.e. mixed with stones in a gourd]?

Bukko: Yes that's how the children ate, scraping the stones for food and throwing them away. Throwing them away all the time. And that man said, 'Ay! Are you giving the children something?' The woman said, 'What do you mean, giving them something; of course the children are given something, the children are always given something'.

W.D.: And didn't he ask the children?

Bukko: He asked the children. The children, they didn't tell him. The children didn't tell him. They waited and told him later when he went to search for them after they had left in anger.

W.D.: They left for the bush?

Bukko: Yes they left for the bush. They stayed for a while, and then climbed up [trees]. They lived up there. He later went to search and found them and said, 'Ay! Please come down. Please come down'. They said, '*Çaah!* Father, we are not going to come down, we have grown tails. We are not coming down when we have grown tails. Your wife ill-treated us. She gave us just stones'. If it were me I would go back and beat her up with stones. 'Are my children becoming *çiŋkina*/ to me?'

The children remained for ever there. They gave birth to those black monkeys, the ones you call black monkeys, but they are really people. And the red type are Arabs.

Uduk mythical stories cannot be arranged in a clear sequence; they do not represent an unfolding development from a unique primal beginning. There is no agreement on a first created thing, or the first man or woman. There are no personal names, and no genealogies connecting the first men with the present. There is no attempt to account for the origin of more powerful and foreign peoples, from whom in the beginnings of their own society, they sometimes received protection, help, and knowledge. Human differentiation seems to have existed before the foundation of their own society; they do not see themselves at the centre of the world and its creation.

Partly because of this acceptance of their relative lack of power and competence, the Uduk do not claim to have final

answers to philosophical or religious matters. Even in relation
to the beginnings of their own society, they claim only partial
understanding. A consciousness of having lost former homelands, former wealth, former companions pervades the general
picture of the remote, as of the recent, past; people frequently
say, 'We know nothing. All the people have died; we are only a
few, only a few children left now'. They may say 'We are all
çiŋkina/. We have lost our fathers, only a few of us remain outside' (meaning 'outside the grave'). These comments are sometimes given in a provocative, even a defiant way—as if the
picture of themselves as weak and ignorant is a sort of cunning
defence, a ploy to deflect enquiry and avoid admitting to any
knowledge, in case it should be taken from them. There is
wisdom in such defensive tactics from their point of view; but it
remains annoyingly difficult to elicit a complete account of any
matter, even apparently straightforward historical traditions.
Those who knew are gone, and have taken their knowledge
with them. The people of today have only partial scraps of
knowledge—which therefore convey little if taken from them!
—just as they see themselves to be scattered remnants of a
larger whole in the past. By surviving only in part they have
preserved what they claim is only a fragmented knowledge of
the world, and of their place in it.

But through the mythical tales of the Uduk, there run a few
coherent central ideas, which in many cases are not confined to
them but represent variations of themes found widely in the
Nile Basin. One of the most insistent themes, which supplies an
answer to questions of the origins of life, of social institutions and
customs, is that of the way in which people have managed to
remain alive, at least a few of them, in spite of disaster, and with
the support, even blessing, of Spirit, *arum*. In a very general
sense, all existence and life derives from *arum*: *arum* created us,
and everything around us; and *arum* may destroy us, or allow
us to be destroyed. When we die, we return to the realm of *arum*
which is located primarily below the world that we know, in the
earth. That is why people often say, 'We know nothing of these
matters; for there are only a few of us left up here now.' In a
sense, though I do not wish to press the implications here, the
Uduk see themselves to be living, and to have survived, not by
their own efforts alone, but 'by the grace of God'.

One of the most widely known tales, often quoted and always mentioned among the northern Uduk when origins are discussed, is that of the Birapinya tree. This great tree reached up to the sky, which in those days was close to the earth. There were villages in the sky, and people used to go and dance up there, using the tree as a route (and some say that the people of the sky in turn would come down to visit the villages on earth). After the tree's destruction by an old woman who considered herself wronged, or in some versions insulted, people were stranded up in the sky, which retreated very far above the earth. Death, which formerly had been followed by revival, then became a final end for humankind. I must mention that there are a host of other stories which I have no space to discuss here, bearing on the same themes. But as the Birapinya is of especial interest in the present context, I quote two versions. The first was given to me by Tente, a shrewd man of about forty, who lived in Waka'cesh and was a continuously invaluable friend and source of new and often surprising information. The vernacular text and a close translation may be found in Appendix 1.

'Many people used to go up from the earth to dance the *barangu*[38] up there. A certain woman built a house near the path and she cooked food on the fire. She called some girls back: "You girls, come and grind some okra for me." And the girls said to her, "Oh no, we will lose our boyfriends to other girls." And again some others came and she said, "You girls, come and grind okra for me." And the girls said to her, "No, we are going to lose our boyfriends to others." And again some more came. She said to them, "You girls, come and grind some okra for me." "No we will lose our boyfriends to others."

'But another was being led behind by her brother and at last the two of them arrived. She said, "You people who've come last, you two come and grind the okra." And they agreed and they went to grind the okra. They cooked the food, the food was soon ready, and they served it out. They ate a meal and washed their hands, and then departed. The woman said to them: "Go on up. But don't stay there very long. Very soon I shall set fire to the Birapinya." They heard her warning, danced a little, and soon returned.

'And the people went on dancing the *barangu* for a very long time. When they had danced enough they came away. They found the

---

[38] The *barangu* is a dance of the old days, performed to gourd flutes. It is remembered by many people, but scarcely danced at all today, having been replaced by other dances.

Birapinya was burnt by her. And then they were asking, saying "Oh, where is our path?" The path was not there, and some suggested, "Let us go. There's a wide path down there. Let us jump down, to that big open, wide place there."

'A great tall fellow straight away jumped first, falling over and over; he broke into pieces which scattered all over the ground. And another followed him and smashed onto the ground with the first. Then another, a very short man, hoisted another tall one on his back and they came down *shuur!* to land upright, *thup!* and to remain alive. Another carried one on his back, and they came down *shuur!* *thup!* and they remained alive. And another came after, he jumped down by himself and broke into pieces.

'And the others remaining, refused to jump, and stayed up there. One said, "No! I'm staying here", and the others heard him, and they stayed up there. There are many still up there.'

Another version, given to me by 'Tima who lives in the Yabus valley, represents the old woman at the foot of the tree as the mother of a girl who is insulted at the dance, and who sides with her daughter against the rest of the people, destroying them by burning the tree. The reason the girl was insulted was that she smelled bad; and this was because she was *arum*, having died, and having then reappeared from the grave, as people used to do in the days before death was a final end. Everyone used to be reborn in this way.

'A woman stopped her daughter as the daughter was on her way to the dance. It was just as children behave these days; children don't hear what their mothers say. She went on up in spite of [her mother], thinking she would follow the others to dance the *barangu* up there.

'The mother stayed there, toasting grain for beer. She sat there, just sat there.

'People said, "What is it smelling like that? What is stinking so badly? What is stinking so badly?" The daughter took offence and left [the dance] crying as she came. She came and found her mother there. Her mother asked, "Why are you crying?" She said "I was with those people when they started criticizing me; people said I stank. Why should those people dance the *barangu*, those nasty people?" She then went.

'The mother was angry. "Is my child going to be insulted like this? What business have people to insult the child? Great fat-arsed louts to insult people up there. My child must not be insulted like this." She was angry and went to bring fire. She acted against those people, right at the foot of the Birapinya, *thi'b*.

'People were preoccupied dancing in a great joyful party there, while the fire was swirling up like a whirlwind from the foot of that tree, *'thek̲*, *'thek̲*.

'People were in for a big shock. They were all enjoying the great dance, on and on, and suddenly it fell *dushur*! to the ground, with a great *bushur*! on the ground there. Then they came to peer out at the great open space, looking and saying "Where is that tree that we climbed up on foot? Where has it gone?" While the tree was split on the ground, *bug*!

'They came down like a swarm of bees, heavy with wet wings, *shuur*! The big tall ones went *k̲ushur* [sound of breaking]. And the little short ones came, jumped from there and landed on their feet, *thi'b*. They came on their feet, *thi'b*! Came on their feet, *thi'b*.

'Some were afraid, and remained up there. Others jumped, and some died. There was no place to remain alive. They jumped and broke into pieces. Others remained up there. There are people still up there now.'

A phrase which recurs in these tales and many others is that 'there was no place to remain alive'; and many are presented as accounts of how people, in the face of impossible situations, in fact managed somehow to remain alive; accounts which therefore explain how it is that the community of the *'kwanim pa* exists at all today.

The story of the dance in the sky, from which only a few returned after the burning of the connecting tree, has many features which recall other stories of former links between sky and earth, especially among the Nilotic peoples. There is in fact a strong likelihood that the story is an adaptation of an imported Nilotic tale. I have tried to find parallel tales among the Komo and the Gumuz, but without success. The Birapinya seems to be found only among the Uduk, of all the Koman peoples—and the Nilotes are probably better known (mainly in the persons of the Meban) to the Uduk than they are to the other Koman groups. The story is particularly well known and accepted among the northern Uduk, although the southerners do know it (the second version above is from a southerner). But Sheikh Puna Marinyje, from the southern Uduk, preferred other stories of the people's origin (for example, that of the *'thikath̲* grass quoted in Chapter 4 below, and the famous story of the coming together of men and women), and told me not to take the Birapinya very seriously; 'That story of the Birapinya appeared for no good reason. It appeared for no good reason . . . It's just a tree.' This suggests to me that it was the northerners who introduced and popularized the tale. Moreover, most informants in the north say the Birapinya existed in what is now Meban country (in a text quoted below, Bu<u>k</u>ko names Pumke, beyond Boing, as the site), and that you can still see the signs of the former burnt patch on the ground. Some refer to the birth-group Bonyaŋgadhe as the 'owners' of the tree. This is a northern Uduk birth-group living close to the Meban border where many people are bilingual and intermarried. It is true that Tente himself told me that the tree used to be at Jebel Bisho, in the south of Uduk country, the mountain from which the northerners maintain they migrated. But this could well be merely the latest modification of a story, originally Meban, in order to accommodate it better into northern Uduk tradition—a tradition which is certainly still in the making. The very name Birapinya is meaningless in the Uduk tongue, and to the Uduk as far as I know. One informant, I believe bilingual, told me it was called thus 'from going up'; but this is one of those questions that I now regret not having pursued more energetically in the field. But after discussion with Nilotic specialists, it now seems to me almost beyond doubt that the name has a Nilotic derivation, and has probably come to the Uduk from the Meban. The phrase *bir piny* means to 'come down' in Nuer, is used of *kwoth*, Spirit, coming down to earth, and has cognate expressions in various Nilotic languages. The coming down of divine powers is sometimes associated with trees; in the Zeraf island, Douglas Johnson tells me that there is a *kwoth* in a tree, known as *mar piny*, 'shake the earth', for when it speaks it shakes the earth like thunder. In an early article by Evans-Pritchard on the Nuer, he writes: 'If rain is very heavy and is accompanied by thunder and lightning a man takes the mallet with which he beats cattle pegs into the ground, and lays it in the doorway of his kraal, and says to God, "*Kwoth bir piny goaa, eghondu*", "God rain well, it is your universe"' (1935, p. 45). I understand that a literal translation of *kwoth bir piny goaa* would be '*Kwoth*, come down well' or '. . . come to earth well'. A similar usage from the Shilluk has been pointed out to me by Walter Kunijwok Gwado in the following song:

Ce ya biä piny, ö	When I come down
Deng piny ko-rëny ɛn.	Deng has spoiled the earth
Ce ya döga mal	When I go back to the sky
Abuk man-Deng döm piny ki riäk	Abuk, the mother of Deng, help the people in this time of disaster

In the first and third lines, it is Deng, or the rain, which is speaking, and the second and fourth lines are the people's replies. The meaning is that when it rains heavily, the people on earth below suffer; and when the rain disappears to the sky, and there is drought, the people on earth suffer too, and must call on the rain again. The Shilluk *biä piny*, when pronounced, sounds very like the Birapinya of the Uduk; and of course the Meban and Shilluk languages are very close. From evidence of this kind, I would guess that it is very likely that the Meban language is the source of the name 'Birapinya', and quite possibly of elements of the tale as told by the Uduk. Unfortunately we know next to nothing of the Meban or their myths and legends. But we can consider briefly some interesting contrasts between the Uduk story and apparently related stories from the Nilotic peoples and their neighbours.

There are many tales in the Nile Basin of the original separation of sky and earth. But these are usually told to account for the primal break between mankind and God. Well-known examples include the Nuer story of the severing of a rope between heaven and earth, thus opening a gulf between men on earth and *kwoth* in the sky;[39] and the Dinka tale of the woman's pestle which struck Divinity on the chin and caused his retreat to the heavens.[40] But the Uduk story is not about the separation of mankind and God. It is primarily about the breaking up of the people themselves. One part of the people is divided from the rest, and though a few make the transition, most are cut off permanently from their former fellows.

Douglas Johnson has pointed out to me that quite a number of versions of the separation story among the Nilotes do involve human movement, but that the emphasis is on people who originated in heaven being kept down on earth. As a result they

[39] See Evans-Pritchard, 1956, p. 10.
[40] Lienhardt, 1961, pp. 33–5. Compare Dr. Lienhardt's treatment of a number of themes in Nilotic myth in his article of 1975.

are unable to return to the sky and are thus obliged to augment communities on the ground. In the Nuer version I have just mentioned, people are prevented from visiting the sky as they used to; and in another version also mentioned in Evans-Pritchard's first book on the Nuer, one Gaawar ancestor, Kar, cut the rope so that another, War, could not return after being enticed down with the smell of roasted meat.[41] In a version collected by Douglas Johnson, Kar actually cuts down a tree to prevent War from returning to the sky.[42] The trapping of ancestors down on earth, so that they are absorbed into the communities on earth, seems to be the main systematic difference between these stories and the Uduk tale of the loss of people from the earth because of the tree's destruction, a loss which left their own communities diminished. The tale which most closely resembles the Uduk one in this respect is not from the politically and culturally expanding northern Nilotic peoples, but is reported by Jean Buxton from the Mandari. After the severing of the rope, most of the people are reported to have remained above in the Mandari Bora clan version of the story, which does not even refer to God (Creator) at all.[43] Other versions do mention Creator, who was separated by the severing of the rope, and now remains above together with a proportion of the people.[44] The human focus of the Mandari stories, and their calling attention to the division of the people themselves at an early stage of their formation, remind us of the Uduk tales. The Mandari are marginal to the more powerful northern Nilotes, and have like the Uduk absorbed and transformed elements of Nilotic culture in the process of reconstructing their own communities after repeated disruption.

The story of the Birapinya then seems to be a case where the northern Uduk have taken over a theme from the body of Nilotic myth, probably from the Meban, and adapted its details to their own political and moral experience. It is certainly characteristic for them to adopt something foreign and to make it their own. In this case, as with the Gurunya rites, which are described and analysed in Chapter 7, they have taken elements of foreign origin and made them into a core representation of themselves, and of their own origins as a divided and disrupted

---

[41] Evans-Pritchard, 1940, p. 230.   [42] Personal information.
[43] Buxton, 1963, pp. 19–20.   [44] Buxton, 1973, p. 23.

people. Disruption and foreign contact is central to their self-image; and it is apt that a tale, or a rite, of foreign origin should become an emblem of their inner incompleteness, the overcoming of which made of them a distinctive people, the *'kwanim pa*. For the Birapinya story also shows how, through co-operation between people with differential characteristics—young and old, brother and sister, tall and short—the community may survive. Beyond the divisions and structural differentiation of place and category in this tale, the moral message of survival through mutual aid seems unmistakable. It is particularly clear, perhaps significantly so, in the version from the northern Uduk I have quoted, where those who survived include the brother and sister who helped the old woman at her grinding-stone when others had refused; and also the people who jumped down in pairs, a tall one on the back of a short one.

The beginning of death, referred to obliquely in the versions of the Birapinya above, is dealt with more explicitly in the story of how, originally, there was no final death; like the moon, people died for only two or three days and reappeared to live again. In a sense there was everlasting life, which we are now denied. It is sometimes said that the continuation of life after 'death' was possible because people were treated with the oil of the moon, or the spittle of the moon, which had this property of ensuring revival. However, in some versions through a quarrel between two similar but contrasted lizards (one rough and one smooth) the gourd of the moon oil was broken, and death became final. The theme of the need for mutual support and the disastrous consequences of a quarrel between what is almost certainly seen as a complementary but brotherly pair of animals, echoes the moral lessons of the Birapinya myth. Bukko's version mentions the two lizards (p. 78). Tente's goes as follows:

'Listen. The moon spat out his spittle for the *wuṭule/*. The lizard was to swallow his spittle, but he refused. And Moon again spat for him. Again he refused. And Moon said to him, "Ay! You are now refusing my spittle, so you are going to stay on earth in a very cold place. And you, if you die on earth there, you will not appear again. You will not appear. You will die for ever and stay for good. And those people who look after you on earth there, will be together with you for ever, they will die with you for ever. They will not appear and see the place outside [the grave]. They will stay for ever. Die for ever, and ever, and ever, always, always, always, and will not appear to see the place.

' "Because I wanted you; if you had swallowed my spittle, you would have returned back up again and we would have lived well for ever; if you were to die, you would reappear. And your people would die, but always reappear as I do.

' "As when I die, I appear outside and they see me. You see me, all of you, and the place is lit up very well. For I do not want darkness to stay for ever there. I want there to be good light. But your action is very bad for me. Perhaps you are angry with me. Perhaps you would like to stay outside yourself alone. Because there are many of you on the earth. Are there not many human beings? They were created by *arum* like this one after another.

' "And that is why I wanted you to catch the spittle from my mouth with your mouth, and you would have helped them well, and kept them outside well. They would have gone as visitors into the earth and then come back, as I do. As I go as a visitor, and come back again. Then they see me, to light the place up brightly." '

'Tima, from the Yabus valley, gave this version:

'These are things of long ago. People used to return to live again. People were cut off there. And again, people spat spittle from up there, it is said. It was given to that bad little lizard. It was given to this little thing, in order for it to swallow the spittle. The lizard then dodged quickly and evaded the other's spittle. He evaded the Moon's spittle by moving aside. He first spat the moon spittle there, and Moon swallowed his spittle, *'kolo'c*. And Moon also spat his spittle and told the other 'Swallow my spittle too.' The lizard immediately dodged the spittle of the other, stepping aside.

'Moon was angry. He was angry, angry; and that is why we die finally for ever, without coming to life again. If it were not for this, we should have died like the dying of the moon, and again appeared.

'He said, "Now you are avoiding my spittle. You will die, even you yourself will die, and you will not re-appear. Your people will stay in the earth in future; in the place you sit here, you will not appear again, at all." He [the moon] alone will reappear. People now die like that on the earth here. A face which is known will not live again. It will die for ever and ever, become dust, and become a great tree again. And then the tree dries up.'

One of the favourite myths told by the Uduk, and one which is well known among neighbouring peoples too, is that of how Dog brought fire to people in the beginning, humanizing them and helping them to establish a proper home life by using fire for clearing the bush round the villages and cooking their food. Here is a straightforward version of the story from Tente:

'People just used to dry their food in the sun, in the years long ago. They just ate sun-dried food. They peeled the hardened crust of food from the pot and filled the bowls, keeping some for the children who looked after goats in the forest. And they would come in the late afternoon and eat food. In the past people had no fire; but then Dog came and said to the people: "How do you cook your food?"

'They said, "Oh, we just dry food in the sun and eat it." Then he said to the people, "You wait here and you will see something. One day I will bring something here for you to see."

'And so they continued to dry their food. And Dog went as far as another place where fire was used. And the other people remembered and said: "Is that the thing of which Dog spoke, that he said he would bring? That must be the thing!" People shouted: "Waaah! What is that bright red thing? Ooh!"

'People ran away at the sight of the bright red stuff on Dog's tail. He took this stuff round all the villages where there were people. Then at last Dog settled in a certain village, made a fire and brought a cooking-pot. He took it and put it on the fire, and said, "This is how you must do it. This is how it is done. It is done like this."

'Then the pot became hot, and he brought a little ground flour and wiped it round the pot. "Wait a moment until the water froths up and then put it all in." The water frothed up and he said, "Bring the dough and pour it in the pot. Do it like this. Pour the dough and bring the paddle."

'Then he stirred it with the paddle, *gudush, gudush, gudush.* At last the food was ready. "Bring the scoop and serve it out." Then they ate the food, and he asked them, "How does it taste in your mouth?" "Oh, it is very delicious. Where did you get this thing from?" And he said to them, "Oh, it is in a very distant place, over there where the sky ends. I brought it from that place far away."

'"Why did you not come long ago to tell people of this thing? You should have brought this thing much sooner: the villages are overgrown with grass." Then he burned the grass for the people. He burned the tall grass from around the huts at last, for the people in all the villages had been living in a forest of grass just like antelopes. At last the villages were clean, because Dog cleaned them up for the people with fire.'

The tales I have so far quoted are well known, and fairly standardized. They may be told without elaboration or comment, and often are, especially perhaps by younger people, for entertainment. But people may reflect on them at length, meditating on the connections that can be made between these mythical tales and the world of experience. Bukko, the elderly man of Beni Mayu, well known for his sharp tongue and memory for tales, opened a world of speculation about the materials of myth and history which illuminated my understanding of both. I shall now present at some length excerpts from conversations with Bukko, in which in fact I played a minor part, but left most of the exchanges to William Danga, who as a younger man was interested in what he had to say. Our aim was to persuade Bukko to give us as many of the stories of the old times as he remembered; but we couldn't stop him switching from retailing 'myths' to giving us his opinions on present-day affairs; nor could we stop him from inserting, quite gratuitously as I first thought, his own extra anecdotes and historical snippets into 'traditional' symbolic folklore. As time went on, and we made further visits to Bukko, it became clear to me that this linking of direct experience and memory with the tales of old was the key to understanding what he was trying to tell us, and that to separate his version of the 'traditional texts' from his personal interpolations would do violence to his wisdom and indeed to the nature of 'tradition'. To convey something of the way which he would switch from a well-known story to a speculative aside, these latter are printed in italics. At the time, I was still trying to sort out the chronological sequence of the various stories, and he quite rightly became annoyed with me for doing so.

He gave the impression of casting about to find satisfactory explanations; and in trying to convey to us what the early days were like, he brought in the origins of language. I had not heard any mention of language from other informants. It was Dog, possibly in his wild form of Fox (*mak*, which may also be translated 'trickster'), who in the beginning helped mankind become physically human and brought him fire. Dog also taught mankind how to speak; at least Bukko assumed he must have done:

'For people were *arum* [spirit] long ago. . . . Did people speak proper language [*'twan gana*]? . . . It was just a wild gabble [*'twan thus*]. . . . Their speech was not the same as the proper language we speak now. No! They spoke just a gibberish, which didn't make sense. . . . People all spoke like that. *And from where was language discovered? Was*

*it acquired at the time when fire was brought by Dog? Perhaps it was acquired
at the time fire was brought by Dog. . . .*

'Yes, [fire] was brought while people were without language . . .
They didn't know it. They were ignorant of the Uduk language.
People spoke just gibberish, *dumpulu, dumpulu* like that. And people
then improved themselves with the Uduk language, when they had
made fire. People then spoke a little real language, while formerly
they had spoken just gibberish. It was just the speech of wild people
['*kwanim bwasho*]. . . . It was the Dog who spoke. The Dog showed us
the way, all the time. . . .

'Yes, they began to give birth properly, and speak proper language;
that is how they knew the word for 'mother's brother' [*shwakam*] at
last.'

The conversation ranged far and wide; and Bukko was never
at a loss for explanatory connections.

Bukko: *You can see the place where the Birapinya was burnt in Meban
country . . . The place of the Birapinya is not far, at Pumke, beyond
Boing. It is a great burnt area, my own uncle has seen it, Kaya. It
looks a good place for maize.
I wonder why that old woman behaved badly like that, and burnt
the Birapinya? Was she a witch?* [bo/o'd].

In discussing the story of the oil, or spittle, of the moon, Bukko
demands to know why this is not the same substance as is used
by medical doctors; he was thinking particularly of the use of
anaesthesia for operations, which must have taken place occasionally at the Mission clinic, and also is known to take place in
the hospital at Kurmuk. In operations people are made un-
conscious in order that they should recover again, healed. This
is what the secret must be, according to Bukko. The Uduk just
use the name moon oil, moon oil, without really knowing what
it is.

W.D.: What happened to the moon oil?
Bukko: The gourd was smashed by that nasty, evil *wutule* [the rough
lizard]. The gourd was broken by him because he snatched it
away from the *sukule/* [the smooth lizard] saying the *sukule/*
had very slippery hands. He, that *wutule/*.
W.D.: Where were they taking it?
Bukko: It was snatched by him, he broke this thing for us for no
reason; for it had been used for our healing [*thoson*]. *The
Bunyans don't like the wutule/ now.*

W.D.: The Uduk too.

Bukko: Yes, because it caused us to die for ever. People died like that, people were helped with this moon oil, and they remained alive. They were revived.

 . . .

> *It's called moon oil; but isn't it the oil of white people? It's that oil of theirs used for helping people with medicine. It's just called moon oil while the Uduk people don't understand it. That's why it's called moon oil. It's called that while it is really your oil, your oil with which you revive people who are dying. Some people nowadays who are treated by you, don't you kill ['kosh] them and help them with medicine which revives people? That is what this is. People just invented the name moon oil.*

W.J.: Does the moon use this oil to appear again each month?

Bukko: Maybe, that's why it dies and comes to life again.

W.D.: Yes, it renews itself [*lulu'd*] like a snake.

Bukko: We call it dead, when it's not dead. It is just renewed, and we speak of it as dead, while it's not dead. We calculate the time with it.

Before people became human, Bukko said at times that they were birds; and at others, that they were hoofed creatures, one with the wild ancestors of the cattle, goats, and sheep that we know today. The Dog helped them in a fight against the wild animals, and they became creatures of the homestead together with the other hoofed animals. He told us also the much loved story, of the days when men of the wild and women of the village did not know each other (compare the story in the Prologue).

Bukko: *Men used to live by themselves and women also lived by themselves. . . .*
> *When people joined together, when people joined together, perhaps people were just birds.*

 . . .

> Woman went to bring *'tash* wood, they say. Man threw down a fig to her, he threw a fig down onto her neck, *pu'k.*

W.D.: We men were birds?

Bukko: *We men were birds.*

W.D.: And women were human beings [*'kwanim pa*].

Bukko: *Women tied up branches of* 'tash.[45] *They lit fires in their place where*

---

[45] The ashes of *'tash* wood and leaves are used as a salty flavouring for the stew which accompanies meals of porridge. One of the women's regular tasks is to collect this kind of leafy branch.

they also lived by themselves. They made fires of 'tash. Woman said, 'What's happened to this bird that it throws things on my neck like this?' While Man was the one throwing things on her neck. And then Woman looked around saying, 'Ay! Is this person Man then? What is that penis doing on him, *bolo'th bolo'th?'*

And Man came down, down, caah! came down, and Woman understood, and tried the penis, and bundled up Man in the leafy branches of *'tash*. Carried him on her head and dragged him into the hut. She untied him and hid him in the hut. She found the *yisayis, yisayis.*

W.D.: *Yisayis?*

Bukko: Yes, that Woman who first tried the penis spoke like that. 'I've found the *yisayis, yisayis!*' She kept him in the hut like that, while the others didn't know at all. She kept her husband in the hut like that.

W.D.: She went on hiding him?

Bukko: She hid him; people knew after some time, the belly in which she had conceived gave birth.

W.D.: Then the others asked about it?

Bukko: Yes, the others asked: 'From whom have you conceived? From whom have you conceived?' She told the others: 'I have found the *yisayis, yisayis, yisayis*'. Caah! The others came running to him there, *dhoro'th*. That man, they soon finished him off. 'Tell us about the others. Didn't you leave them behind? Didn't you leave some others behind?

He said, 'Ay! Listen: go over there and bring *'tash* from there. Go right to the fig-tree there. That fig-tree over there; they're living in that fig-tree. Yes, go to that fig-tree.'

She prevented the others from getting her man.

For people [men] then lived and cultivated just wild things. They came and found grain eventually, from the womenfolk. Ay! For people were *arums* long ago.

And could people talk properly then? It was just gibberish.

W.D.: Was there no special language of theirs long ago?

Bukko: Yes, their speech was not the same as the proper language which we speak now. They spoke just gibberish which was not understood.

W.D.: What was it like?

Bukko: *Ay! We can't know about that gibberish. Has it ever been heard?*

W.D.: And were women the ones who spoke properly?

Bukko: Çaah, people all spoke like that. *And from where was language discovered? Was it discovered through the bringing of fire by the dog?*

It was perhaps discovered through the bringing of fire by the dog. For people were drying things, and scraping just a piece to eat, because the dough was just like that, there was no fire to cook anything.

W.D.: Did people of old ever drink beer?

Bukko: *Caah! What could they brew beer with? It was a wretched business, making things without fire.*

They ground the grain for food, soaked it in water, and carried it to dry in the sun, just for the dried crust. Then they would soon eat the crust, and dry the food again for the people who were looking after the goats, the goat boys. *What a miserable life for those people of old. It is we, who created a proper home-life later.*

People then were giving birth properly. Over the whole country, giving birth properly. *Over the whole country, with Bunyans too; the Bunyana Turuk were there, when people came to give birth properly, for that state of affairs came from . . . that came from there. It came from those clothes-wearing people, those Turuk.*

That is why the Turuk were so unhappy when we were attacked here, when the Bunyan Gwami were attacking us. The Bunyana Turuk were unhappy and came to attack the Bunyan Gwami for denying us the country which they had given us. Were not the Turuk the ones who gave us this country? The white people gave us the country now. These 'Sudan', the Bunyana Arab, have changed things now, and are in charge of us now. Are they the ones who gave us a home? No. They didn't give people a home. They changed things, saying they are now in charge. They keep the other from our home, who brought us home. While the other is our own friend.

We Uduks! We Uduks are silly stupid, powerless. How did we become so silly? It was from that camel. For we were the owners of the camel. . . . and cows too.

We Uduk, they say we didn't know how to put the camel saddle on the camel's back. We were just nailing it on, *'du'b, 'du'b*, and the camel fell, *wuup*. And again, we knocked wooden nails onto another, *te'b, te'b*, and the camel fell, *wuup*. The Arabs then came and said, 'Please bring them here. Give them to us to try too'. The Arabs then carved [by chipping the wood] the wood for the camel saddle [properly]. Then they denied it to us, while we are the real owners of the camel. Yes, things were often mistaken by the people of old. We Uduk are really the owners of that animal.

These are direct references to the historical facts of the 'Turuk' having saved the Uduk from being wiped out by the

Bunyan, and to the technical incompetence of the Uduk themselves as they laughingly and ironically see it—they could not
even look after their own creature, the camel, properly, and so
lost it to the Arabs. Dogs, on the other hand, are Uduk creatures;
but they are not just things of the Uduk. They helped people in
the beginning; and Bukko maintained that dogs should be
better treated by the people than they are these days. In telling
us the story of Dog bringing fire, Bukko added his own thought
that Dog must have gone as far as the country of the Turuk to
find fire in the first place. It was the Turuk who gave Dog all
the necessary instructions to pass on to the Uduk.

Bukko: People were eating that stuff, eating that stuff [uncooked
  dough], and Dog then went *as far as the Turuk*. That burning
  stick which was knocked off, *'dow*, it was tied to him on his
  tail. They [the Turuk] said 'As you're taking it, go and see if
  there's grass on the road, go and knock embers on it. Dog
  heard this. He knocked embers off. People saw a lot of smoke,
  and said, 'Where's all that smoke coming here? What's all
  that smoke coming here?' The fire burned through the night
  and for several days. For people were surrounded by the long
  grass. And he brought this thing, 'You people! Please prepare
  some straw. He spoke to people thus. Yes; 'Prepare a little
  straw' he said, 'I've brought a little something.' While people
  were eating dough in that awful way [*ka jinthus*]. Then people
  knocked off some embers *ta'b*, and lit a fire. Everyone saw that
  smoke, çaah, and flocked there in a mass, because of the thing
  which was burning. 'This thing that burns' they said, 'Where
  did you bring it from? Where did you get this burning thing?
  Where did you get this burning thing to help [*waç*] people so?
  We are just eating dough.'

W.D.: And he told people, 'You must light a fire like this and cook
  food'?

Bukko: Yes; they eventually lit a fire, and put a pot on the fire. He
  heated water. He heated water. 'The meaning of all this has
  been explained to me', he said. And a proper fire-stick was
  given to him, was tied to his tail from that place. He brought
  fire like that. 'This thing you must drill like this', they said. It
  was all explained to him. Then we cut the fire-stick for ourselves, to drill fire. While Dog, he's the one who showed us
  the way. Yes, Dog, he showed us the one way to do it like that.

W.D.: And at the time fire was brought by Dog, did people know
  how to speak Uduk or were people still talking gibberish?

Bukko: Yes it was brought here while people were without the Uduk language.

W.D.: Were they just ignorant?

Bukko: They didn't know it. They were ignorant of the Uduk language. People spoke just that gibberish, *dumpulu, dumpuli* like that. And people improved at last at the Uduk language when fire was made by them. People then were able to speak a little real language. While just gibberish was spoken by people at that time. It was just the speech of wild people.

. . .

The dog is treated badly by people now, but it is Dog which has civilized (thoson) *us. People behave like that but I know if Dog had not done as it did, we would be extremely wretched. It is the Dog who helped us, and so we have it in the village.*

The discussion moved on, as Bukko began to complain about the way in which today villages keep splitting up, when in the past everyone lived together, and helped each other. Today, he thought, people didn't help each other as they should, implying that each one selfishly looks after himself. I asked him about early marriage and kinship:

W.J.: When marriage took place and the first baby was born, did people go to live with their mother's brothers—did that child have a *shwakam*?

Bukko: What sort of mother's brother would he know? People lived in disorder. What kind of mother's brother would be understood? What kind of mother's brother would they find? They had to find their mother's brothers with their heads [i.e. looking around and organizing themselves].

W.D.: People married haphazardly at that time, didn't they?

Bukko: They married in a scattered fashion, haphazardly.

In those days, people were not properly human; Bukko kept returning to the idea that we were developed from hoofed creatures, and that Dog helped us from being attacked by the other wild creatures, by giving us spears.

W.D.: And what were the people like at that time, when wild animals were about to kill them?

Bukko: *We were wild animals ourselves.*

W.D.: We grew feet like them?

Bukko: *Yes, it was these feet* [*pointing to his hand*] *which enabled us to go upright. These feet here. They made us go upright at last by growing like this. Our feet were just like those of hoofed animals.*

W.D.: At the time of the dance were we still going on all fours?

Bukko: Yes, it was while we were still in the form of hoofed creatures.
. . .

> We went upright when we spoke real language. . . . Our hands were all the same, like hoofed animals. Our hands split up later. They split up when we spoke proper language. We were still hoofed animals. For Dog, didn't he bring fire, when we at last spoke proper language, from Dog. Dog is the one who came and taught us how to speak.

I returned to the question of the early relationship with the Turuk, who Bukko had said so clearly were the friends and helpers of the Uduk in the beginning; were they one people with the Uduk—did they also come from the Birapinya? Bukko's answer was that not only did all people come from the great dance in the sky, but he assumed that the Turuk know more about it than he did. For, as he said, they keep talking about *arum* in the sky; and here he was accommodating in his own mind the teachings of Christianity, which had filtered through to him although he had never joined the mission community. The neologism *Arumgimis* was coined by the S.I.M. missionaries to refer to God (literally '*arum* in the sky'), and talk of angels, of the dead being raised up and so forth, made sense to Bukko in terms of the village traditions of people remaining up in the sky after the burning of the Birapinya. The relative ignorance of the Uduk, already pointed out by Bukko, in telling us for example of their stupid loss of the camel to the Arabs, and their dependence on the Turuk, the source of knowledge, leadership and support in the early days, is also explicit in the following exchanges. William Danga put the question:

W.D.: Did the Turuk people also come from the Birapinya?

Bukko: *Agi! Didn't everybody gather up there? But they will know about that. The white people, aren't they the ones who speak of Arumgimis, Arumgimis, like that? . . .*

After a question as to who looked after those who survived the Birapinya, he said:

Bukko: *You white people, the Turuk are the ones who looked after them, and washed people's burns, and the skin healed up and came off. Why are you asking when you are the ones who cared for people. They are the ones who washed people and removed the worms completely with their [medicines]. That is why the Turuk are interested in what we have to say.*

Myth and history are clearly not 'the same thing'. But nor is it permissible to separate them, regarding history as what actually happened and myth as its fictional representation. The Uduk representation of immediate historical experience bears a very close relation to the way in which they see the total character of their society in its moral relations with other peoples. There is a close intertwining of the imagery used in mythical accounts of the early days of mankind with that used to represent the periods of destruction of their community, in particular the late nineteenth-century upheaval. In both contexts, people are described originally as running in the bush, with no fire, no homes, no cultivated food, living on wild roots, like antelopes. They are without kin and in a state of disorder. They are helpless waifs whose survival, and particularly their survival as a community, is only possible through the intervention of the Turuk who come to their aid. Bukko's rethinking of the early myths incorporates this political and historical reality; language, fire, medicine, were all with the Turuk in the beginning, who conveyed these means of civilization to the Uduk through Dog (Bukko once suggested that the Turuk must have given the Dog fire in the form of matches!). The miraculous moon oil, which enables people to recover from the door of death, is with their doctors now. My own interest in the people's past was interpreted in these terms: for Bukko, it was a further example of the interest that the Turuk have always taken in the Uduk.

We recorded Bukko in the act of modifying, of rethinking the traditions of the northern Uduk people, and of tacking on to them fragments drawn from direct experience, from historical memory, and from foreign traditions. But he is not the only story-teller to have done this. Among the northern Uduk perhaps more than in less disturbed communities, this has been a general and continuing process, which has itself produced the ferment of contradictory and partial tales that constitute the 'mythology' of the people. There are certainly 'ancient' and authentically Uduk elements in the stories I have collected—for example, the story of human origin from the family of hoofed species. Even though this specific story is unknown to many informants, its echoes are everywhere (for example in the insistent image of people's running about in the forest like antelopes in accounts of the turn of the century when homes, possessions and kin were lost). But most Uduk tales are versions of themes found quite widely; the story of Dog bringing fire is quite common (found for example among the Nuer),[46] and even the story of the woman finding a man in the forest has analogues elsewhere (for example among the Murle).[47] The Birapinya is probably however a fairly recent importation from the Meban, following the northerly migration of the Uduk and their settlement in the Ahmar and Tombak valleys. It is one example among many of the way in which the Nilotic languages and cultures have been an important recent source of symbolic and mythical material, which the northern Uduk have used in the building of a new imaginative world.

[46] One version is quoted in Huffman, 1931, pp. 88–9.

[47] See Lewis, 1972, p. 20. There are comparable themes in Komo myth. David Turton tells me that there is a similar story among the Mursi in Ethiopia, and Patti Langdon has recently collected a tale about the Lotima (monkey) generation among the Longarim. The men of this generation were very big and hairy and preferred to live in the bush with the animals, until the women sent for them to come home. Another analogous tale comes from surprisingly far afield – from the recent fieldwork of John Burton among the Nilotic Atuot. In this tale the men lived among themselves in the forest looking after buffalo, while women lived by the river keeping cattle, fishing and growing millet. A man followed a lost buffalo trail to the camp of the women, and encountered a woman. After they mated, the other women rushed upon him; eventually he died. (See Burton, 1978, pp. 16–17.)

3

SUBSISTENCE

We 'kwanim pa work together.
We do not buy and sell between
brothers, as the Arabs do.

The Uduk think of themselves as a cultivating people, as hard-working grain producers. Although they love to spend time hunting and fishing, and also raise a few animals, the hoe cultivation of sorghum, maize, and sesame occupies most of their time. They have become quite important as grain producers in the region, supplying among others the nomadic Rufā'a el Hoj with considerable stocks of grain when it is on hand, and obtaining mainly through the *ad hoc* barter and odd cash sale of sorghum and sesame most of their own needs in the way of metal tools and weapons, additions to their domestic stock, clothing, salt, and so forth. But they are not traders in an entrepreneurial sense, and do not produce for trade as such. They are suspicious of merchants and of the commercial way of life. Their economic attitudes hinder the appearance of trading and the entrepreneur in their own society, and restrict trade relations with outsiders to a necessary minimum. Money, that is Sudanese currency of pounds and piastres, plays a negligible part in their lives.

The cultivation of the earth is the prime duty of every *wathim pa*: it is a collective task, and it constitutes the base of community life. Not only should those living together hoe together, but the fruits of this work are supposed to be shared out in a brotherly spirit. In practice of course each person must look out for himself, put aside a little of his grain secretly, hide a few luxuries like tobacco from his friends and pretend they do not exist. Small pots of beer are discreetly put aside before a large beer-party, for quiet drinking when the last guests have been convinced the beer is finished and have gone home. Individuals may hide the odd gourd of beer or tobacco from guests—corners in my premises proved useful for this purpose. Everyone knows that a certain secrecy is maintained about possessions, and on the whole it is harmless. But real individual greed and jealousy is strongly disapproved of, and sometimes suspected behind the pleasantest of appearances. Ill-intentioned resentment and jealousy are feared and not a few witchcraft accusations, violent incidents, and homicides can be attributed to a complex of tensions built up on this basis. A community of equals, and ideally of willing partners, is known to be a fragile thing. An appearance of generosity thus becomes an obligation. Not only should there be public evidence of a fair distribution of the community's work and a just redistribution of its product, but participation, morally enjoined though not enforced, should appear free and willing.

Any mode of production is related in the first place to natural conditions of the environment, and in the second to local technical knowledge of that environment and the possibilities of its exploitation—including expertise in the use of tools and implements and traditional skills in the management of available crops and animals. But beyond geographical and technical possibilities, it is the way in which human effort is organized and applied to production and the way in which this work, and its fruits, are evaluated, that give a mode of production its essentially social character, and it is in these terms that we may relate it to other social facts. For the Uduk, we may ask particularly whether their present mode of production has historical roots. Whether, that is, in the course of their past experience, they have formulated a distinctive tradition of social and economic thought which makes intelligible their practice of tight-knit co-operation and sharing, and their resistance to otherwise 'rational' principles of market exchange.

The conscious rationale behind production and exchange in Uduk society is that of satisfying the present needs of the community. A general surplus is not aimed at, and individual effort at surplus production is condemned. Even when a small surplus is produced, and exchanged with non-Uduk, the competitive bargaining spirit is rejected, in practical and symbolic manner. The Uduk do not do very well out of the fact that they are significant suppliers, particularly of sorghum and sesame, to others. They prefer to keep outside competitive markets, and restrict quite harshly the appearance of competition among themselves. Any transaction between Uduk partners which smacks of profiteering on one or both sides is gossiped about, while those involved attempt to represent the deal as a fair exchange.

Equality, partnership and reciprocity are more than a liberal dream among the Uduk. The standards set by public expectations impose rigid obligations on the individual. On the other hand through the same network of conventional obligations, the individual can rely on help from kinsmen and neighbours for the completion of the necessary work on his own fields. He can also expect support in illness and old age, and in times of personal trouble. The self-sufficiency of the Uduk as a whole in relation to the outside world is complemented by the interdependence of people within the society: the interdependence of young and old, of men and women, of the matrilineal kin of a father in relation to those of his son, of neighbour and neighbour. Between persons in relations such as these, there are conventional expectations of co-operation and sharing in terms of which the Uduk judge individual behaviour.

THE DUTY TO WORK FOR THE COMMUNITY

Not only do Uduk spend most of their time cultivating, but they know that they must, in order to survive. The lifelong obligation of each man is to cultivate; and of women, not only to cultivate a little for themselves, but more importantly to provide food and beer so that the men who work on the fields can be fed and sustained. A man must cultivate the three main staples; a man who does not grow sorghum, maize, and sesame is not a real man, and would not be able to keep a wife, or to contribute properly to the sustenance of the hamlet community. Moreover, a man has a duty not only to cultivate fields for himself and his immediate dependants, but a duty also to assist in the cultivation of other men's fields, especially those of the hamlet he is living in, and the immediate birth-group to which he belongs. He must also cultivate fields for any of his young children, or sisters' sons, living with him; and for a sister or mother living with him. The general word for cultivation is *kor*; and in particular, it refers to weeding. The weeding over of fields, using a hand-hoe, is the heaviest and most demanding task involved in Uduk cultivation; it is also regular, and obligatory. There are other heavy jobs: the occasional clearing of new fields for example involves chopping down trees with a hand-axe; but the weeding goes on inexorably. It is particularly vital in the meadow fields near the river, where the thick heavy clay soil supports grass and other vegetation which would easily choke the delicate growing maize. These meadows have to be weeded over at least three times in the early rains. The idea of weeding, and cultivation in general, represents work for the Uduk (*tuç*); when a friend asked why I spent so much time reading and writing, another suggested that 'Paper-work is weeding for her!' Most of the food and beer prepared by the womenfolk is for work on the fields; they spend much of their time gathering firewood, collecting water or cooking for *asum ḵor* (work beer) or *maaŋ ḵor* (work meals).

A man who does not work very much in the fields, or who does not pull his weight in the communal cultivating parties of the hamlet, will acquire the reputation of a *nyoŋḵor*. This is a scathing epithet, implying laziness and lack of manhood. Although there are many individuals among the Uduk who spend a good deal of time practising specialities such as healing the sick, they must take care not to neglect their fields, or the work-parties organized for their relatives' and neighbours' fields, or they will be sneered at as *nyoŋḵor*. A diviner who used to visit the villages of the Uduk, from the Jum Jum, was known to live well off the fees and hospitality he received from his patients without cultivating; but this way of life is scorned by the Uduk. People told me that it would not be allowed in an Uduk community. From time to time, my household included one or two young men who were from one point of view employed by me as research assistants and general helpers; but they usually took good care that this did not appear too obvious, and spent a good deal of time cultivating their own and other people's fields. The possibility of my paying for them to get others to cultivate their fields while they stayed at home all day working with books and paper was quite out of the question. I therefore found myself spending time too in the fields and scratching out small maize and vegetable patches of my own.

A person has to work in the fields, but at the same time has to take care not to work too hard on his own fields at the expense of others'. He must be generous with his capacity for work. A man whose fields appear to have done surprisingly well will be criticized just as much as one who has shirked his duty. It will be thought that he has put far more of his time into his own field, and consequently less on others' than he should, in order to try and get rich. This is a crude way of putting what is actually a most subtle and delicately-judged matter. It is all right if all the fields of a whole hamlet or preferably a neighbourhood have done rather well, or rather poorly; but if there are discrepancies between the fields of individuals, without any obvious natural reason such as a flood to account for the contrast, something has gone wrong; for ideally the labour of the community should be evenly distributed between the fields of all its members. Has someone been putting in too much work on his own field? Or has someone's wife been neglecting to cook food and brew beer for work parties on his field? An unmarried youth I knew cultivated a proper meadow for the first time; the planting and weeding of the maize was finished early, and well done; when he became sick shortly afterwards, it was strongly rumoured that he had brought it on himself, by working so hard on his own field. Others were, perhaps, resentful; and some people's resentment is dangerous. Any appearance of superior efficiency, or of private innovation and enterprise, is to be avoided. A man who tried planting onions fell sick with lumps behind his ears; another who thought he would plant a handful of coffee beans to see what would happen, was interested to find that they sprouted and grew up into strong plants. He then pulled them up and threw them away. I asked why he did this; and I was told that he was afraid that people might think he was trying to get rich. The problem is that if one person appears to be amassing wealth or possessions, or benefiting somehow from his fields, it may be at the expense of others. It takes a man of very strong personality to experiment with growing onions, or other unusual crops; and when such crops as tobacco or yams are grown, which are possible only in specific areas, the grower must expect to give away a proportion of his crop to relatives from less-favoured areas.

The accumulation of a surplus, either in the hands of a single person, or collectively, is difficult, for these and other reasons which will appear. An individual has to avoid the appearance of conspicuous plenty on his fields or in his granaries. If he does not, he will be relieved of his stores by others, who will unexpectedly find themselves in need of extra maize here, and sorghum there. This happens on a large scale sometimes. For example, when the harvest has been poor in the territory of the Meban, to the west of the Uduk, where the rainfall is even more unreliable, the Meban come on begging visits to any Uduk hamlet with which they can trace a tenuous link of friendship or past kinship.

The public willingness of the Uduk to consume or give away what they have produced works against the accumulation of wealth, individually and collectively. It must be a contributory reason for their over-all poverty.

Even the normal processes of exchange between the Uduk and the Meban, Berta, nomad Arabs, and various merchants, whereby the grain of the Uduk is timidly bartered for animals and equipment, or occasionally sold for cash, are somewhat lopsided; I do not consider that in the aggregate these exchanges compensate the Uduk, and similar cultivators, as much as they might for the loss of their spare crops. Without a tougher attitude to the value of what they produce, people in the position of the Uduk will scarcely improve their economic or political strength; and yet, if they were to do this, the community of equals which they have constructed would be threatened. In their weakness lies a certain strength: and they are conscious of this.

LAND AND LABOUR

Production is shaped mainly by the working arrangements of the Uduk community. The vital matters are the services of men, to plant and to weed and to harvest; and of women, to support them by providing food and beer for work-parties. Above all, women bear children who will join the working community when they are able. The local community consists of a core of people who regard themselves as matrilineal kin. This locally based birth-group, or *wak̲*, described in detail in the next chapter, usually observes a common rule of exogamy, and may occupy several hamlets. The local birth-group has joint interests in cultivable land; in the labour of its men and the fertility of its women; and in a small cattle herd, which represents the exiguous joint 'savings' of the community. Whether a man settles with one or other of the hamlets of his birth-group, or with his father's people, or with another birth-group for some reason, he will always be found space to cultivate with them, and his assistance in their fields will be welcome. You must help in the fields of those you live with; and even a guest, staying two or three days, will join in the work-parties that happen to be organized on the days he is there. Helping hands are always welcomed.

Each local birth-group has general rights to cultivate in the nearest stretch of river meadowland, and the nearest stretch of higher savanna woodland. The fields of members of each local birth-group are usually together, but where close links exist between one birth-group and its neighbours, their fields may be partially inter-mingled. Individuals may if they wish carve out and cultivate fields some distance from their kinsmen, perhaps in an area generally recognized as 'belonging' to another birth-group, but this does not often happen, partly for the practical reasons that the people from whom you expect most help in the collective work-parties on the fields are your matrilineal kinsmen and therefore it is easier if everyone has their fields in the same area. There is also greater security in cultivating near your kinsmen, and helping to keep an eye on the ravages of birds and other hazards.

Although rights in areas of wild bushland are very general, once an area has been carved out from the bush and cultivated, the birth-group whose members have done the work has very clear rights over the fields. If a man dies, his closest brother or sister's son (within the birth-group) will normally take over his fields. No objections are raised by the Uduk to the use of the wild woodland by passing nomads, or to the clearing and cultivation of virgin areas by outsiders, such as merchants, or visiting Berta who may clear a bush area for growing sesame. It is the work involved which gives men a right to lands carved out of the bush; but the bush itself is there for anybody to utilize. This also applies to the resources of the wild: water, firewood, small game, ironstone, etc; though control over large-scale hunting and fishing is vested in certain people over specific territories.

Individual fields 'belong' to specific persons; and their

owners have full rights over the main crops harvested. It is a serious offence to take grain from someone else's field. This does not apply to certain crops, such as pumpkins, which may be removed from anybody's field. A married man is expected to cultivate at least one field of sorghum and one field of maize in the name of each of his wives; if he has two wives, he is likely to have one large field of each type, divided down the middle. But he may have more than one of each type, particularly in the meadows. Although these fields are in the name of the wife, and she prepares the food and beer for work parties on them (using grain from the previous harvest) and maintains herself and her children on their produce, the grain is regarded as his. If the marriage breaks down, he keeps the harvest. A man without a wife, whether young, deserted, or widowed will also cultivate fields, the food and beer or work-parties being prepared by his sisters or his mother. Fields, especially of sesame, may be culti-vated by a man in the name of his sister's son or daughter, if they are still young children. Extra sesame fields may be planted if money or wealth is needed for some reason, such as the payment of a big debt to diviners. Women may also cultivate; but it is usually only deserted or widowed women who cultivate sorghum and maize fields, often with the help of their brothers, to feed themselves and their children. Married women usually limit themselves to small sesame fields; and if their marriage collapses, they retain the produce of these fields. If they die it passes to their brothers. Other minor cultivating activities of women include patches of cotton, groundnuts, and beans, but all in small quantities.

There is little specialization of labour, except on the basis of age and sex. Even those people who spend much of their time on ritual activities, and who may gain substantial rewards for their services, or (meagrely) paid Sheikhs, all cultivate fields and depend largely on them for subsistence. There are no specialized craftsmen; all men are able to fashion the wooden parts of weapons, objects and implements, and all women can manu-facture baskets and simple clay pots. Metal goods are obtained, however, by barter or purchase.

All men, including young boys, are expected to spend most of their time in the fields. Nearly all the hard work in the fields is carried out by men, even on those fields which nominally belong to women. An old woman's sons for example will weed her sorghum field, in return for beer or food cooked by her and her daughters from her own grain of the previous year, or from grain which one of her children or brothers has given her. House building is done almost entirely by men, apart from the carrying of materials.

Cattle and goats are looked after by boys and unmarried men, who are responsible for seeing that they are not lost, do not damage crops, are adequately watered and tied up or sheltered at night. Thorn stockades may be constructed for cattle, near to the hamlet, especially in the rainy season, when wild animals are a danger at night.

Women's work includes all transport, not only of building materials from the bush, but of firewood (which they chop down themselves), and harvested crops from the fields. They carry all these goods, as well as gourds of water, once or twice daily from the river, on their heads. Sometimes the maize has to be transported across a flooded river, in which case men will assist. Women spend a great deal of time at the grinding stone, preparing flour for food and beer, or sesame for oil. They do all the cooking. They also collect wild roots and leaves, mushrooms and herbs from the woodland; and if a large animal is killed, or if the nomad Arabs make a gift of a camel or cow which happens to have died naturally, the women rush down with axes to chop it up. A good deal of effort and co-operation is required from the women of a hamlet, including its own members and wives married into it, when a big occasion is planned. This may be either of a purely practical kind such as clearing a new field, or more usually of a social or ritual kind. They have to prepare for many days beforehand, grinding and regrinding, bringing firewood and water, brewing and cooking. The Uduk method of making beer takes three days (the Meban method which is less popular takes two days) and so even the smallest work-parties take some advance organization. The planning of work-parties in a hamlet, and to some extent the planning of rituals, is in the hands of the women, who make the domestic arrangements upon which they depend. They have to agree between themselves upon a rota for work-parties on the various fields of the hamlet, since not only are all the men supposed to co-operate in these communal parties, but whenever possible several of the women (wives, daughters, and resident sisters) should co-operate in the preparation of the food and beer. Social and ritual occasions, which are usually bigger than the ordinary hamlet work-parties, require even more organized co-operation, and the women have to arrange to fit in such occasions with the sequence of work-parties. The management and planning of economic and social activity, on a day-to-day basis, is thus the responsibility of the women.

A woman's place is at the grinding-stone; lazy women are criticized for not grinding as lazy men are criticized for not cultivating. Little girls learn to grind very young; they even practise as toddlers, with a couple of stones and a handful of mud they have collected from the bush, or with small gourds, singing in unison, with gusto:

Yorka yorka yee	It's ground by me, ground by me,
Yorka ki dush dush	Ground by me, *dush dush*!
Ayo ma ta'da	My mother's grinding-stone.
Yorka yorka yee	It's ground by me, ground by me,
Yorka ki dush dush	Ground by me, *dush dush*!
Ayo ma ta'da	My mother's grinding-stone.
Ayo go'di miiyata	Why's it sounding loud, the stone?
Ka yo go'di ḳor pos	To grow the grain, it's sounding!
Ayo ma ta'da	My mother's grinding-stone.

Production in the fields is thus the result of co-operation within the hamlet, men doing the bulk of the actual cultivation but women preparing the food and beer necessary not only to feed their own husbands or brothers but to repay those who assist them in their fields. The minimum working team is a man-woman pair; the most stable and probably productive combination is a brother-sister unit, and as the Uduk recognize, a hamlet composed only of brothers and sisters would be a sounder economic unit than one which relies on fickle wives!

There is a definite seasonal character in the tasks of men. The appearance of the rains (April–May) marks the start of the season of hardest work, of planting and weeding in all the fields; on most days there is a communal work-party. The maize is harvested in August–September, and then the sesame. There is a relatively slack period just before the main harvest of sorghum, in November–December. After the main harvest, in the middle of the dry season, men's work is minimal, though this is the time for hut-building. This is the main season of ritual and social activity, for which there is no time in the rains. Figure 6 summarizes this cycle of seasonal activity. Women's work, however, continues at much the same intensity through-out the year. In the rains, women spend most of their time cooking and brewing for work-parties on the fields, and in the dry season, they continue cooking and brewing mainly for ritual and social occasions (though funerals, which create a lot of work, can occur at any time). Their hardest tasks are search-ing for wild roots and other foods in a year of grain shortage, especially at the end of the dry season and in the early rains; and carrying water from distant sources, possibly two miles, in a very dry year.

A good part of the work necessary on a field is carried out by its owner himself; but perhaps three or four times a year for each field he will get his wife or sister to make beer or food for a work-party to finish a particular job. He will try to take advan-tage of suitable weather conditions; for example, weeding is much easier just after rain, when the ground is soft. The sequence of work-parties is worked out within the hamlet, and each man or boy in the hamlet is expected to join in, unless he has a special reason for not doing so. If a next-door hamlet does not have a work-party on a particular day, people may come to join in their neighbour's party, especially if the hamlets are of the same birth-group or closely allied. If there is a particularly onerous job, such as the clearing of a new field, the owner and his wife or sister may make a point of passing the news round widely, so that helpers may come from distant hamlets. They will expect plenty of beer. A man may also send the news to his grown sons, living elsewhere, who will be glad to come and help. The beer or food provided for a party is not regarded as a 'wage' or a direct payment for labour, but as hospitality; guests are usually welcome at the beer-drink after work, even if they did not turn up to help in the fields. Most everyday social life centres on beer parties, people sometimes moving on through the afternoon from one hamlet to another for a taste of the beer and the gossip in each place.

A man's working day, in the early rains, may start at dawn with a few hours' work on his own weeding, and then he will move to a field where a work-party is being held, and if that field is finished early, the party will either move on to finish someone else's field, or the members will disperse to their own fields until the beer or food is ready, when they will assemble back at the hamlet to eat and drink. This may be near midday, in which case the men may go back to their own fields afterwards, or it may be nearer sunset, in which case they will relax. The shorter the supplies of grain for cooking and brewing, the smaller the work-parties are likely to be—each housewife will provide just enough food for the men of the hamlet; and even if it is not sufficient, they will go on working out of a sense of duty and the knowledge that if they don't work there will be even less food the next year. If grain is plentiful in a particular year, the work-parties are likely to be provided with large quantities of beer, and non-working guests will be warmly welcomed.

THE SHARING OF FOOD

The hamlet, with resident wives and sisters, is not only a unit within which there is a duty to work, but it is the unit within which you are obliged to share food, and conversely you may expect shares of others' food. It is true that a woman does occasionally cook a little porridge and sauce inside her hut, which is intended just for her husband and children, or for her mother and herself; but if anyone sees her cooking, she will have to share it, or risk being thought selfish. In an Uduk hamlet, you can't easily cook in private; if you creep out to collect a few twigs for a fire, a couple of sharp-eyed women will call across the hamlet: 'What are you going to cook? Are you going to make some coffee?'—and I was not the only one observed in this way. So usually, when a woman cooks, she tries to make enough for a dozen to two dozen people to share. When the meal—basically two dishes, porridge and sauce—is ready, towards sunset, she calls everyone in the hamlet to come and eat: '*Iiyu shwa maa!*' Three bowls of porridge, *maam pos* (sorghum porridge) or *maaŋkoba/* (maize porridge), each with an accompaniment of sauce, are usually served, one for the men, one for the women and one for small children. A meal may be offered daily at several houses in the hamlet when grain is plentiful. When it is short, there may be no communal meals at all, and people eat what titbits they can in their own huts. In the mornings, food or beer from the previous day, or snacks such as roasted maize cobs or seeds, may be eaten for 'breakfast'; or the coming day's beer may be sampled before going out to work.

The importance of eating, of a full belly, and the assurance of grain supplies, cannot be over-emphasized in describing Uduk life. Work is undertaken to ensure a supply of grain for food and beer; and many social and political discussions use the idiom of grain production and consumption. 'We drink beer together' means 'We are friends, allies.' The imagery of eating flows over into all sorts of contexts, not only of a social or economic kind. For example, the stomach is the seat of the will, of conscious thought; happiness is *ki bwam 'boro'd* (with a good stomach); generosity is suggested by the expression *bwaŋ kush* (a white stomach).

In a time of hunger, or when a man's wife leaves him, if he incurs a debt or if he has to spend the planting season in prison, or if for any other reason he has no grain, a man's security lies with those whom he has worked with for years and with whom he has shared his food; he can rely upon his matrilineal kinsmen (especially those of the hamlet where he lives) to support him as they would themselves. This potential security could be regarded as a right deriving from the investment of one's labour in the commonly worked fields for many years. In this perspective, what 'corporate solidarity' the local birth-group possesses derives from the economic support it can give its members in return for their long years of loyal work. One member temporarily in difficulties can be helped out, as by an insurance company, or a benevolent society. But security cannot be obtained by other means, such as possession of land or property; it can only be earned by long continued labour, at least in theory. The idea is implicit in the concept of the birth-group as a working and productive unit. A man who is scarcely known might be supported by a particular hamlet, on the grounds that his mother's brothers worked with them, and all members of one local birth-group should have equal claims.

Since the Uduk economy turns upon the arrangement of people's labour, rather than on scarcity of land or other resources, one problem of the hamlet is to attract more individuals, for the larger the corporation, the greater the security for each member. There is a particular need to secure and retain the services of as many women as possible in the hamlet, both sisters and wives, and the services of their children. It is not surprising that in an economy of this type the question of men's relationships to individual women and their children is of focal importance.

CONSUMPTION AND SAVING

No attempt is made to store crops from one year to another, and even after a good harvest the Uduk farmer disposes of the whole of his produce. Most of it, and in poor years the whole crop, is consumed, but a small proportion in good years is converted into animal wealth. Animals, unlike grain, grow in value by natural increase, and are treated by Uduk farmers in a way analogous to our treatment of savings.[1] Unless there are special circumstances, those animals occasionally killed for sacrifice are the males, castrated males or aged females. Fertile females are kept to multiply. Animals are needed mainly for sacrifice at times of sickness, rites of passage, and particularly funerals; they are a certain guarantee of social and spiritual security. Uduk do not keep cattle for themselves to eat or enjoy; they keep them 'in case of funerals'.

The word used by the Uduk for all forms of disposal of the harvest is *shwa*, to eat, or consume. Some types of consumption enable a man to maintain good relations with others, within his hamlet and between hamlets. The holding of large beer-parties is one of the main forms of such social reciprocity. The giving of presents or tribute to religious men, or the holding of religious sacrifices and feasts, serve both social and spiritual ends. The payment of taxes, another way of 'eating' the crops, helps to maintain political security. But an Uduk farmer knows very well that he can put a surplus harvest to greater use by converting it into animals and keeping them for some years, than he can by 'eating' it in any of these admittedly beneficial ways.

The most valuable crop grown by the Uduk, in terms of its

---

[1] The term 'savings' is far more appropriate than the term 'capital' in this context. The amount saved is extremely modest by any standards, and in no way can Uduk 'savings' be invested in the labour of others, or in cumulatively productive projects.

market value, is sesame. It is usually through the sale of surplus sesame that savings are made in animals; the commonest pattern is for sesame to be exchanged for pigs, often from the Meban; pigs for goats, from other Uduk or the Meban, or sesame directly for goats, especially from the Berta; and finally, sesame and goats for cattle, from the Berta or the Meban. Pigs and goats usually belong to one particular person, who has obtained them from surplus crops from his own fields, though if there is a need, the owner will hand them over to anyone in the hamlet. But cows are usually purchased for goats collected together from several members of a hamlet. They therefore belong jointly to the members of the local birth-group and the cattle herd represents the accumulated savings of its members, as a group. The herd is visible evidence of the local birth-group as a socio-economic unit. Its increase is the result of the joint labour of the birth-group members, and of the series of transactions by which they convert their small crop savings into a permanent animal herd. Joint purchase of an animal with people outside the birth-group would not be considered. The herds of closely allied birth-groups may be jointly cared for, and although cattle may be loaned out to more distant allies, or to the son of a member of the owning birth-group, they must eventually be returned. The herd rarely becomes very large. I am told that a generation ago, there were many more cattle in Uduk land than there are today. The decrease might be accounted for by the spread of anthrax by 'Fellata' cattle, which according to officials are a source of this disease in the region. Besides the various diseases which affect all types of animals, there are many calls on the animal resources of a hamlet. Sacrifices must be made on a large number of occasions, and although the male animals should provide for these, sometimes females have to be used. Building up a herd is therefore a slow and often discouraging business. But the significance of the herd remains, as the external symbol of the joint activity of the local birth-group as a productive unit. Even if its members are scattered among distant hamlets, as long as they continue to contribute to the herd, they may claim matrilineal brotherhood, and its privileges, such as help in meeting their own debts. The herd, though modest in size, represents the future security of the local birth-group, in a substantial sense as well as 'for funerals'.

TRANSACTIONS, GIFTS, DEBT

The circulation of wealth in Uduk society is marked by two main characteristics. The first is that the main pattern of circulation is between Uduk and non-Uduk partners. Circulation between Uduk partners is minimal. This must be seen in relation to the position of the Uduk in the social hierarchy of the southern Funj region; they are important suppliers of grain to several other peoples, and rely upon 'external' trade for specialized goods. The lack of differentiation within the Uduk economy is a partial explanation of the weak internal circulation of wealth; but a further factor is the lack of convertibility of rights over persons and goods, commonly found in other societies in forms such as bridewealth and bloodwealth. It is only possible to compensate the loss of a life in Uduk society by another life, and not by bloodwealth; and extensive rights over a wife and children cannot be secured by paying bridewealth. There are also inhibitions on trading one class of goods for another within Uduk society. It is not so much an extreme form of 'spheres of exchange', as the exclusion of certain modes of transaction within the community. Each productive unit has to survive in virtual isolation. Circulation in general is therefore relatively stagnant. Just as the continuance of the matrilineal birth-group depends on the fertility of its women, so the continuance of the cattle herd depends on the natural increase of the cows which compose it, and apart from its own fertility the herd can be added to only through the labour of the owning birth-group. The birth-group, like its cattle-herd, is a remarkably self-contained corporation, and has to thrive from within.

The second characteristic of most economic circulation in which Uduk partners are involved is that it takes the form of reciprocal gift-exchange, or redistribution with the aim of satisfying the other partner, rather than transactions aimed at maximization of material profit.[2] This applies even to major transactions with outsiders, for example the purchase of cows, which is usually concluded with a sacrifice; and sometimes even to monetary transactions. I have seen an Uduk friend in

---

[2] The *locus classicus* for this distinction is of course Marx (for example, the early chapters of *Capital*); and within social anthropology the key discussion is Mauss (1925; trans. 1954).

extreme embarrassment after being given a loaf of pressed tobacco by a neighbour who hoped he would sell it in a distant village where he was going as a visitor. My friend made no efforts to advertise the fact that he was trying to sell the tobacco; but the news was passed around by others, and several people including non-Uduk approached him at different times and made offers. He was reluctant to discuss the matter at all, and late in the day quietly gave the tobacco to someone who had offered six *riyals* (60 pt.), although he had been offered more by others, including myself. The man he sold it to was a stranger. Evidently, my friend was anxious not to appear a profiteer. This incident could be paralleled many times.

Two main types of exchange transaction are verbally distinguished in Uduk. The first is *wan* or *wan e*, which means to exchange one item for another of the same kind, to substitute or swap. It implies a replacement, and not a transaction. Thus, two men may *wan* goats; for example, a female may be exchanged for a male, if it suits both parties. Or two throwing sticks may be exchanged. This type of exchange is the commonest which takes place between Uduk. It also occurs between Uduk and others; for example *Bunyan* (arabized Berta) bring female cows for direct exchange with castrated young oxen from the Uduk. The Uduk of course prefer female cows because they give birth; and the Berta prefer oxen for meat and for trade. The social range of this type of trade may be wide or narrow, taking place both between strangers and between close relatives, who often exchange chickens or puppies. But it is the only form of material exchange proper within the body of the birth-group, or indeed between relatives or friends of any kind. It is always a substitution of articles regarded as being of the same type.

Wan is used also in contexts which carry strong moral overtones. For example, it can sometimes have the sense of 'redeem', as in the historical song (above, p. 59) which pleads for Mis-Mis to go and redeem the country, *wan pa*; and in another song mourning the loss of a sister, it is demanded 'What can redeem the grief of Tirko?' (*Tirko goki'di wan ka ta yee?*) In the S.I.M. *Uduk Dictionary*, *wan* is given as 'exchange'; *wan bwa*, 'to be reconciled', *wan 'ba/* 'to redeem, ransom', and *wan is* 'to buy off, like "greasing the palm"'. In discussion with Shadrach Peyko Dhunya, it has seemed to me that *wan is* is closer to the idea of mellowing and softening up a person through giving him presents, rather than 'buying him off'.[3] In another song, it is used of a would-be lover, an older man, approaching a reluctant girl with a present of sweet food in the hope of gaining a little affection. The exchange is not supposed to be of a commercial character, but one which establishes a bond where perhaps there was none before. In the histories of birth-groups, it is sometimes mentioned that in times of trouble, when links of mutual support were formed between two groups, they would exchange children; and the exchange is described as *wan* (*'kwani wan uçi e*). After such a *wan* exchange, a permanent tie remains between the parties; and the concept of self-interested profit, to one side or the other, would be quite out of place, especially as it is an exchange of *persons*, rather than commodities. This does not mean, of course, that a cynical onlooker might not describe a given exchange as *yol*, when the parties to it regard it as *wan*.

Yol has always the commercial implications that *wan* denies. The *Uduk Dictionary* gives 'price, bargain, cost; to trade, to sell, to bargain . . .' In a historical song of the same period as that which yearns for the redemption of the country (*wan pa*), there occurs a line *Aa mudha bunyan e gu yol mo* (I was tricked by the foreigners and taken to be sold) (quoted above, p. 59). Sometimes, the payment of bridewealth is criticized by the Uduk as a form of *yol*, of buying and selling people as though they were objects, and on this matter they take a firm moral stand; they will not, they say, put their women up for sale as though they were animals. The idea of exchanging one woman for another in marriage, though, as practised by the Koma and Ganza and occasionally by the southern Uduk, is not *yol*; this is not a market transaction, but the forming of a bond between families, and I believe the traditional form would be regarded as *wan*, as were the exchanges of children between birth-groups in history.

Whereas *wan* is in its most material sense an exchange of objects of similar type, *yol* refers to the exchange of goods of different types, with the implication that their value, not

---

[3] Interestingly, all three of these expressions have reference to the body, or rather to the person, as do many Uduk verbal expressions; *bwa* is the stomach, *'ba/* the neck, and *is* the body as a whole. *Yol* on the other hand, as far as I know, is not made into any compound expressions of this kind.

intrinsically commensurable, has been compared and calculated, and the implied calculation cannot be dissociated from an element of self-interest and profit-seeking, which itself is potentially damaging to the relationship between the parties. All money transactions come under the term *yol*, and it applies impartially to both sides—to buying and to selling. The exceptional money transaction would be the exchange of notes for small change, which might be *wan*, or might be *nyith*, a term which implies exact equivalence, without the formation of the moral bond, which *wan* connotes. Not only are the categories of goods different in a *yol* transaction, which necessitates the agreement of a 'price', but the parties to it should properly belong to different communities. The *yol* transaction should certainly not take place within a birth-group or between linked (allied) birth-groups, or between a person and his father's people. From those in your own birth-group, there is no need to buy anything anyway, for you have so many rights in common with them; from a linked birth-group you may borrow if in need; and you may make what demands you wish upon your father's people. Cross-cousins may take each other's property freely. To buy or sell within these limits would destroy the social bonds upon which these relationships are based. If a *yol* transaction does take place within these limits, people will say *'kwani yolon cem buni* (people are selling among themselves) in the same tone of disapproval as they would say *'kwani mashan cem buni* (people are marrying among themselves) or *'kwani asan cem buni* (people are fighting among themselves). The actual social limits of the community from the point of view of selling, marrying, and fighting, respectively, do not coincide (you may marry into your father's birth-group, for example); but these are qualitatively associated judgements which may be made on the behaviour of those who are supposed to be of one community. Buying and selling, in many contexts, is incompatible with kinship and neighbourly interests, although 'swapping' is not. One of my friends remarked with great distaste that the northern Sudanese buy and sell among brothers. Even between unrelated Uduk, transactions are limited. People may *yol* minor items such as chickens and small pigs, for money, with unrelated neighbours, and very occasionally cows for goats.

But major transactions, involving cows, goats, sesame or grain and money, take place usually between Uduk and non-Uduk (especially Meban, Bunyan, nomad Arabs, and miscellaneous merchants). The biggest common transaction of this kind is the buying of cows by Uduk from the Bunyan petty traders of the villages south of Kurmuk. Even this transaction is not of a brazen commercial character, but contained within a frame-work of moral relationships. Neither party is profit-seeking in a crude manner, for even the Bunyan, whose economic sophistica-tion is undeniable, values the personal connections within which his trading is carried out, and knows very well that if he were to abuse them, he would find no business. The individual Bunyan may be well-known among the Uduk, and have long-estab-lished trading connections with them. The transaction is ulti-mately one of sesame grown by the Uduk for cows reared by the Bunyan. He sells the sesame later for cash in the markets of Ora or Kurmuk, and is familiar with the annual price cycle (highest in the early rains, just before the new harvest). On the Uduk side, there is a considerable degree of trust, and a desire to satisfy the visitor so that there will be no question of resentment or later claims. The transaction is not direct, but mediated by the use of goats, which are used in this context as a medium of exchange locally, and it is concluded by a sacrifice.

The transaction takes the following typical form: the Bunyan usually takes the initiative, perhaps after hearing that a particu-lar Uduk hamlet wants a cow, and leads the animal there. He then states how many goats he wants for the cow. This may be discussed by the Uduk villagers among themselves, and is subject to negotiation. Thus, eight may be offered, and accepted, when ten were originally suggested. The goats are then collected from various members of the birth-group in the hamlet. The Bunyan then says: 'Good. Now would anyone like to keep his goat? I will sell the goats back for sesame.' Some people will buy back their goats, and maybe the goats of others as well; some people leave their goats with the Bunyan. He then goes off with some sesame and some goats, tours round some other hamlets until he has sold all his goats for sesame, and then goes home.

After negotiations are completed in the first hamlet, one of their small male goats is taken (extra to those involved in the transaction *per se*) and sacrificed. If there is no goat, a chicken is used. This sacrifice is known as *roroço*, and is to 'make blood', to welcome the new cow into the hamlet. The goat's carcass is cut in two, the front half being roasted and eaten by all the parties to the transaction, and the back half is given to the Bunyan to take home. The goat's blood is touched on the rump of the cow, and she may wear the goat's skin on her horns for a while.[4]

There is a further meaning of the Uduk word *roroço*. It is used of a man at the scene of battle who for one reason or another is left behind by his fellows as they retreat from the enemy. He gets killed gratuitously. His death is extra to the formal confrontation of battle, and yet there is no retaliation or vengeance possible in the peace following the battle. The people I discussed this question with were reluctant to admit a link between this usage and the *roroço* sacrifice which may follow a *yol* transaction. But it is tempting to see an implicit analogy here, between the sacrifice of a life over and above the formal opposition of the battle and the market-style transaction respectively. The analogy is a sharp reminder of the element of hostility and danger which the Uduk certainly see in the commercial transaction, and suggests strongly that there is a need in both cases for some kind of sacrifice, at least the giving up of the pursuit of an eye for an eye, in order to achieve the social peace.

The *roroço* following the purchase of cattle also recalls the gifts and offerings made to gods of the market-place in many parts of the world. The gift element in the *roroço* leads us on to consider gifts in general among the Uduk, which are more common than nakedly interested transactions. But the circulation of gifts has limitations, from an economic viewpoint; for except within the birth-group, gifts are not proper items for keeping, for adding to one's savings. They should be consumed.

Within a birth-group, small gifts are given; for example a mother's brother will give his sister's son some seed sesame to plant, to start him off in life. This gift has the same character as the sharing of food within the birth-group community; it does not involve a transfer of ownership. But gifts which pass from one birth-group to another are of a different character. They do not form part of what is ultimately shared property. It would therefore be wrong for the recipient to add such a gift to the common stock of wealth and animals in which he invests

---

[4] This description is based on an account given to me by William Danga, for I have not witnessed the transaction.

jointly with his matrilineal kin. Like the sacrifice which is one form of gift, any gift should be consumed and not stored away for future profit. Or perhaps the yield on the gift may be consumed, and its original substance returned, as with cows loaned by a father to his son, for him to drink their milk. Even if a father gives his son a gift of sesame, which quite often happens, this seed is of a different character from that given him by his mother's brother, and to which he has a right. The seed from his father may be planted, but the crop should be sold for money which can then be spent on coffee or clothing, or it may be used to buy a pig or goat which must be killed and eaten. The animal bought with it must not be kept to give birth, and thus to contribute to the future purchase of a cow; if this should happen, the father and his birth-group would regard the cow as belonging to them, at least partially.[5]

The same rule, that goods passing from one birth-group to another are not proper for converting into permanent savings, applies to the payments received by ritual specialists. These payments, often of chickens, goats, sesame, or money, should be shared out and consumed by the matrilineal kin of the specialist. Thus if a man received say a goat and 20 piastres for his services as a healer, he should spend the money on some coffee and invite everyone for a cup, kill the goat and roast it for everyone around, including visitors, to eat. It would be immoral to keep the goat, especially if it were female, so that one's wealth would increase. The original donors would say, 'The man is getting rich at our expense', and come to lead away their goats, or complain that a debt was owed to them.

These rules of economic morality insulate the birth-group as a self-contained working and investment unit, inhibit circulation within the Uduk economy, and restrict the activity of entrepreneurs, as the price of preserving fairness and security in social relations. It is against this background that the significance attached to debt, and the effort put into the recovery of wealth from creditors, may be better appreciated.

[5] This does not apply to sorghum, a staple food grain rather than a high-value market crop. The principle parallels closely Sahlins' re-analysis of the Maori *hau*, Mauss' 'spirit of the gift', which Sahlins convincingly argues is the principle whereby any yield or profit made from a gift should be given to, or shared with, the original donor of the gift. See Sahlins, 1974.

There is a particular class of obligation between birth-groups which gives rise to substantial transfers of wealth, a class termed *amure* and translated as debt. Debts between birth-groups are pursued with some vigour, as this is the easiest way of increasing the possessions of a community from external sources while preserving the fiction of social equality and balance. Goods transferred in repayment of an old debt are not regarded as gifts, to be consumed, but as replacements of savings, permanent wealth lost or due at some previous time. It is in the nature of savings, as animals, to multiply, and therefore, the longer a debt has been due, the larger it becomes. The sphere of manœuvre to regain old debts is of considerable importance in local politics.

Debts arise from two main sources: first, the failure to return animals which die or are lost while on loan, or the direct killing of others' animals when they trespass; and, second, from the ritual healing services of diviners, men of *arum* (spirit power) and other specialists. Fees are due to those specialists who cure a disease (nothing is due if the patient dies), for the recovered patient owes his life to the doctor. Usually they are paid at a special ceremony of 'shaving the head' a few months later. Before the fee is paid, the patient should allow his hair to grow long, as a sign of his state of debt; the word for hair (*amur*) is related to that for debt. Occasionally, the fees do not get paid; perhaps because the patient's people cannot raise the necessary grain and animals, perhaps because the specialist dies, or one of the parties moves to a distant place.

It is thought that grumbling over such a debt by creditors will activate their rainstones, if they possess them, and a storm will damage the property or lives of the birth-group in debt.[6] In practice, when the storm damage occurs, a diviner (*ŋari*) is consulted, and he diagnoses the particular debt which caused it, according to his knowledge of current grumbling and past history. The debt should then be repaid, with sufficient extra items to satisfy the creditors completely. Some of these items are symbolic prestations, rather than payments; for example, spears, tobacco, oil, bangles, and arrows may be requested or voluntarily given in addition to the goats which usually form the substance of a payment. Moreover, certain counter-payments

[6] This is explained in detail in my article on rainstones and debt; see James, 1972.

are made by the recipients, and the whole transfer is sealed with a series of sacrifices. Although the recouping of debts is the main means through which a politically active birth-group can add to its wealth, it is represented ideologically as an effort to restore the *status quo* and regain the fair and proper equilibrium which should obtain between communities.

The Uduk perceive very clearly the social and moral dangers of the commercial transaction: that is, the transaction in which each side avowedly aims at a profit, in the light of his own self-interest. Profit they assume to be gained at the expense of the other party—indeed, wrung out of his very person. The crops a man has grown represent part of his own life and labour (quite apart from other people's) and to sell them means selling a part of himself. A hired labourer, who is giving all his life and labour for money, they see as reduced almost to a commodity himself. A person of moral integrity can become damaged, and in the extreme enslaved, by the business of buying and selling. Among *'kwanim pa* there is a deep aversion to the calculations of price and profit which must go with commerce, for persons are inevitably dragged into the calculations. Crude calculation of the wealth, power or other assets of persons are distasteful and threatening to the Uduk.

Why should this feeling, which dominates their economic life, be held so strongly? It is not a mere matter of custom or unconsciously accepted tradition, nor of an undeveloped economic rationality. The Uduk do not hold these opinions naïvely or unquestioningly. They sometimes speak of them with sharp intelligence and passion and would appreciate some of our classic debates on political economy. For they know, better than most, what can be the consequences of commerce run wild. Not only are they aware of being done down by outsiders in material transactions all the time, but they know by received tradition and in a few cases still by direct experience what it is for a person to be totally reduced to a thing, through literal enslavement. Persons reduced by commerce, who have sold themselves or been sold merely for the sake of their working capacity, are not *'kwanim pa* but *ciŋkina/*. To become dependent on cash income or even trading by barter for the essentials of life, and thus to put their survival in the hands of others, would leave the Uduk people as a whole as *ciŋkina/* in relation to the richer and more competitive peoples around them. This is precisely the condition of which they have past knowledge, which they abhor, and from which, historically and morally, they are trying to free themselves. They do not regard it as straight dealing to make a profit; there is an evocative phrase *'ce'da po/*, glossed in the *Uduk Dictionary* as to 'Go around another way; also not to sell for right price – may be used of making a profit; profiteering'. An example given is *Wathi/ 'ce'd gu'ba po/*, 'The man has gone around the house, the other way'; and of profiteering, *Nuur 'ce'de'da guurusha po/ mmoyol to*. This could be translated literally as 'Nuur [the main Chali merchant] goes around the money, the other way, in selling things'. It is the concealed thorn of hostility in the commercial transaction which the *roroço* sacrifice is designed to avert, even to exorcise; and it is the past ravages of this thorn which the Uduk language of reciprocity and mutuality is designed to heal.

4

WOMEN AND BIRTH-GROUPS

*We all had one mother in
the beginning.*

Through the interrupted history of the Uduk, through their
scattering and coming together, and through the shifting relations of their present society, one outstanding principle of continuity and connection persists. This principle is the physical
continuity of substance of those born to the same woman: the
female line carries the bodily inheritance, in particular the
blood, from one generation to the next. The language of social
organization uses this theory of natural connection to some
extent, but also employs concepts which cut across it—such as
marriage and affinal connection, fatherhood, patronage and
protection, friendship and alliance. Bonds of this kind, which
constitute the political fabric of Uduk society at any given time,
are historically constructed; they are thought of as man-made,
of temporary duration, and replaceable. The continuity of the
female line, and the connection between its members, on the
other hand, are thought of as natural and inevitable, and if once
destroyed, as irreparable. The natural growth of the matriline
supplies the raw material from which society is built. The raw
material itself may be wasted and lost historically; if only one
girl is left of a line, and she is lost or dies without children, that
line is finished for ever, unless of course someone rescues the
girl and gives her children. The idea of continuity through
the fertility of the female line provides a language in which the
persistence of life through time and history can be discussed—
not only human life, but animal life as well. Animals in general
do not have historically constructed societies (apart perhaps
from dogs), but they do live in natural groupings or 'species'
called *wak̲*. The same word is used by the northern Uduk for the
natural kinds of humanity—as differentiated by matrilineal
descent. Genealogical history is represented in terms of these
natural lines, but patrilateral links are not thought of as

continuous lines in the same way. Although patrilateral links are extremely important socially and politically, they are spoken of as particular individual connections of fathers and children between one natural line and another. There is no concept of a patrilineage, as an enduring group of people. But everyone belongs to a natural matriline, which may have sprung from very early times and survived the vicissitudes of history, or may have entered history later, from a newly-assimilated foreign woman or from a rescued girl waif. The enduring quality of the female principle, its natural strength and steadiness by comparison with the male principle, recurs in images; for example, when a double rainbow is seen, the bright and dominant bow is spoken of as the female, and the paler second bow as the male. The main rainbow is the mother of all the snakes. The moon is male—a small star often by his side is his wife; and the sun is female—when she sinks at night, people say she has gone to suckle her child. When speaking of the fingers of the hand, Uduk describe the thumb as the female, or mother finger; the forefinger is the male. In every field of sorghum grain, there should be at least some black, 'female' or mother plants, for the sake of the fruitfulness of the field as a whole. These examples could be multiplied.

It is difficult to translate the Uduk *wak*. 'Clan' might at first suggest itself, but this word connotes in English, and in anthropological jargon, social association rather than natural descent. It is true, as I shall describe, that the Uduk *wak* may be represented as the proper basis of local groupings, and indeed may constitute that basis; but it is not necessarily a social group of any kind. Indeed, the concept of the natural *wak* is sometimes placed in antithetical opposition to the institutional relations and group structures of political society. There are similar difficulties with the terms 'lineage' and 'descent group', which do not in themselves discriminate between naturally and socially relevant connection, and have not always been used without ambiguity in anthropological analysis. The phrase 'birth-group' suggests itself as a happier translation of *wak*; it is not only truer to the Uduk concept than clan, or lineage, but I hope will make for clearer analysis of the way in which the Uduk see the nature and the history of their own people.

It is generally accepted that one particular birth-group, the

Lake, appeared very early and has been central in the growth of the Uduk people. Sheikh Puna Marinyje, himself a Lake from the Yabus valley where more coherent traditions about early times are current than are found further north, gave me a mythical account of the beginnings of humankind, identified with the appearance of the Lake. The first creature was a female in this story, the ancestress of the Lake. The first part of Puna's account is as follows:

'And now, the place from which people appeared long ago. The people who appeared long ago came from a clump of '*sikath* grass, the same grass which exists today. It was that from which people came. There appeared a female person long ago. Then she bore children. She bore little children: and one child was a boy, and then she gave birth to a girl. And those children lived. The person who married her, at that time long ago, at the beginning of human life, is not known. That man is unknown who married her and begot those children. Perhaps she conceived from her *arum* alone. She bore those children; and those children married, brother and sister. The people were called Lake. They gave rise to this story of long ago.

'They appeared from a clump of '*sikath* grass. After a while, that woman alone was waiting, and she gave birth to a girl child. And then she next gave birth to one *golga/* [tiang cob]. A real hoofed creature, it was born from that same woman. They were called Lake, Lake, because they were wild people, together with the hoofed creatures. They were *arum* from the bush.'

Puna regarded Kolop as the place where the Lake appeared, far to the south, in the real home of the Uduk. For many Lake, the Lake are themselves the real '*kwanim pa*. There are other ancient birth-groups; but the newer ones are regarded as still foreigners. For example, the birth-group Baggara, who look like any other Uduk to me, were dismissed—'Those people . . . their mother is a Baggara, from the beginning. They came from the land of the Baggara there. They came from there and live now in Beni Mayu, on the far bank. They are not Uduk ['*kwanim pa*], they are Baggara. Haven't you noticed, their ears are different. They are a red colour.' There is a physical, almost racial, undertone in the discussion of birth-groups and their distinction from one another.

Birth-groups are represented not only as enduring through time, after emerging from the womb of one woman, but as growing and expanding, through the fertility of generation after generation of daughters. Expansion goes with branching, one sister going one way, and one sister another, and their brothers building in different places. People say, 'We all split and divide up, building separate villages here and there, but we are all from one mother in the beginning.' The more fertile the women, the greater the expansion of the birth-group. If you ask why there are so many Lake, people will say that it is from their great fertility, and they will name some of the branches of the Lake. There are the Yap Yap, for example, who are fast-moving and quick to join in battle and to die in fighting, also known as Ka'd Shoush, 'soft-nosed' people who die easily if sickness comes; and also the Golga/ (tiang), Ulmany (stork), and 'Per E (red-eyed). Other birth-groups formerly famous but under-represented today, such as the Pa'dwosh (flat hill), are said to have no fertile women and to be dying out.

Natural metaphors are often used in speaking of *wak*. Sometimes they are represented on the analogy of species—especially species of hoofed animals. The connection of at least some Lake with the tiang cob has been mentioned; Bukko told me that his own people were hartebeest, and the people of Yabus and Borfa were waterbuck; they all became humankind, as the gazelle became the goat, the *yul* became the sheep, the roan antelope became the cow, the warthog the pig, the giraffe the camel, and the francolin the domestic chicken. The growth of individual *wak* is compared to the growth of plants from seeds; the Yap Yap division of the Lake was once described to me as the original plant of the Lake, from which seeds were scattered to grow into the other Lake divisions. The *wak* may also be spoken of as *tor*, a term applying both to the afterbirth, and to the vine of the squash plant, both images suggesting the linking of a new individual to the continuing source of growth. A very common metaphor is that of a body, *bungwar*, for the birth-group as a whole, or a branch of it, with primary reference to the common blood which its members share, not merely in a 'metaphorical' but in a substantial sense. Other bodily images abound: for example, the matrilineal descendants of a man or woman may be described as *apo*, 'back', which refers both to the backbone and to a train of followers behind a person. The descendants of a woman may be called her *'pen*, 'buttocks', which can also mean literally the little ones following behind her. The birth-group is often represented as a whole organism; for example, it is said that a child has been 'borne' by such and such a *wak*. The normal word for giving birth is used (*dho'th*), which more commonly describes the actual delivery of a child from its mother. When used of a *wak* 'giving birth', rather than an individual woman, it refers to the children that birth-group has *begotten*—not the children of its womenfolk, but of its menfolk. When a person says of a whole village or birth-group, 'They gave birth to me', he means that he was fathered there; the people of that village or *wak*, thought of as a body, gave birth to him. The children of the womenfolk of a *wak* are a part of the birth-group itself; they do not represent something new which has been created, apart from the body of the *wak*.

The image of shared substance within the birth-group has profound consequences for social relations. For instance, since the birth-group is the life-producing group, and its members share the same blood, it is easy to understand that when this blood is spilt, and a person is killed, it is the duty of his fellows in the same birth-group, his matrilineal kinsmen, to avenge his death. It is also easy to understand that those of the same birth-group may be susceptible to the same diseases. A mother and her children are often treated together for a complaint that is affecting one of them. The matrilineal kinsfolk of certain ritual specialists are likely to be affected by the medicines and powers which they employ, and frequently become ill or possessed by them, while others, equally close neighbours but not of the same birth-group, will be less open to their contaminating influence.

The transmission of blood itself through the matriline can have effects on the people born to it. The most dramatic and serious of conditions transmitted in the female line is that of 'witchcraft'. The *dhathu/* condition, so fearful that it is rarely discussed in the open, is one in which a person involuntarily causes harm and evil consequences to those around him, particularly to his own matrilineal kin. This is not merely the capacity of an individual; a man or woman acquires it from an evil birth, from the mother's womb which has gone bad. It is the capacity of a whole matriline which has been contaminated. There are visible signs of this contamination, notably the birth of monstrous children and of twins. To give birth to twins is a sign to the mother that she has been contaminated by *dhathu/*. Very often, one child is disposed of so that people will not know of the monstrosity. It is said that in the past, both children, and their mother too, were killed in order to eliminate the evil. Today, because of the secrecy surrounding birth (women often give birth in the grass, not in the hut), it is assumed that there may be *dhathu/* anywhere, even close to home. Children born to a woman who has already had twins are even more dangerous than the twins themselves, and if they or the twins are female, they will pass on the contamination. Sometimes whole birth-groups are suspected of being *dhathu/*. The language used of a monstrous or twin birth is not that of ordinary human births; to bear twins is *wol*, not *dho'th—wol* is otherwise used only of the multiple births of certain animals, and a comparison is most commonly made with goats. A woman is not a goat, that she should bear two at the same time. The effect might be shadowed in English by a whispered 'She's littered.'

But the representation of *dhathu/* is more complicated than this. I have been told that in the past, *dhathu/* were not necessarily evil in nature; their special capacities were used for the benefit of their fellows—for example, they could direct people to find game in the forest. The ambiguity adheres to birth-groups like the Lakeŋ Golga/, associated with a former antelope-birth; to some, it indicates a witch condition, but to others, a spiritual capacity to which people looked for help in the past.

THE BIRTH AND GROWTH OF A PERSON

A man's contribution to the birth of a child is quite distinct from that of a woman. The term *dho'th*, to give birth to, is not normally used of the fathering of a child, except in the sense mentioned, of a whole *wak* begetting children. Giving birth is the job of women, though it is well understood that sexual relations are necessary for conception.

It is considered that the substance of the baby is derived from the mother's blood, the normal monthly flow, but that the child is 'formed', moulded or created, by his father. The word *uk*, used of this act of creation, is the same as that used of a potter moulding clay, or of *arum* (spirit) creating the world in the beginning. A man does not sleep with his wife during her monthly period, but by having relations with her soon after, is able to stop the next flow by moulding it into a child. The embryo is considered to be 'just blood' for the first few months, and if the mother has a miscarriage it is said that 'the blood has come down'. Or the embryo may be referred to as 'just meat', or as a little bird. After about three months it is thought to develop a real body (*buŋgwar*). Spirit (*arum*) plays a part in the conception of a child, which cannot be understood; so that although it is correct to say the man creates children for the woman (*wathin gwath uk uçi gom a'bom*), this is not a complete explanation. Rapka explained the part played by both man and *arum* in the actual creation of women's children:

'Men marry us to give birth to children. Children are present in men. Children are present in their fathers, they are not present in us. We produce monthly blood which is nothing in itself. The children are present only in their fathers. If we marry, then we conceive a child. If we remain as girls, we don't conceive. . . .

'*Arum* says, "I am going to give birth to a girl child."

'Another *arum* says, "Ay! That person will give birth to a male child, as the first born . . ."

'Some men can't impregnate a girl: that man is dried up, they say, he has no children, and never will.'

While the baby is growing in his mother's womb, the father should go on sleeping with his wife, for semen is thought to nourish the baby and make him strong. If the husband is absent or does not have relations with his wife, the baby will become weak (*kushakush*, literally 'pale'). During this time, he is also being nourished indirectly from the food that his mother is consuming in the hamlet of her husband. If a woman is deserted by her husband, and is expecting a baby, she should eat plenty of *a'tash cuk* (stew flavoured with the ash of *a'tash* wood, which occurs significantly in Bukko's version of the story of the finding of the first man, pp. 79–80 above), and this will nourish the baby. The production of a baby is thus a joint effort; and at the time of birth, both parents are regarded as being in a 'hot' or ritually vulnerable state, and various restrictions are placed on the activities of the husband as well as the wife.

Children are thought, on the whole, to resemble their father or his (patrilateral) kinsmen, not only in physical appearance, but also in character and behaviour. Uduk informants, pragmatic as ever, will always point out some cases where the opposite holds, and a person resembles someone in their own birth-group with whom they do not have patrilateral kin in common; but these cases are treated as interesting exceptions, and the general rule of partilineal transmission of character and appearance remains valid. It will often be remarked that little John's ears are just like his father's; or the baby girl Dhayina looks just like her *iya*,[1] Nathir (this man being her father's patrilateral, but not uterine, brother); or that another boy has a temper like his father's, or a girl is beautiful like her father's sister. In cases of doubt over paternity, people say that the matter will be cleared up when the child is born, and its features can be examined, for it will resemble its father; though I have not come across a case where this was actually done.

The father is usually responsible for the continuing nourishment of the child after his birth, and until he is ready to join his mother's brothers. While he is at his mother's breast, she is able to provide him with milk because of the food she eats; and she is normally living and consuming food in her husband's hamlet. The child is therefore being nourished, through his mother, on food grown by his father, and the people of his father's hamlet. When he is weaned, he of course begins to consume their food directly, as long as he and his mother remain with his father. The child is thus created by the father from the mother's blood, and nourished in the womb, at the breast, and later directly, by the father, until he is mature. The social consequences following from this picture of the growth of a child will be described below.

Close to Uduk concepts of matrilineal connection are images drawn from the physiology of the body; in particular, blood circulation, consumption of food, and health.

The body is said to be kept alive physically by the circulation of the blood, which is pumped by the heart (*kwasinjama*) in a circuit to the head and back, and to the limbs. If a person or animal is wounded, it is thought that death results from loss of blood. If a person's throat is cut, the vital circulation between heart and head is cut off, the blood escapes and the person dies.

---

[1] *Iya* is a reciprocal term between 'father's brother' and 'brother's child' (male speaking).

If he is stabbed near the heart, or in the stomach or liver which are near the heart, there will be a serious loss of blood and he will die. The heart itself, as the centre of blood circulation, is extremely vulnerable and if pierced even by a small instrument will cause death. If a person is hit hard on the head, which is not regarded as a vital centre in itself, the blood will all go down to the heart, and this will cause death. If a person is speared in a limb, far from the heart, not much blood will be lost and so he will not die. Unhealthy blood (sometimes described as 'black') may cause pain and illness, and blood-letting is practised for some headaches and other complaints.

Circulation of the blood is stimulated by exercise and hard work, which are therefore health-promoting. A sick person will not lie down and rest if he can manage to get up and struggle to work, for if he were to rest, his blood would slow down and he would get weaker. Strength and health are further equated with a well-built body, and plenty of weight—though of course obesity is unknown. Shortage of food, leading to loss of weight, is itself thought to weaken and sicken the body. I have often heard remarks: 'Look how thin I am. I shall go to the Dispensary to drink some medicine.' Shortage of food is of course often just round the corner, and alternate hunger and satiation are part of everyone's life.

The really nourishing foods are those made from plain grains: sorghum and maize. If you do not have enough of these, for making porridge and beer, you are struck by hunger (*'kosha ṭe*/). Starchy roots may appease this basic hunger if grain foods are not available; but a person may die eventually if *ṭe*/ is not satisfied. Desire for meat is in a different category; one is said to be *'kosha ḵwa/a*, struck by meat-hunger. This can be satisfied by meat, or fish, or eggs; but its satisfaction is not, I think, regarded as essential to preserving life and health. Meat and fish are extras, luxuries which one could strictly do without. Relishes made from herbs, mushrooms, vegetables, and spices, and sweet things such as honey, are also luxuries, which satisfy the taste but do not nourish the body. Indeed, for people who are not strong and healthy, all extras such as meat, or sweet foods, or strong sauces, or even sesame paste, are thought to be dangerous; and invalids are supposed to eat only the plainest and safest of food, that is grain porridge and beer. Nursing mothers, whose milk is produced by the food they eat, should also avoid exotic and strong-tasting foods, most meats, and so on, because they would affect the milk and make the baby ill. Most infant illnesses are ascribed to this cause.

Life and health therefore depend on a body nourished by the crops of the field; and the very act of hard physical work stimulates blood circulation, fitness and the growth of the body. These images of life and growth depending upon the circulation of blood and the production of grain for the nourishment of the body enter the representation of the naturally-based matrilineal birth-group.

RESIDENCE

The idea behind the birth-group is one of natural connection through the blood. There is no reason why this principle of physical connection should necessarily form the basis of social and political community life. The Komo, for instance, also have a theory of natural connection through women, but do not live in communities according to this principle. However, on the whole the Uduk do—their small hamlets, and even clusters of hamlets, are primarily communities of matrilineal kin, and are identified with particular birth-groups. This is the characteristic pattern today, although as I shall explain, there is evidence that it has not always been so.

The general expectation among the Uduk is for a boy to leave his father's hamlet about the time of puberty, and join his own hamlet, the hamlet of his genealogically closest *ishwakam*, mother's brothers. Here, he will later build a home for his wife, and their young children will be brought up in it. However, a man is not obliged to live with his closest mother's brothers; he may settle with another hamlet of his own birth-group, sometimes many miles distant, or in the hamlet of a birth-group closely allied to his own. Or he may live with his father's people, sometimes remaining for life in the hamlet in which he was born, and bringing his wife there. Occasionally, two or three patrilaterally related men will form a small hamlet together. Very rarely, a man may build with his wife's people. And in extreme circumstances, a man who is excluded by his relatives may seek protection from strangers and settle with them. A man is likely however to move at least once in his life, from his father's to his mother's brothers' hamlet; and in very old age, he may leave his own hamlet to live with one of his sons—who will care for him in old age as he cared for his son in childhood. Some men utilize several of the possibilities open to them during their lives, moving round frequently from place to place.

Women are even more mobile as individuals. The simplest pattern consists of two moves instead of one. Whereas a boy usually moves from his father's to his own hamlet and remains there, a woman moves from her father's, where she was born, to her husband's hamlet, and then in old age to her own home— the hamlet of her mother's brothers. This basic pattern is complicated by a young girl's moving with her mother as her mother remarries several times; by her own complex marital career; and by the repeated periods she and her mother spend with their own matrilineal kin in between marriages, or in illness, or when their brothers are without wives and need them. Women may also, if they wish, move back to their father's people and spend time there.

A young woman, Shara, of the Yakan birth-group, for example, about 25 years old, was born in a hamlet in the northwest of Pam 'Be (see Figure 3) where her father's people lived (they were of the birth-group Ça'ba). Her mother died there while she was still a child, and her mother's sister took her fifteen miles north to Bellila, where I believe her husband lived. After several years, Shara returned to her father's people, who had by this time moved across the Tombak river to the south bank. She married her first husband, who also lived in southern Pam 'Be, had a child who died, and later left her husband. She rejoined her mother's sister, who had by this time also left her husband and was back in northern Pam 'Be with a group of their own people (Yakan), and after a few months Shara married again, into a nearby hamlet of Waka'cesh.

Another young woman living in Waka'cesh, Buthe, who was about 20 years old, was born in nearby Pan Gathe with her father's people. Then they moved site, to Paŋ Ça'ba, further west on the northern bank of the Tombak. Her father then left her mother, who took the child Buthe to their own people at Pam Bigin, even further west, where she grew up. Her mother then married into Pany Çaran, and they moved back upstream to that hamlet. Buthe went to mission school for two years in

Chali, after which she rejoined her mother in their own hamlet of Pam Bigin, for her mother had left her second husband by this time. Her mother then married again, for a second time into the same hamlet of Pany Caran, and they returned to live there. Then Buthe herself married, into Waka'cesh.

A third young woman, Thayke, of about the same age, was born in north-western Pam 'Be, with her 'grandfathers'—her father was living with *his* father's people, of the Gwami birth-group. Then her mother became sick, and she took the baby Thayke to their own people (Kunthuk) living at Yilejada, beyond Beni Mayu. She died there, while Thayke was still very young. One of her mother's brothers moved to Pany Caran, and brought her too; and the hamlet moved site several times. She married a Bitko man, and would have joined him in Waka'cesh, but he died before the house was built, and she remained with her own people, until she married again, for the second time into Waka'cesh (but this time a Lake man).

The brief histories of these young married women in Waka'cesh are quite typical, and give a characteristic picture of the frequent movements of Uduk women, and the pull which is exerted by their own 'home', the hamlet of their own birth-group, throughout their lives.

A 'typical' Uduk hamlet is thus likely to consist of a group of perhaps half a dozen men who regard themselves as close matrilineal kin (although they are probably unable to demonstrate full genealogical links), one or two others who come from a more remote branch of the birth-group or from an allied birth-group, perhaps a couple of adolescent sons who have not yet left for their own people, and perhaps an old father. Half the women will be 'sisters' of men in the hamlet, that is women of the birth-group—either old women who because of sickness or widowhood have returned home for good and live in huts built by their sons and brothers, or young women temporarily without husbands, or sick, or simply 'on holiday' from looking after their husbands, and looking after their brothers for a change. The other half will be outside women married into the hamlet, together with their young children from current and previous marriages. There is a good deal of coming and going, with wide options of settlement as well as the instability of marriage; moreover, the hamlets themselves are often splitting up and reforming, and moving site, as I have described earlier. In spite of this high degree of mobility and apparent confusion, the hamlet remains in ideal conception and in statistical description based upon a core of matrilineal kin, close members of one birth-group.

Hamlets are often known by the name of one or another of the individuals who live there; thus one speaks of *pan Tente*, the home of Tente. But a hamlet may also be known as the home of a birth-group, for instance Pai Bitko. Place-names of some geographical permanence are also in use, and often used inclusively of a locality which is settled by people of several allied birth-groups living in a series of hamlets. Waka'cesh is such a name, embracing today hamlets of the birth-groups Lake, Bitko and Koro. But even such place-names are ephemeral, and do not provide a fixed framework for describing Uduk settlements. Appendix 3 shows details of the residential structure of a typical hamlet in Waka'cesh for February, 1966, together with genealogies.

MARRIAGE

As a prologue to this book I have quoted Emed's version of the story of the beginnings of marriage, and Bukko's version is quoted also in the second chapter. This story has many echoes; besides richly imaging the centrality of women in the emergence and continuation of the society of the *'kwanim pa*, it directly illuminates Uduk attitudes to sex and marriage, in which women are by no means the passive creatures of men's pleasure and socio-economic transactions.

The northern Uduk of the Tombak and Ahmar valleys, the main body of the people, pride themselves on always having, according to them, married 'freely'. The women in particular criticize and deprecate the marriage arrangements of neighbouring peoples—the bridewealth of the Meban, Berta, Arabs; the bride-service of the Hill Burun and Ingessana; and the sister-exchange of their fellow Koman speakers, which they know from first-hand contact with the Komo and the Ganza to their south. They regard bridewealth payment as equivalent to the buying and selling of animals, and sister-exchange as restricting to women and a cause of fighting. They can see that these various systems give women and young people little say in their own marriages, and one thing they value strongly is the freedom of young people, and of women in particular, to make and break their own marriages.

Although the northern Uduk refuse to contemplate any connection, present or past, with exchange-marriage, the southern Uduk in the Yabus valley and in the hills to the south of it do occasionally reciprocate a marriage. It is not by formal arrangement between families, as is the proper tradition among the other Koman peoples, but a tit-for-tat elopement—something the other Komans also know, and disapprove of. A young fellow whose sister has been eloped with may feel tempted to gather a few friends and kidnap a girl in return. This style of marriage is called *ri'c mash* by the Uduk, 'revenge marriage', an apt term. The southern Uduk say that they, as distinct from the northern Uduk, used to practise a thoroughgoing exchange system, but have given it up as it leads to fighting; and when an occasional 'revenge marriage' happens they regard it as something of a joke. I shall return to the interesting connections of sister-exchange, southern Uduk revenge marriage and historical speculation in a later chapter.

Uduk marriage, at least in its early stages, is the concern of the two principals themselves; their relatives have little say if any, and are put under no particular obligation by it. A couple who wish to marry usually stage an elopement; there are no long-drawn-out negotiations or other preliminaries. The couple are bound by personal interest and affection, and either may terminate the relationship if they wish. Young people often speak of romantic attachments, and *mmoen*, to love, can mean specifically sexual love.

The neighbours of the Uduk, the local administrators and magistrates, and the missionaries who used to operate at Chali, have all found it difficult to take Uduk marriage seriously, and have often regarded it as hopelessly 'primitive'. In 1963 the local Omda, with the backing of the missionaries and the administration, instituted a new policy for marriage among the Uduk: marriages should be registered, and bridewealth should be paid, at the rate of £4.000 (Sudanese) for a girl, and £2.500 (Sudanese) for a widow or a previously-married woman. The idea was to stabilize marriage. The new system, which could not be enforced anyway, did not last long; within a year, it was abandoned, and the bridewealth which had been paid had in most cases already been returned. Nobody was happy with the payment system—especially not those who received the money for their girl, for she could not return home when she wanted to. It was like selling her as a goat; and if she did return home, demands would be made for the return of the money, which would have been spent by that time, and the girl's people would be left in debt. After the first year, the authorities gave up trying to enforce marriage payments.[2]

Marriages certainly seem to any outsider to be remarkably unstable. But this impression is gained partly from the lack of distinction between what an outside observer might call 'marriage' and what he might call a love-affair, for all sexual relationships are termed *mash*. The term may be qualified as *mash thus* or *çal*, bad marriage or adultery, if it refers to secret affairs where the man makes no attempt to build a house for the woman or take her away from her present husband. The word *mash* may refer simply to the sexual act itself, though only in reference to people. The mating of animals is termed *ha'k*, which may on occasion be used of human beings, but it is a crude usage and carries none of the social implications of *mash*. Sexuality is a relatively open matter, and not hedged around with secrecy, shame, and taboos. It is a topic for straightforward discussion or for loud bawdy joking. Uduk men and women seem to radiate enthusiastic heterosexuality; there is no tradition, even discreetly accepted, of homosexual activity, which is regarded by those who have travelled as an Arab practice.

In spite of the range of short and long term sexual relationships covered by the term *mash*, and more or less accepted, there are criteria for judging what is proper marriage (*mash gana*) from casual affairs. Proper marriage requires that the man build a house for the woman, and that he cultivate fields for her and generally look after her properly. She too has domestic obligations, and if she does not observe them, her marriage will not be regarded as a proper marriage. When the domestic side of the relationship is properly set up, people will speak of the couple in relation to one another as *kath* and *ash* (husband and wife). Or the woman may be referred to *a'bom piti*, literally

2 I have described the background to this situation in an earlier article (James, 1970b).

'his woman', with the sense of 'his wife'. The use of these terms
confirms the social recognition of the existence of a proper
marriage; they would not be used of a pair of lovers who did not
settle down as a domestic unit.

In selecting a spouse, Uduk say they like to marry 'far out'.
They say they should not marry anyone they call *'bwaham* or
akam: these terms apply to siblings and to parallel cousins, and
we can with careful reservation translate them as sister and
brother, or 'sister' and 'brother' if we wish to indicate parallel
cousins (mother's sister's children or father's brother's children).
For a man, the category *'bwaham* includes, to begin with, all the
girls of his own generation who belong to his local birth-group,
and is also applied sometimes to those of a closely allied local
birth-group; and on the patrilateral side, applies to all the
girls of his generation who share the same father's people—
and who were therefore, on the whole, brought up in the same
hamlet or cluster of hamlets. Although he may marry a cross-
cousin (*'kwaskam*) on either side, if she were a first cousin it
would be slightly frowned on. I have heard a young man teased
by the girls for hanging round his father's hamlet—they taunted
him for not having the courage to go further from home to find
a girl for himself who wasn't a cross-cousin. Across the generations, there are parallel prohibitions on marriage; a man should
not marry, for example, anyone called *'bwaham* ('sister') by either
of his parents.

Marriages do occur within the proper limits, especially
between allied birth-groups. In one case I know, where the
members of two local birth-groups applied kinship terms to each
other as though all were one, a man of one married a woman of
the other whom he called *ara ta'da* ('mother's sister'). No such
marriage between the groups had occurred within living
memory, and it evoked mild disapproval. It was said by outsiders: *'kwani mashan çem buni*, people are marrying among
themselves. Marriage sometimes occurs even within a local
birth-group, and this is regarded with scorn by outsiders. It
may lead to fighting within the group—that is, a man's brothers
are likely to fight and possibly kill him if he has sexual relations
with a girl or woman of the local birth-group. However, as far
as I am aware, there is no special word for 'incest', and there
appear to be no standard mystical consequences of marriage or

sexual encounters between close kin. The Uduk do not speculate much on these possibilities. When asked why an *akam* and *bwaham* should not marry, informants are likely to give a highly pragmatic reply: for example, that if siblings or parallel cousins within the birth-group married, their children would not have any father's people. It is also said that they would be weak and sickly, whereas if the parents come from different birth-groups, with different blood, the children will be strong and healthy. However, if the men of a birth-group do fight an offending brother for sexual involvement within the group, this fighting like any other hostility within the birth-group can itself lead to sickness and death, through the anger of the spirits of the dead.

A man may be married, that is, count as 'husband' (*ka̱ẖ*) to as many women as he can keep in adequate domestic comfort. In practice, it is very rare for a man to be able to keep more than two women at the same time, for they are sexually jealous and demanding, and each requires the provision of a house and the cultivation of fields, which may become a burden on the husband. If a man marries a third woman, one of the existing two is likely to pack up her things and go home. Unless the husband makes great efforts to get her back, she will soon cease to be regarded as his wife, but as a *dalla*. This is a special word for women who have been married, but are separated ('divorced' would be too formal a term) and are available for re-marriage. A woman can be regarded as a wife (*ash, a'bom*) to only one man at a time. Thus a woman passes from the status of *nyara* (girl), to that of wife, and then on to *dalla*, back to wife again and so on. A man whose marriage is recognized as finished, and who temporarily has no wife, may also be termed *dalla*, or *washana dalla* (young man *dalla*).

Since there is no rigid distinction between what constitutes formal marriage and more informal liaisons, it is not surprising to find that the Uduk make no distinction whatsoever between *pater* and *genitor*; one's father (*baba* or *com*) has the same relationship with one whether he remained attached to one's mother for years and years or not. Although a child may be born of a secret affair and termed *dhothu ki 'kus* (born in freedom) or *dhothu 'peni bwasho* (born from the bush), he suffers no disability and this origin will be forgotten as he grows up. When paternity is uncertain, as I have mentioned, it is likely to be decided from the appearance of the child. It follows, of course, that among the Uduk marriage cannot be defined as a social relation providing for the birth of legitimate children. It is a personal relation of mainly private concern in which sex is important, and which develops wider social consequences only through the birth of children. Women in particular, who often take the initiative in courtship and sex, are anxious for children in marriage; and if they do not conceive after a few months of marriage will seek advice from a diviner, and perhaps think of leaving their husbands. They are jealous of other women in whom their husbands may be interested; and an Uduk practice which has gained some notoriety is that whereby women fight each other, in a style of formal duelling or jousting, over the men they love. Long staves, up to six or seven feet, are used in a style of face-to-face combat which recalls the ceremonial duelling of men among the Mursi of south-western Ethiopia.[3] Each woman approaches, crouching, with her stave held horizontally but swung diagonally as she moves forward, feigning attack; then one actually smacks down her stave on her opponent's, trying to force it to the ground, in two or three rapid strokes if it can't be done in one. The pair then separate, to crouch and approach again. It is a spectacular performance to watch, though the real thing usually takes place very early in the morning and in private. Women may be injured, although the aim of the jousting is not to hurt your opponent seriously but to vindicate your honour, display your skill in women's arts and defend your rights in your man. If it is not easy to see the real thing—and villagers themselves tend to keep away from the early morning fury of offended women—there is plenty of friendly practice which a visitor will find quite entertaining. Little girls start practising with each other at an early age, and men and boys sometimes take a turn with the women's jousting staves for a joke. Here is a missionary's description of the women's jousting, for which the Uduk are understandably notorious.[4]

'It was just getting light and from the direction of the village female voices were pouring out wild sounds . . .

'We wanted to find out all we could about the Uduk people, so we went to the village. As we neared the scene, the shouting grew louder

[3] See the unpublished L.S.E. Ph.D. thesis of D. Turton.
[4] Forsberg, 1958, pp. 127–8.

and angrier. One of the men had taken a second wife the day before and his first wife was giving vent to her wrath.

'We found the two women standing ready for battle in a clearing between the huts. They glared at each other across a distance of about fifteen feet. Both were stripped of beads and other decorations and each held an eight-foot bamboo stave. They were furious; as they shrieked insults, a second woman stood dutifully behind each dueler to shout further curses and insults at the opposing fighter. The fiery talk of the second exceeded that of the injured women. Male onlookers were absent and we learned that the men were disgusted because wives would not live together, so they never watched these fights. It was time for the duel to begin.

' "You'll take my husband away from me, will you?" shouted Wife Number One.

'She lunged forward and took two quick cracks at her adversary, one with either end of her stave. Wife Number Two deftly swung her stave into action and defended herself, then the first woman stepped back. Apparently there were rules for this kind of fighting. The second wife poised her mouth and her stick.

' "You with the face of a hyena, you aren't going to drive me away from the man who wants me", she screamed.

'Then she let loose the two blows allowed her as Wife Number One warded off the attack. The sticks cracked like rifle shots as they met. There seemed to be no rules to govern the war of words, as the seconds kept up a machine-gun stream of vituperation. They were profane, with no evil deed of either contestant left unmentioned. The insults added fury to the already fiery emotions of the fighters.

' "Nobody will have you", shrieked the first wife, "so you try to steal my husband!"

'Her stick came down—one, two!—as the defender warded off the blows with her stave . . .

'Wife Number One, who had the most to fight for, was tense and efficient. When her turn came again she poised, swung her stave and the first blow fell with animal-like dexterity. The second came with the speed of lightning. Wife Number Two did not move fast enough and her opponent's stave got inside hers, skidded down the length of it, and tore the skin from her wrist. She looked dismayed at the blood on her arm. The fight with staves was over but not the war of words. We wondered if anything had been decided. It was later that we learned the two wives had settled down in separate houses and avoided each other. Eventually, when Wife Number Two could endure it no longer, she picked up her few belongings and returned to her mother.'

If a man takes a second wife, there may be some weeks of early-morning jousting between the two women before things settle down to a routine. The husband will have to build a hut for each wife, close together with the doors more or less facing each other; he will have to spend alternate nights with each wife and be meticulously fair in his affections; he will keep his bows and other weapons in or outside the senior wife's hut; and he will have to attend to each task of cultivation on the senior wife's fields before seeing to the second wife's. Small arguments may easily escalate at any time, and the women will fight again; or one may go home in a temper. Married life is often stormy, and hot-headed spouses may come to blows. I found this apt comment in some anonymous manuscript notes on Uduk customs:[5] 'Wife beating is far less common than it is among the arabised tribes, but only among the Uduk is husband beating by the wife no cause for astonishment.'

A wife who is extremely angry with her husband and who wishes to end the relationship will sometimes set fire to the hut her husband built for her, and then depart. A number of such cases are taken to the court in Kurmuk, where indeed the Uduk are a byword for cases of arson.

Sora once did this: she burnt the hut her husband had built for her in 1966, and was sentenced to three months in Kurmuk jail. But this experience did not seem to cool her passions, and she later told me how she had acquired a bruise under her eye:[6]

'We were jousting, Tamke and I, at night, when Belo was married to us and was keeping us both. Belo struck me because we were jousting at night, Tamke and I. Maybe we were fighting over sex. We were fighting, Tamke and I, at night, because he would go to sleep with one of us.

'Then I took a cane which was going to be used for weaving a door, meaning to beat Tamke *mush*! and then Belo immediately came up and knocked me on the ground, *bush*! I got up, and then I took another stick to beat Tamke, *ṯug*. Then Belo immediately caught me and I fell, *dhus*. Have I any strength? He went on knocking me down, just me.

'Dapka asked him, "Why do you keep on knocking Sora on the

[5] A copy of anonymous typescript 'Notes on Uduk Customs', found in Kurmuk Hospital and given to me, has now been deposited in the Central Archives, Khartoum.
[6] In this case, which is developed below, I use pseudonyms.

ground like that? You're hurting her terribly." That's what she said to Belo. And Belo took hold of his throwing-stick from its place; and I got hold of him, about to bite him on the elbow, meaning to bite Belo here. Belo swung his arm back, the one holding the throwing-stick, and it hit me under the eye, with a great *'dwal*. Wendy, it was right here below my eye—here is the scar! It hit me, *bup*. I cried, "My eye is burst, my eye is burst! You must bring me another eye— you must pick out one of yours for me!—for me to go and see to dig up roots in the forest." Because he had struck me.'

It is not only the wife who is prepared to defend her marriage by direct action. A husband who discovered that another man is paying attention to his wife, would traditionally be entitled to fight, injure, and even kill him. The fighting between women is usually contained within the rules of the formal stave-jousting, but conflict between men over women is not restricted by such conventions. In the past, there was plenty of violence in defence of marriage, according to informants. Quarrels over women were the main source of conflict in the past, people insist. Today, ironically, with the presence of police and courts, Uduk men are less ready to take physical action to deter adulterers; and the establishment of 'law and order' may paradoxically have contributed to increasingly casual marriage relations among the Uduk. However, cases of violence do still occur; in one case of about 1965, a husband returned home to find a man with his wife, and unsheathed the short dagger which all men carry at the elbow. The adulterer managed to escape with only a minor wound in his side, but might have lost his life. He was taken to the Chali dispensary, from where it was inevitable that the case should reach the court in Kurmuk. The husband was furious because he had already taken this man to court over his adultery, and he had emerged unreformed after six months in prison. The situation was particularly serious because the two men were 'brothers' of allied birth-groups and supposed to be friends. If the adulterer had been killed, direct vengeance would have been sought, and perhaps a large-scale fight would have developed, with the two traditionally close birth-groups each recruiting supporters; and the courts might have made a number of serious convictions. However, the adulterer managed to persuade people not to start a general fight. He was given a further three months in jail, I understand, but the offended husband after spending some time under arrest went unpunished, as the violence was not severe.

According to genealogies (see, for example, Appendix 3), which of course represent what is reported of the past rather than what actually may have taken place, it was unusual for a man to marry more than one or two wives a couple of generations ago, whereas today many go through four, five, or more marriages. This apparent increase in the frequency of marital unions is further attested by older informants, who tend to remark, 'In the old days, you found a good wife and stayed with her; nowadays, these young people behave like dogs.' Similar comments are of course made in most societies by the older generation; but coupled with the evidence of genealogies, I consider that there probably has been an increase in the fragility of marriage, which can be attributed partly to the increasing official discouragement of physical self-defence.

Further evidence suggesting a decline in marriage stability was provided by a remark of William Danga, who said that it was formerly a general custom for a man to build a special extension to the hut he prepares for his first marriage, in the form of a circular enclosure which gave extra privacy to the new bride during the initial period of the marriage, when she and her in-laws practise discreet avoidance. This enclosure, or *bem*, is only rarely seen today among the northern Uduk, though it is fairly common among the southern Uduk and standard practice among the Meban. The disappearance of the *bem* among the northern Uduk would be consistent with an increasingly casual approach to marriage, and the declining importance of associated ceremony.

The rights and obligations involved in 'proper marriage' are a matter of direct give-and-take, lasting for the duration of the marriage relation and not involving any longer-term commitments. The husband is expected to provide a hut for his wife: if this is his first marriage, he should build a hut with his own hands, except for the help his wife may give in transporting materials. For subsequent marriages, both husband and wife can expect help from others in building. The husband should cultivate fields for his wife; at least one sorghum and one maize field, in the *bunto* and *bangap* belts respectively. She uses this grain to cook for herself and her husband, others of his community, her children, their guests, and to provide refreshments (beer especially) for work parties on her husband's fields. A wife who does not grind, cook and brew energetically is not welcome among her husband's people. A wife acquires no long-term rights in her husband's property or the land of his hamlet area; she may cultivate small plots while she is there, especially sesame or maize, and these crops remain her own property which she will take away with her if the marriage breaks up. The grain grown on her husband's fields, although partly produced by the work parties for which her cooking and brewing is essential, remains her husband's property.

A woman remains an outsider in her husband's hamlet, and her place there derives only from her personal connection with her husband. The relation between her and her affines never merges, as in some societies, into one of increasingly close ties approaching those of kinship. If a husband dies, his wife no longer has a place in his community; after his final death rites, she is ceremonially chased out of the hamlet.

It seems that marriage ceremonial used to be more elaborate in the past than it is today. There was no bridewealth, it is true; but Bukko explained that there used to be beer parties at the groom's and at the girl's father's hamlet, and there was the sacrifice of a goat. Spears would be brought as a gift for the bride's father. But as for bridewealth, Bukko said, using the Arabic *mal*, the beer was our bridewealth! The grain was provided by the groom from his own people, given to the bride's father and the girl herself would grind it for the beer. The position of the groom's people seems to have been that of begging outsiders in relation to the girl and her father's people: some of the beer was separately strained for the groom, and placed on the ground for him to drink. I believe the implication is that he had to lap it like an animal. They also scooped out a little porridge for him to eat separately. When the goat was sacrificed, the groom had to sit, or as Bukko later suggested more specifically, a couple of the father's sisters of the groom— women from the people of the groom's father—had to sit wafting away flies from the meat with branches. 'If you are that one you mustn't rest and put your hands on the ground. The sun will go down on you chasing off the flies. . . . The meat is deliberately put there to keep you occupied chasing off the flies. . . . It is just kept to test you . . . There will be two people to sit there chasing off flies. The women are paternal aunts, they are the ones put on this job . . . Paternal aunts, from the people of the boy's father . . . They are kept there like that, very wretched, apart from the others. Do you consider this a good thing? The custom of treating us like this is like the *çiŋkina/*. Ay! *Çaah!*' Bukko was thankful that this ceremony had been given up, and that people now 'marry freely'. When he expostulated about the manner of 'treating us' as *çiŋkina/*, he meant we, suitors who wish to marry girls, and our own relatives. The image of the suitor and groom as *çiŋkina/*, as a worthless and helpless beggar seeking out the favour of the girl and her relatives, has analogies in myth and history and although this particular ceremony is abandoned, Bukko's memory of it illuminates modern practice. Bukko regretted modern ways at times. He sometimes said that nowadays, people married too young, they were not sufficiently serious about it, the young girls who marry don't even know how to brew beer, and so forth.

Certainly people do marry young, usually in their mid-teens. A song, sung by young people, playfully takes up this idea; it has the form of a flirtatious exchange between two sweethearts. The girl doesn't want a boy lover who will soon leave her but a grown man who has already settled down, and the boy teases her for not spending enough time at the grinding stone:

> *Aa atha is ki 'daŋ 'daŋ oki mashi com pa yee*
> *Dhan nyara is ki yogom dara yo me'doo*
> *Aa atha is ki 'daŋ 'daŋ oki mashi com pa yee*
> *Dhan nyara is ki yogom dara yo me'doo*
> *Kara 'bom Gwara gi mi'da yo*
> *Ba ti kara 'bom Gwara gi mi'da yo*
> *Nyara is ki yogom dara yo me'da*
> *Aa atha is ki 'daŋ 'daŋ oki mashi com pa yee*
> *Nyara is ki yogom dara yo me'da*
> *Ba ti kara 'bom Gwara gi mi'da yo*

Roughly translated to catch the varying tones of voice, this would read:

Girl What I need is to catch an established family man, oh yes!
Boy These great lazy girls who never go near a grind-stone
Girl What I want is to marry an established family man, yes!

Boy   These great lazy girls who never go near a grind-stone
Girl Well get yourself a Meban woman who'll grind all day.
    Just get yourself a Meban woman who'll grind all day.
Boy   These slack untidy girls who never touch a grind-stone
Girl But I'm going to marry an established family man!
Boy   Lazy girls who never go near a grind-stone
Girl Then please find a Meban woman who'll grind for you!

The girl and her friends have had enough of young men who love them and leave them and cannot be relied upon. She is teasing her lover by threatening to become the second wife of some older man who will settle down and look after her. The young man in reply suggests that girls like her are not interested in housework and cooking anyway. She tells him to find a Meban woman for himself—Meban women are more 'house-wifely' than their Uduk sisters.

Today the ceremony involved in marriage is often minimal, especially for subsequent marriages, and is treated casually. The ceremony through which a marriage relation is initiated is in any case less important than that which marks the birth of the first child, for it is at the latter that the people of the husband and wife meet together formally for the first time.

First marriage takes place at an early age, often soon after puberty, and is entered with a sense of spice, adventure, and competition, especially among the young men. Tales are told for years afterwards with great relish, of the hazardous courting expeditions of one's younger days, when a boy went 'weasel-crawling' (*ya leheny*, to go as a weasel, i.e. secretly to steal) to exchange endearments with his sweetheart through a small hole in the wall of her hut, at the level where special beds are constructed for unmarried girls at the back of the hut. Whispered conversations, Pyramus and Thisbe style, may lead to further trysts; a bold lover may creep into the girl's hut to continue the flirtation in greater comfort; but all the time there is the danger that her relatives will wake up, and beat the boy or chase him far out of the hamlet. When he eventually arranges to elope with her, they spend a few days in a friend's hut, as secretly as possible. The girl's people find out where she is, and come and collect her; both the girl and boy are separately treated with a black oil cosmetic at their homes (*jiso*, the substance often used in rituals of separation, made from charcoal or burnt sesame and oil). The boy begins to build the hut, and when it is completed brings his bride to live in it. A beer party is held (this should be, but is not always, at the boy's father's hamlet), and there may be dancing; and the central element in the ritual is the anointing of the new couple with red ochre (which often marks the completion of a rite of passage, and at the same time suggests health and strength). The wife returns to her own hamlet for the birth of her first child, and after a few weeks a double ceremony is held, with beer and sacrifices at the wife's and the husband's hamlets, and the child is conducted in a formal procession from its birthplace to its father's home. This is known as *kal a'ci pa* (taking the baby home). It does not matter where subsequent children are born, though it is usually in the husband's home.

There is no formal action or rite marking the termination of a marriage.

Ceremony involved in later marriages may be reduced almost to nothing; though a beer party may perhaps be held. On one occasion, an older woman who had been married several times was brought to her husband's hamlet without any ceremony; when she brewed her first beer for work on her new husband's fields, some of the rituals of a marriage celebration were carried out (for example, her in-laws guided her hand on the grinding stone); I asked whether she was going to be anointed with red ochre, and she exclaimed: 'My goodness! What do you think I am?—a young bride?' The ritual of first marriage marks the entry into the state of sexual maturity and adulthood, rather than entry into the married state as such.

I will describe something more of the marital career of one young man, whose age is probably in the early thirties, and whom I have called Belo. He arrived in his birth-group hamlet in Waka'cesh a few years before I met him in 1966. He had come from Bellila, from another hamlet of the same local birth-group to which he was in fact more closely related. I asked him why he had left Bellila, and he replied joking, 'I was tired of being beaten by my wives there!' He had married, in succession, three women there, of whom only the first bore him children. By 1966 he had broken all relations with these women, and was married to two more from hamlets near to his own in Waka'cesh. The first of these, Tamke, he must have married in 1963–4, because he had paid bridewealth for her under the Omda's official policy of that period. He paid £1.000 (Sudanese), four goats and two pigs, although she had been married before, briefly, but had not borne children.[7] The other, Sora, whose account of a fight I have already quoted, he had only recently married, and no bridewealth was paid, for by this time the Omda's policy had failed. Sora had also been married before.

In February 1966 there was a crisis: Tamke, a relatively quiet girl, was reported to have run off with a man in Chali. Her people applied pressure on her to return to Belo, largely because of the bridewealth payment, which they could not easily return. However, Sora was very jealous of Tamke, and early morning jousting often took place between them; Tamke sometimes used to stay at home with her mother in the next-door hamlet, and Sora would be furious with their husband when he went off in that direction to a dance. When Tamke returned, Sora was so angry that she burnt down the hut that Belo had built for her, and went home. There was a court case over this; Belo was angry because in the fire, not only the hut itself but also the grain stored in the roof was destroyed, and I believe a chicken was killed as well. In the court record (20 April 1966)[8] Sora is said to have wanted revenge on her husband for going to sleep with his other wife, when he had promised her, on marriage, that he would desert the other wife completely for her. The court noted that mischief by fire was common among the Uduk, and that severe punishments should be imposed, so that the Uduk would feel the force of the law and not violate it. As I have mentioned, Sora was given a three-month sentence, and also a year's bail on good behaviour.

While Sora was in prison in Kurmuk, Tamke lived with Belo, but went for increasingly long visits home to her mother, where Belo sometimes went to spend the night. But by the time Sora came out of prison in mid-June, people were saying that the relationship between Belo and Tamke was probably over. Belo planted fields for Sora that summer, but not for Tamke, who remained in her mother's hamlet. Sora lived with Belo and kept an eye on his movements. As the rainy season wore on, she

---

[7] The bridewealth rate had been fixed at £4.000 (Sudanese) for girls, and £2.500 (Sudanese) for widows or divorced women; the value of the payments in this case were nearer the upper than the lower figure.

[8] A note on this case was provided for me by Kamal Abdel Rahman.

discovered that he was still seeing Tamke, and on several occasions the two women had combats with their jousting staves. A nasty scrap took place between Sora and Belo themselves on one occasion, and as she told me in the account quoted above, she received an ugly wound from his throwing stick. At some point during this period, the people of Tamke managed to repay the bridewealth that Belo had given them; they didn't want to have to force Tamke back to Belo in the circumstances (they couldn't anyway); and they didn't want to remain in debt, which is how they saw the situation.

Tamke remained at home; the one child she had borne Belo grew sick and died in September, and Belo's relationship with Sora began to improve. She bore a child about January 1967, and he built her a new hut on the site to which the whole hamlet was moving. But his roving eye led to another big quarrel, and Belo himself destroyed the roof of the new hut, causing Sora to go home temporarily. However, in May 1967, Tamke remarried; her new husband was Nabak, a 'brother' of Belo but from a different, though closely allied birth-group. Belo was dissuaded by his brothers from fighting Nabak, on the grounds that his marriage with Tamke was finished anyway, and that it would be very dangerous to risk a general conflict between the two friendly local birthgroups, between whom there had been an incident of the same kind a couple of years back. But some months later, Tamke came back from Nabak and spent a night with Belo. This made Sora very angry indeed; but Tamke seemed to settle down with Nabak after this.

Sora gave birth again, I think in early 1968; and her relationship with Belo remained calm until about November 1968, when he unexpectedly married another woman (also previously married). In spite of stormy scenes with Sora, he built the new wife a hut in early 1969; but things were so difficult that he abandoned her by March, and he, together with Sora and the children, left the area for Bellila, where, it was rumoured in the summer of 1969, they intended to settle permanently.

I have no space to quote many similar stories; but the information on some 158 marriages over a period of three and a half years, in Appendix 5, tells its own story, and suggests that the experiences of Belo in the case I have described are not at all unusual. But we should remember that very few sexual affairs can be carried on in secret, and that the record of Uduk 'marriages' should be considered in relation to another society's record not only of marital, but of all extra-marital sexual relationships as well. There are no separate categories of wife, mistress, girl-friend, prostitute, in Uduk society; and I do not consider that the Uduk practise an unusual degree of promiscuity. It may very well be less than in a society where the very social rigidity of the marriage relation, on one level, makes possible a variety of casual, non-public sexual relationships on another.

5

AFFINITY, PATERNITY, AND OTHER BONDS

The relation of affinity consequent upon the establishment of a new marriage does not have much material significance. It is not associated with major transfers of wealth or with substantial economic co-operation, as in many other societies. It has nevertheless interesting symbolic aspects which seem to underline the bodily difference between each spouse and the birth-group he or she has married into, and the dangers of bodily contact and contagion across the bond formed by their sexual union. An awareness that the fragile relation of marriage and in-lawship may eventually mature, through the birth of children, into much closer and economically and politically more co-operative relations seems to lie behind the care with which spouses and their in-laws treat each other.

But the relationship of affinity itself, with all its ritual dangers, exists quite independently of the birth of children, and does not cease if the marriage link is broken. Thus a man who has been married five times, but is only living with the last of the five wives, will have five sets of in-laws to be respected. In fact there will be ten hamlets, at least, where he will have to behave himself and be circumspect at beer-parties, for there are two sets of senior in-laws for each woman he has lived with—her own people, and her father's people. In a society where the relation of affinity is compounded by material services and exchanges, such a situation would not easily arise; but in Uduk society, where the affinal relation is of little material consequence, its ritual observances can complicate a young man's social life considerably.

The main duty in early marriage, apart from the mutual obligation of the two spouses, is the symmetrical respect and avoidance which each should practise towards his in-laws, particularly the senior generation of the partner's own or father's people. The reciprocal kin term between each spouse, and these senior in-laws, is *mar*. *Mar* should greet each other in a special manner, which implies respect. The normal greeting between Uduk, also used by several peoples of the region, is to clasp right hands and then to draw apart until each person retains only the tip of the other's middle finger between his own thumb and middle finger, and then for each to snap the thumb and middle finger as they separate. Or they may merely snap each other's thumb and middle finger, without a prior clasp. When *mar* greet, each grasps not the hand but the underneath of the other's forearm (*mmothe me'di 'bame'd*, 'to greet on the wrist' or lower arm). If you greet your *mar* in the ordinary way, with palms touching, your hand will start to shake and tremble. It is also necessary to avoid mentioning the names of your *mar*; when addressing, or speaking of them, you use a teknonym or the expression *mar pem*, 'my *mar*'. If you do use the personal name, your mouth is said to swell out after your death, and people will see this and know of your disrespect, at your funeral. You should avoid directly meeting your senior in-laws for some time after your marriage; this is less onerous for the man, than for the girl, who has to spend much of her early married life inside her hut, and cannot work together with the other women of her husband's hamlet. Young girls may spend time with her. After the birth of the first child, these restrictions are gradually relaxed; and at the ceremony for bringing the child to his father's home, the people of the husband and wife meet together for the first time, as groups. The most important restriction between *mar* is that on eating together, which may be very dangerous unless ritual precautions are taken.

All these aspects of avoidance are covered by the Uduk word *ga/*. The word also refers to the avoidance by individuals of certain foods which make them sick, which clarifies its meaning in the context of affinity. The underlying notion is of incompatibility; a particular food, such as goat meat or *disha wulul* (a certain pungent mushroom) may not agree with you, and your body cannot absorb it. Even the smell of it may be nauseating, and if you eat it you will certainly vomit. You find out only by experience whether you have this antipathy to any particular food. Both in this context, and that of the *mar* avoidance, the expression *ga/* suggests the danger of contact, and the need for circumspection. If the matter is treated carelessly, sickness results in both cases. If a person does not avoid his *mar* with due respect, he may be struck by a disease known as *gu'th*. If he eats together with his in-laws, even after many years, and after they have taken the proper precautions of ritually feeding him on appropriate occasions, he still may get sick. The dirt on the hands of his *mar* is particularly dangerous for him. Alko of Waka'cesh explains graphically the nature of this disease and its remedy:

Alko: Yes, the disease *gu'th* is found in our country here. It appears like this: if you eat food until you are full, and eat stew with dirty hands, that woman [your daughter-in-law] will be struck by *gu'th*; people will say 'Ay!' The woman gets thin, and has diarrhoea, *du'k, du'k, du'k.*

If you get up, and diarrhoea pours out, people will say, 'That man [i.e. your *mar*] will help you with *gu'th*.'

The man will hold his fingernail like this, to scratch the dirt off, *ko'c ko'c* into a shell, to scratch off the *gu'th*. It is scratched off into some oil. Then he brings a little soot from the roof of the hut, and puts that too into the shell, and you drink it. Then he makes a little paste of sesame in a little gourd like this, after that oil which was prepared for you. Oh! You will take hold of the centre pole of the hut like this; the centre pole is standing here, you go and hold it, and you eat the stuff while standing up. It's always like this . . . This is an Uduk thing [as opposed to an imported disease].

W.J.: Why are people struck by *gu'th*?

Alko: It is from a dirty hand. A very dirty hand . . . My *mar* will come and eat food with me, with a dirty hand, and his dirtiness will strike me with *gu'th* in my stomach. Diarrhoea will pour out, and I will get thin, my head will go dizzy until I'm nearly falling over. I fall over.

In other cases [*gu'th*] is picked up from eating something at the home of your in-laws. If you go and eat something at the hamlet of your in-laws, when they have not done the feeding ritual,[1] you will get *gu'th*. . . .

People then bring sesame. You go to them because you are

---

[1] *Çi 'twa/*, literally 'to give to the mouth', is a formal ritual in which a little food is carefully handed to another's mouth, which often forms a part of ceremonial. The first food offered may be taken in the mouth and rejected, but the second taken and swallowed. The rite is frequently performed between *mar*: young married people and their senior in-laws.

sick with *gu'th*. You go to the home of your *mar*. Your wife will
lead you. People will take a little sesame, to roast and grind,
to squeeze out the oil. To squeeze a little oil. And to scratch
away at the fingernails of all the people of that hamlet; all the
children of your in-laws' hamlet, all of them, together with
your *mar*. They scratch their nails, scratch, scratch, scratch, to
prepare with the oil; and you eat it. You will eat the dirt of
their fingernails. Look at the soot up in the roof of the hut, it
is smoke from the fireplace. The smoke from the fireplace goes
up to make the dirt in the roof. People will scrape it, and put it
in the oil here. Yes, in the shell here; and then you eat it. You
eat it, drink it together with the oil. And then people will
bring some sesame paste, to give you in a little [gourd?] after
that oil of soot which has the fingernails in it.

Danga explained the special danger of being caught by *gu'th*
at funerals. Young spouses may even have to accept food into
their mouths from the hand of the corpse, if he is a *mar* to them,
as part of the protective feeding ritual.

'You can get ill with *gu'th* from your *mar* through eating the meat of
their goats. At a funeral at their place, they will ritually-feed you
with goat meat, and then you can eat. If you eat without this
precaution, and if your body is hot [i.e. if a child has recently been
born to you], you will very soon be seized by this sickness from the
goat-meat which you have eaten.'

The relation of affinity is not only hedged about with dangers
and controls on eating together, continual reminders of bodily
difference, but is associated with certain specific relationships
of the 'joking' type, which embody among others the paradox of
the sexual union of opposites. Verbal joking, *asor*, using insults
of a conventional pattern,[2] is much enjoyed and often takes
place between cross-cousins. Between *imugu* (persons married to
siblings) there is also joking of this type; and in the case of *mok̲*
(*imugu* of opposite sex) it may take the form of serious practical
joking and sexual horseplay. Humiliation of one side may result
in a situation of debt (*amure*), after which 'forfeits' will have to
be paid to equalize.

The 'boundary' symbolism in the definition of the affinal

---

[2] Most jokes play unkindly on a person's unattractive features, comparing them
directly or indirectly with animal features. Most animals are thought very ugly.

1a Hamlet scene, Wa'ḵacesh

1b A Rufā'a Arab passes by

2a Chali Church, 1966
(Abd-al Ghaffar Muhammad Ahmad)

2b A beer-drink

3a Preparation for sowing in the sorghum fields

3b Weeding the maize meadows in the early rainy season

4a Rapka brings home the
sorghum harvest

4b Panyc̲edha/ thickens the
stew with a twist of bark

5a Umpa, a grandmother of the hamlet (Abd-al Ghaffar Muhammad Ahmad)

5b Tente using the fire-stick

5c William Danga

5d Shadrach Peyko

6 Children

7a, b Dressed for the dance

8a, b A demonstration of women's stave jousting

9 Mutkina and her Gurunya 'sitting black'

10a Child-minder and baby Gurunya newly blackened with *jiso* at the *tora ga̱p* rite

10b Presents collected for the Gurunya at the *'thi ku̱p* rite

10c The sponsor carries the baby, and the Gurunya mothers are led like cattle on the begging procession through the hamlets

10d Shaving the head of the child-minder, while the baby, already shaved, waits to be anointed with red oil (see Frontispiece)

relation, especially in the disease of *gu'th* and its treatment, can be of a striking bodily nature. Thus commensality is dangerous, because of the polluting effects of marginal bodily dirt in the fingernails. The incorporation of a person in his birth-group is very closely associated with commensality, and affinity is its opposite. The dangers of eating and even working together define and re-emphasize a difference in bodily kind which is by no means overcome by the union of marriage. Ironically it is this difference which gives the sexual union its *raison d'être* in the first place. The elaborate rituals of affinity are reminders, to the Uduk and to us, of the idea of bodily association within birth-groups and the principle of sharing of substance, including food and wealth, within those groups.

Affinity by itself cannot be described as *alliance* in Uduk society, without distorting the English language, since it has no existence outside the marriage which caused it, and it is not marked by mutual obligation, material reciprocity or political support. It is not even a link between two corporate groups, but between each individual marriage partner and the birth-group and father's birth-group of the other spouse. However, it may develop, in time, into a more substantial relationship. One such development is always potential in affinity, and grows directly out of it: that is the paternal link. When a child is born to an Uduk marriage, it does not necessarily bring the parents closer together, although the rules of avoidance between his parents and their *mar* begin to be relaxed. But an important relation is established and begins to grow between the child and his father and father's people, a relation which has much in common with the relation of affinity, but with greater emphasis on positive reciprocity.

PATERNITY

A child, who is normally brought up in his father's hamlet, is very soon made aware of the division in his world between his father's people who treat him generously and affectionately, and those more distant people to whom he really belongs, and to whom, his mother tells him, he will have to go to live and work when he grows up. Even though this usually happens around puberty, he retains an important link with his father's people throughout his life. There is a degree of respect in the relationship, on the side of the child; he should avoid his father's name. The same term, *ga/*, is used of this avoidance as in the affinal context. He may often mispronounce his father's name, or simply call him by the kin term, *baba*. I have been told several times that this is because small children have difficulty in speaking correctly. However, children do not mispronounce the names of other relatives.

Whereas a person's domestic duty lies toward his own birth-group, and a child is said to fear his mother's brothers, who exercise authority over him in the domestic sphere, great love is said to exist between a person and his father. You can go to your father's people, your *ibaba*, at any time because of this; there is a 'pathway' linking you to them. It would be a terrible thing if there were anger between you and your fathers, for 'the pathway would be closed', and you would have nowhere to go. You are a welcome guest in your father's hamlet at any time, and you can have any small animal to eat, or a piece of clothing, or a weapon that takes your fancy, from your father's people. You are particularly free and easy with the possessions of your cross-cousins among them. However, when you go to visit your father's people, you should take a small present with you, to greet them, such as coffee beans (the commonest luxury item in circulation, and a welcome gift). Your father's people may be so delighted to see you that they will kill a goat, or if you have been away for very long, they will call together some others of their children, and sacrifice an ox.

A man may live, if he wishes, with his father's people, and build huts for his wives there. He will be allocated pieces of land on which to cultivate, and will join the work-party system of his father's hamlet. But his position is that of a privileged and welcome guest; he is an outsider, and remains so, even if he spends his whole life with his fathers. He will not contribute towards the joint purchase of cows with them, but should do so with his matrilateral brothers. He will not share the debts of his father's people, but those of his own. The work he does in his father's hamlet is done 'out of love', and is reciprocated in the same spirit; it is not done as an expected duty, as it would be at his own hamlet. These principles which clearly 'incorporate' a man with his mother's brothers, and not with his father, are explicit in the following explanation by Bukko, which was in response to the question whether you would join with your fathers in buying a cow, if you were living with them:

Bukko: No, you don't join with them [i.e. your fathers] ... No. Your fathers will buy theirs separately. The sesame which you grow, you will use to buy a goat, and rear it with them there. A billy goat will grow up as big as this [indicating]. You will cut [sacrifice] it for your fathers, for them to eat. And if you want to buy a cow with these [goats] of yours, your mother's brothers will come and lead them away and sell them together with theirs.

Danga: Your mother's brothers?

Bukko: Yes; while a male goat you will keep as theirs [i.e. your fathers']. You will say, 'Oh. You must leave me this male, I have kept it for my fathers to eat. Take away the nannies, but save one grown female which has given birth and don't sell it. You must bring it back later.' Yes, and when it has given birth, given birth until it has finished giving birth, you will then cut it for your fathers, for your fathers to eat. You cut that goat because it has finished giving birth, while another one may be sold by your mother's brothers, so that they can rear cows in their hamlet there.

If your goats become very many, and cows are brought for sale,[3] you can buy cows while at your father's place.

Danga: By yourself?

Bukko: Yes, with your own [goats]. And then you can keep your [cows] there, while living with your fathers. They will give birth, again and again and again, until there are quite a number, and then you instruct your fathers to cut one, for them to eat, and to keep the little skin, saying, 'I am keeping the thing of my children.' This is the position.

The duty of giving gifts of animals for sacrifice is significant, for such gifts are not usually made within a birth-group; apart from religious occasions, such as funeral sacrifices for the dead, sacrifices are held for guests, travellers, and others not of the local birth-group. They create a link between people, whose relationship would otherwise be undefined, and form a part of that generous reciprocity which is also the essence of the father-child relationship. Because the father and child belong to different 'natural communities', any transfers that take place

[3] Berta traders often bring cows to sell in Uduk hamlets; the transaction is described in Chapter 3.

between them have the character either of a loan, or a gift—
intended for consumption. It is evident in the account above
that those goats given to one's fathers are male, or beyond giving
birth. If a father transfers fertile cows to his son, as quite often
happens, especially when the boy learned to herd cattle in his
father's hamlet when he was young, they are not for him to keep
permanently and add to his own people's wealth. They are a
loan, for him to drink milk for a while. They must eventually be
returned, together with all their offspring (unless one is given as
a gift for sacrifice).

Ownership of other goods or rights vested in the birth-group
such as rainstones, is similarly non-transferable. Rainstones are
a valuable possession, for not only are they supposed to enable
their owners to encourage rainfall, but they are thought to res-
pond to their owners' grumbling about a debt owed them by
sending storm, lightning, and wind to punish the debtors.[4] The
possession of rainstones therefore means that outstanding debts
can be more easily collected, and influence and political credit
built up. Rights over rainstones, as over wealth received in
payment of a debt, are held by the local birth-group as a whole.
A man may sometimes lend the rainstones he administers on
behalf of his birth-group to his son, an action explicitly compared to the lending of cattle. But the son will have to return
them eventually, even though he may administer the stones and
reap their yield while in his possession, in the form of recouped
debts for his birth-group.

Even the present of some seed grain by a father to a son
should not be regarded as a means of increasing his permanent
wealth, but consumed, as a gift. Thus, if a boy is given some
sesame, he may plant and harvest it; but then he should sell the
crop and buy clothes, or coffee, or pay his taxes, and thus 'eat'
or disperse the proceeds. The very worst thing he could do with
his father's gift would be to use it for serious purchases with a
view to future profit (I have already discussed in Chapter 3
some of the general suspicion and avoidance of profiteering, and
the dangers of *yol*, market-type transactions, as against *wan*,
exchanges of mutual benefit). He should not buy a pig, for
example, which might later be exchanged for a goat, which

[4] See James, 1972.

would multiply and make possible the purchase of a cow. If on the other hand a mother's brother gives him sesame, the transfer is more in the nature of the allocation of a share in the joint birth-group wealth, which he will be expected to multiply and invest if he can. In a discussion with Buḵko, an interesting misunderstanding arose. He was emphasizing how keen Uduk fathers were to give things to their children, and the conversation was about rainstones in particular. Buḵko said he knew that the *Bunyan* (that is, northern Sudanese and clothes-wearing people in general) always gave things to their sons, and that I should understand that Uduk did just the same thing. He seemed unaware of the different character of the transfer in the two cases: that what a *Bunyan* man hands on to his son is his by right but that what an Uduk father hands on is a gift, not a natural right.

Inheritance of animals and other domestic possessions is within the birth-group; but several important ritual specialisms properly pass from father to son. In these cases of patrilineal transmission, the natural distinction between father and son may be significant, and symbolically emphasized. It may sometimes be one of the reasons why a contagious ritual power is passed on in this manner. Ritual responsibilities of this kind include the old agricultural cult of *koŋkoro/*, concerned with bird and insect control and the growth of crops; the organization of hunting and fishing on a territorial basis, to which one has a right if one's patrilineal forebear was killed in the hunt or drowned in the river; and the control and treatment of a sickness resulting from the spirit of elephants, a responsibility passed on patrilineally to the descendants of any man who killed an elephant. The birth-group kinsfolk of a man who administers elephant medicine (*cwany je*) are subject to contamination from him, and under certain circumstances may be caught by the elephant sickness. It is their vulnerability which makes them unsuitable to take over the administration of elephant medicine; and so it passes to a son or brother's son rather than to a sister's son. The large-scale hunt (either in the early rains, or during the dry season, when the grass is burnt) is an activity in which fathers and sons co-operate, and often is compared to a battle; it is perhaps a battle, against the wild (and incidentally fights often develop between men at the scene of the hunt). When a hunter makes a kill, he cries out the name of his father, or his son, in joy.

The most substantial source of the continuing reciprocity between a man and his child is the father's original creation and nourishment of the child, from conception almost to maturity. The father does not receive any direct reward for this; when the boy is old enough to do useful work, he leaves for his mother's brothers' hamlet. They receive, *gratis*, a full grown, well-fed, new working member; or in the case of a girl, a new sister who will eventually replenish their number herself. It is in conjunction with this enormous obligation, which devolves upon the shoulders of the child himself, that the great love of a child for his father is explained. This fundamental fact, that a child owes his life and growth to his father, underlies the central political rule of Uduk society: *A boy's primary political duty is to defend the life of his father.*

If a boy's father's people are in danger, he will go and support them; and this rule holds even in the extreme case, where his own people are fighting his father's. He should fight with his father's people, against his own. If he kills his own matrilateral brother in such a situation, there will be no recriminations. The obligation is reciprocated; if a man's son is in danger, he will go to help him. There is thus a mutual defence pact between father and son.[5] Symbolic of this political alliance are the gifts of weapons, bow, arrows, spears, and throwing sticks, which a father, father's brother or patrilateral cross-cousin should present to a boy. And whereas a man's animals go to his sister's sons on his death, his weapons are formally 'taken home' to his father's people.

Danga explained the mutual obligations of father and son in these words (Appendix 1 contains the original vernacular and a close translation):

'If your father's people engage in hostilities over there, you must, you must, whether you live with your father's people, . . . or whether you

---

[5] Structural parallels are widespread in Africa; particularly clear is the case of the Fanti of Ghana, where partrilineally recruited military companies cut across the matrilineal descent groups which are otherwise basic to social organization. Christensen writes for example, 'The Fanti are very definite in stating that a person's obligation to his father and the patrilineal military company takes precedence over all other affiliations, even to the extent of fighting his kinsmen' (1954, p. 125).

live with your mother's brothers, when there are hostilities over there, you must go to fight together with your father's people. For your fathers looked after you when you were a small baby. Your mother nourished you on things provided by your father. You drank hot water [i.e. ate hot food]; your mother drank hot water to let the milk rise in her breasts, in the house of your father. And then you drank milk, from the things which she ate in your father's house.

'Your father reared you, reared you until you grew up at last. You do not get to know your mother's brother, or go to eat things at his place, immediately. You will stay with your father, and if your father goes on loving you, you will stay on and on until you are a young man. You will marry a wife and stay among them. . . . Until the time comes when you want to go to your own people at last; and then you go and live with your own people.

'If you go as a guest to your father's people, they will cut a goat for you. They cut a goat for you, and you eat it. And if your fathers have a very large beast, a great big bull, and they want to kill it, they will not kill it just for themselves. They will go and gather their children together from over there. They will send for their children, saying "Let the children come." The children come. [The fathers] don't kill the bull with their own hands. They will tell one of the children, "You will be the one to kill this bull." And the son then chops the bull with an axe on the back of the head here.

'These are the children whom they bore. . . . They kill the bull in the morning and eat it together with all their fathers.'

Bukko explained more specifically the obligation to support one's fathers in battle in the following passage. He was asked why you desert your own people and fight for your father's people if they are in danger:

'Because he is your father. I grew up on what? I grew up on the things of my father. Did I grow up on the things of my own people? We wait, and go there when we are grown up, when we have had our fill of the things of our fathers. We get our fill of our fathers' things. Our fathers are the ones who rear [and feed] us while we grow.'

I asked him how it was possible to kill your own mother's brothers; and he replied:

'I kill them because they are killing my fathers. My fathers are being killed by them; how can I ignore it? My fathers, who nourished me [gave me life]? If they are being killed, how can I ignore it? Why should my fathers be killed by them? They are the reason why I am alive.'

'[After the fight, the mother's brothers comment] "Ha! You looked out well for yourself. You were shot at by us, we would have shot you dead at the side of your fathers", they say. "You looked out for yourself well and that's why you're here talking to us now. You would not be left alone by us; you would be killed by us at the side of your fathers, right in front of them. Yes, because you said you would leave us and fight on the side of your fathers. You rotten fellow [joking abuse]; why should you be spared, when you were going to kill people [i.e. us]?"

'Yes, that's the situation.

'I have fought, fought against my mother's brothers, on the side of my fathers, at Kupanyuruny.'

I have said that the alliance between father and son is one of mutual support; but it is in fact an asymmetrical relation, especially while the boy is young and the relationship is still maturing. The political control of a local birth-group over the children it fathered is reinforced by certain mystical sanctions. It is considered that the anger of the father's people can harm their children. Thus, if you are unwise enough to fight against your fathers in battle, you will surely die. For if they wish, they can spit on their spears, and throw them at you: and their aim will be deadly accurate. Your own people have no such 'mystical' power over you.

Even off the field of battle, you may suffer if your fathers are angry with you. For example, if they are criticizing you (or perhaps one of your close patrilateral brothers), you may involuntarily injure yourself. You may trip over your own spear, and hurt your foot, or perhaps chop your hand when axing a tree. It will then be said that you are *'kosha 'twa/* ('hurt by the speech' of your fathers).

Girls and women, and their young babies, are vulnerable to danger from the same source. If a girl, newly married, does not conceive, she will go to a diviner who may diagnose that she is *'kosha 'twa/,* hurt by the critical words of her father's people. She will go to them and they will carry out a little ceremony to withdraw the harmful influence. This includes chewing and spitting *shu'be/* (*heglig*) leaves on her head. If she still does not conceive she will go secretly to her father's hamlet and steal ash (*piny*) from the hearth of her father's hut, and smear it on her belly. The type of critical talk which is thought to harm a girl's fertility in this way may concern her marriage, or her loose behaviour, or that of her sisters. A girl who is already pregnant may be hurt in the same way; and this could result in a miscarriage, or the baby may be born with a slight peculiarity. I know of one baby born with an admittedly odd-shaped head, slightly asymmetrical. The mother was confident that it was because of her own father's people, and she took the child to her father's sister's home, where a number of her father's people spat *shu'be/* leaves to withdraw the influence. The baby's head soon gained a normal shape. The mother said: 'His head has been spoiled by his grandfathers. They have been saying bad things about his mother'; and after the treatment: 'My father's sisters comforted (*malas*) him, and treated him with spittle and with *shu'be/*, and his head recovered.' Sometimes the rite is carried out as a precaution. It is completed, at a later date, by a woman's fathers shaving her head and that of her child (a rite commonly marking purification and completion) and the drinking of beer and sacrifice. The following account by Rapka, a married woman of the Waka'cesh people, describes the dangers which emanate from a woman's fathers and the precautions which have to be taken. It is significant that the pregnant woman has to avoid her fathers, in a manner reminiscent of affinal avoidance; and that the beer prepared later for them is a gift, and not for joint consumption.

'If you are *'kosha 'twa/* you will just wait and nothing will happen; you will marry, and you will not give birth. People will divine the cause and tell you to go to your father's people to let them treat you for *'twa/* [literally words, speech, mouth]. You go, and your father's people will spit on you, after chewing *shu'be/*. They spit *shu'be/* on you. Then you will conceive a child, but remain without shaving your head. You will not go to your father's hamlet yet. You will wait, and your stomach will grow big. Then you go to your father's hamlet. If you go while the child is still just a clot of blood, you will lose the child. You must wait until your stomach has swelled. If your father's people come [to visit your hamlet] you will fear them and keep away from them by hiding in the hut. Your stomach grows, and you give birth, and take the child to your father's people while he is tiny to let them spit *shu'be/* on his head, and they will cut a little hair off the child. That is how it is done.

'Then later, beer will be made, and they will shave your head. Your father's people will come and shave your head. They will take the beer back to their hamlet. *Asum 'twa/* [the beer of this rite] is not drunk [that is, by everybody together]; it is all taken in a pot to their hamlet. Then they will cut a goat.'

William Danga gave me another account of the situation:

'If you are a man, and you are struck by the words of your father's people [*'kosha 'twa/*], you will break [a bone] if you run about fast. You will break [a bone] or maybe you will be bruised too. Also your foot may swell, a small place will swell and give you pain. And a diviner will—you must go and get a diviner to divine by fire, and he will tell you, "You are hurt by the bad talk of your fathers." And then you will go to your father's people's village, and they will *wupun* [ritually brush] you with a chicken, spray you with spittle, spray you with spittle. Spray from the mouth, as they say, with spittle. With spittle. Then you will come home. They do it with *shu'be/*. They chew *shu'be/* in the mouth and spray it on you.

'For a person who is a woman, she has a great deal of trouble. It doesn't affect a man very much. But one who is a woman has a lot of trouble. For if she always miscarries; if she conceives and after two months it all comes down, again she conceives and loses it after one month; from losing her children again and again, she will go to a diviner. The diviner will tell her, "You are hurt by the talk of your father's people." And then you will go there, after waiting for the blood [menstruation], waiting for the blood to come again. You will then go while the blood is there, you won't go for no reason. When the blood is there, you will go to your father's village.

'In the afternoon they will appear in the village, and you will tell them that you have come to do *'twa/*. You always miscarry, you conceive and always lose it. And you will ask them if there is some child of theirs who says bad things about his fathers, and the father's people say bad things and grumble about him; for this thing may come upon one of you who is their sister, without you saying bad things—it is one of your sisters. That is, one of a woman's sisters says bad things against her father's people. The fathers then grumble and say "You children who were born here, are you speaking bad words like that? Why do you criticize your father's people? Why do you say such things? Why do you treat your father's people badly?" From this kind of thing, the words will come upon one of the sisters. It will not strike the one [who has been criticized]. It will come upon one of the sisters who has been behaving well and keeping quiet.

'Her father's people will say to her: "Ay! Why has it come upon you?—you who are our real child. We think of you as a real child [i.e. behaving as a child should]. We have never heard anything bad of you. We have no quarrel with you. Why did it affect you? You go, and give birth to a child. You will go and conceive a child now, and keep it. You will bear the child." Then they will *wupun* you with a chicken. They will spray you, spray you from their mouths [with *shu'be/* and spittle]. And they will give you a chicken in your hand, they will give you a chicken and you will take it home. You will rear it in your home, you will keep the chicken until you conceive at last.

'The woman conceives, and then she waits. She will not go to her father's village yet. She will not set foot in her father's village. Nor will she be able to set eyes on her father's people. She will not look at her father's people. She won't greet her father's people. If she sees her father's people coming over there, she will run and hide in the hut. She will go in the hut and hide. Until she gives birth to the child. She goes and gives birth to the child at last, and then she will love [and not fear] her father's people. Her father's people will come, will come; or if she likes, she can go to her father's village. Her father's people then chew a little *shu'be/* for [spraying onto] her head, and shave her head at last. They shave her head. And she will love her father's village, and go inside it, because she is put right by her fathers by the shaving of her head.

'And if you, a woman miscarry; your own father's people will *wupun* you with a chicken. And a woman who does not conceive after this, she will come secretly another day when people are not at home. She goes in [her father's] hut quietly—or the hut of her father's brother. She goes and steals ash. She runs off. She runs away from there [and rubs ash on the lower part of her body]. She goes away like that, and she will conceive at last. She will conceive. Yes! She will conceive from stealing ash [*piny*].'

The danger of the dissatisfaction of one's father's people, which may damage the fighting capacity of a man or the reproductive capacity of a woman, is a strong reminder that everyone owes his existence and early nourishment to his fathers, and can never fully repay that obligation. In relation to men, the power wielded by the father's people, especially on the battlefield, is in the nature of a curse, sanctioning political rights. In relation to women, a more abstract interpretation suggests itself, which would include the political obligations of their brothers. An Uduk birth-group has no substantial economic or political existence, for although it reproduces itself through the fertility of its women and feeds itself through the work of its men, each new member is created only by outsiders, as a free gift, and usually fed when young at their expense. As a corporation, the local birth-group therefore exists 'on credit', by grace of the various people who have fathered its members. Its potential political strength is never realized. It never succeeds in paying off the series of obligations incurred towards the fathers of its members. What resources it does accumulate are largely dispersed through the activities of its own menfolk in fathering and feeding other children, belonging to other birth-groups. There are chains of such obligation running along patrilateral links through the whole society, and since these obligations relate to the creation of life itself and the duty to give it up on the battlefield, they have a stronger pull ultimately than everyday duties arising within the 'natural' community of the birth-group. For much of the time they remain potential only. The supreme obligation to one's fathers rarely has to be met, and people's reciprocal activities remain largely within the local birth-group. But the birth-group operates on credit; it has never secured the complete allegiance of its own members, and is politically weak. There are no transactions equivalent to the Trobriand system of *urigubu* payments, from a wife's brother to his sister's husband, which might be regarded as a means of securing those rights over the sister's children which would otherwise remain with the father, and as thus contributing to the real economic and political strength of the matrilineal group.[6] The Uduk birth-group might be compared to the nominally independent but underdeveloped country, struggling for real political independence but tied by manifold indebtedness and living on borrowed time. The corporate weakness of the local birth-group is founded in the lack of direct reciprocation at the time of marriage and the birth of children, which might otherwise reduce the lifelong obligation of each of its members to his or her father's people. The continuation of the matriline is dependent on a series of gifts from outside, or the 'sum of its paternities', to borrow an idiom from Kronenberg's description of the Didinga patriline as the sum of its uterinities.[7] The control which the father's people are represented as having over the fertility of their daughters is easier to understand in this light; their anger can break the continuity of a daughter's line altogether.

[6] See Malinowski, 1922.   [7] See Kronenberg, 1972.

Affinity and paternity are more closely related than their formal comparison suggests, for together they compose a developing relation between given parties on the ground. In a time perspective the political alliance which may result from the birth of a boy is already potential in the tie of affinity created by his parents' marriage; the relation comprises one whole developmental sequence, with a growing emphasis on co-operation and alliance. The natural difference is overcome, practically and politically, through time, and transformed into historical association.

The paternal relationship remains, like affinity, a cleaving between different natural kinds marked by ritual reminders of the dangers of contact; but in addition it comprises reciprocal obligation, a sentimental tie and potential political alliance. It is contrasted with the domestic authority but politically limited relationship of natural substance between maternal uncle and sister's son. Conceptually, the two relationships make sense in conjunction with each other; the logic of the paternal connection follows on from the theory of matrilineal substance and the Uduk reluctance to regard marriage as a transaction breaking the continuity of that substance. Ironically, the paternal tie makes sense because of the matrilineal thinking of the Uduk—they accommodate it through 'matrilineal spectacles' and do not see it in the abstract as a competing or contradictory principle. In practice, individuals do find themselves in a dilemma of conflicting loyalties from time to time, and the matrilineal and patrilateral connections have varied in their relative practical importance in history. As I shall explain in the next chapter, the matrilineal principle has on the whole gained in practical consequence over the last few generations. But first it remains to show how, beyond the particular tie between child and father, the matrilineal thinking of the Uduk colours their view of other relationships of the 'kinship' kind, regardless of their material consequence or even the classifications implicit in their formal relationship terminology.

SOME 'RELATIVES' AS THE UDUK SEE THEM

Sometimes a person may speak of whole birth-groups which stand to him in a particular relation. He may refer to 'my fathers' or 'my father's people', *ibabam pem*, or 'my grandfathers', *idhan babam pem*—this is applied to the birth-group of either of one's grandfathers, or that of the father of a mother's brother. Individuals of these groups may sometimes be addressed by these terms—a father's sister's daughter of any age, for example, instead of being called *'kwaskam* ('cross-cousin') may be addressed as *baba* or *babam pem*, 'father' or 'my father', and she will reciprocate the greeting with the same term. Any member of a 'grandfather' group can be greeted as *dhan baba*, and will reply in kind. This usage is not restricted to the birth-group in question, but may extend to its allied birth-groups. Indeed it is most commonly heard as a reciprocal greeting between individuals who do not see much of each other, and meet as virtual strangers, but have between them a traceable link of this kind. The language of individual kinship links thus provides a way of talking about relations between birth-groups themselves; whole clusters of hamlets can be referred to as *mar pem* by a married person, 'my in-laws', employing the term used in the individual sense for in-laws of a senior generation to oneself. A whole birth-group is sometimes spoken of as the offspring of another, especially where the tradition of an original or early patrilateral link is preserved, and an individual man may be spoken of as the 'father' of a whole series of birth-groups (once protected by his people). When speaking of their own people, Uduk sometimes use the first person singular. Birth-groups can be thought of thus as persons; and the individuals in them collectively classed accordingly.

But people are more often addressed and spoken of in their individual relation to oneself or to another. The set of terms used, the 'kinship' or 'relationship' terminology, is listed in Appendix 6. The form of the terminology is very similar to that used by the Komo, and also the Gumuz, though I do not have sufficient information to make further Koman comparisons. The terminology makes explicit certain distinctions which are very important to the Uduk, such as that between 'mother's brother' (*shwakam*) and 'father's brother (*iya*); between mother's sister' (*ara ta'da*, literally 'little mother') and 'father's sister' (*so'b*), and between parallel and cross-cousins (the former included as 'siblings', *akam* and *'bwaham* or 'brother' and 'sister', and the latter separately termed *'kwaskam*). However, these distinctions are not sustained in generations above and below one's own; 'grandfather' (*dhan baba*) is used as in English of both mother's and father's father (and applied to their brothers as well) and similarly with 'grandmother' (*dhan ta'da*). The children not only of one's brothers and male parallel cousins, for a male speaker, are *iya*, but also the children of one's cross-cousins; and the children not only of one's sisters and female parallel cousins are called *nam*, but also those of one's female cross-cousins.

One feature, which is evident from the list, is that many terms for kin are self-reciprocal, like the English 'cousin' but even cutting across the generations. Thus, if I am a man speaking, I call my brother's children *iya*, and they call me *iya*. Any child that I call *iya* will call me *iya*. If I speak as a woman, my brother's children are *so'b* or *diṭi* to me, as I am to them. If I, whether male or female, marry, my spouse's parents and mother's brothers are *mar* to me, as I am to them. These terms would be difficult to translate and comprehend if they were defined by listing all the genealogical positions they might cover from the point of view of an ideal Ego. But they are easier to understand as terms for describing relationships rather than persons; *iya* is a term distinguishing the relationship between men and their brothers' children from *so'b* or *diṭi*, the relationship between women and their brothers' children.

Although some of the distinctions made in the terminology are relevant for distinguishing the quality and content of different social relationships, the terminology itself is not a satisfactory guide to the patterning of those relationships. A description of Uduk thinking about kinship mapped onto the terminology alone would give a misleading picture, and fail to represent not only the crucial distinctions they make in social behaviour towards kin but also their intellectual and moral understanding of 'kinship' itself. The terminology is built on a few mechanical principles, which by logical extension and repeated application can be made to bring almost anybody in to a recognizable category; odd bits of genealogy can be fitted together to make a connection across a void, so that a man you have never seen or thought of before can be announced with delight as *'kwaskam pem!*—'my cross-cousin!' from the back of beyond. But although this may represent a warm welcome and the establishment of a friendship on the basis of a generalized cross-cousinhood, there are different kinds of cross-cousins; as there are different kinds even of 'brothers'—*ikam*, distinctions which are not explicit in the terms used to describe or address these relatives. The crucial distinctions arise in the latter case from the difference between those who are matrilineally related, and those who are related in other ways—through marriage connection and paternity in particular. In English, there are real uncles and uncles by marriage; paternal and maternal uncles, and uncles who are 'just called uncle'. The category 'uncle', if not broken down, does not get us far in understanding English families. Similarly with the Uduk.

The terminology is built up on the basis of a few simple relations. The key categories used to define other terms in the system are the parental terms and the 'sibling' terms. The parental terms are specific; *baba*, or *com* and *ta'da* or *kum* are normally used to refer to particular individuals. But the sibling terms are wide in reference, and socially ambiguous. *Akam*, 'brother', is used of half brothers and parallel cousins on either side—patrilateral and matrilateral; and similarly with *'bwaham*, 'sister'. It follows that the terms *akam* and *'bwaham* cover relationships of rather different kinds. Matrilateral and patrilateral siblings (or parallel cousins) are different sorts of people, physically and morally. Matrilateral *ikam*, of the same blood, are a man's workmates, with whom he jointly invests in cattle, and with whom he often has cause for dispute. If this happens, a man may fight, although other brothers will try to settle the quarrel. Quarrels between 'brothers' of the same birth-group may split the community; and this is recognized in the saying that only full brothers should fight, if people have to fight in the birth-group, for that is their own affair and it does not affect anyone else. But patrilateral 'brothers', that is half-brothers and parallel cousins, of a different natural community and living elsewhere, are ideally friends for life, and should not fight against each other. Indeed, if there is a conflict you are likely to find them on the same side, helping to defend your common father's people. A similar pattern is found among *i'bwaham*, 'sisters'; matrilateral sisters have competing interests in the hamlet community where they retire as old women and rival grand-mothers. Patrilateral 'sisters' on the other hand are friends in childhood, and at least in theory remain so.

Various rules concerning sex and marriage affect matrilateral but not patrilateral 'siblings'. For example, it is said to be very bad for a man to marry two matrilateral 'sisters', at the same time or successively, for it will lead to jealousy and fighting between them, which may disrupt the birth-group. In the converse case, if two matrilateral 'brothers' have sexual relations with the same girl, they risk an affliction called *piyan*. If one of the men cuts himself, the blood will flow out uncontrollably, and people will say that it is *piyan*. If his brother comes near him, he will die, and so others must help him to bind up the cut. When a man dies, if his body swells up and bursts and the intestines come out, that is *piyan*. This does not affect patrilateral 'brothers', or other men who are rivals over the same girl.

The domestic co-operation between full brother and sister is one of the closest personal relationships of Uduk life, and something of this closeness extends to any 'brother' and 'sister' of the same local birth-group (that is, matrilateral parallel cousins). If the man is in need, and deserted by his wife, his 'sister', even from a different line within the birth-group, should be prepared to come and help out in the preparation of beer for the fields; and he will take care, when necessary, of her children. This closeness and practical co-operation is not looked for, or found, between patrilateral 'brother' and 'sister'.

I have explained something of the quality of difference between matrilateral and patrilateral *ikam* and *i'bwaham* because these are two of the key terms which are used to build up the rest of the relationship terminology. Thus *iya* can be defined in the first place as the mutual relation of a man and the children of his *akam*. The social relationship which first comes to mind is that between a man and the children of a brother in his own birth-group; these are the children who 'love' their fathers, exchange gifts with them and will come running to help them in battle. But the term covers many other children; there are the children of patrilateral parallel cousins, who may, it is true, be looked to for military support in a major conflict; but the term *iya* also covers the offspring of male *'kwaskam* (cross-cousins), who are more distant socially and have no defined 'social relationship' or obligations to one. These people are not 'real *iya*' (*iyan gana*).

Similarly, the term *ishwakam* refers most often to the senior men of your own birth-group, who have authority over you and from whom you inherit. But there are other *ishwakam* who are not of your birth-group and do not stand in the same social relationship: these are your mother's patrilateral half-brothers and male cousins, both parallel and cross. The application of the term *shwakam* to such people may be a consequence of the internal logic of the terminology; but they are not regarded, or described, by the Uduk as 'real mother's brothers' (*ishwakam gana*). Sometimes when a distant relative, perhaps a cross-cousin of your mother, is called *shwakam pem!* in greeting, it is almost a joke—people may laugh and use these normally serious terms as a friendly way of greeting guests and as a conversation topic. But there is no mistaking who your real *ishwakam* are; as Danga explained:

'Your mother's brother is your real kinsman [*shwakam pini ta wathim piniŋ gana be*, literally "your mother's brother is your own real person"]. That's why you live with them. Your mother, when you are so big, she will tell you to go to your mother's brothers' hamlet. She won't tell you to stay here [with your fathers]. When you grow up a little, she will show you the way, saying, "Those are your mother's brothers. Go and look after the animals. Go and cultivate with them."

'All this is from our mothers. From the mother. They command you, saying, "Go home and look after the animals of your *ishwakam*."'

You receive no such instructions about your mother's patrilateral brothers, let alone her cross-cousins, and the fact that you also call them *ishwakam* is rather an academic point.

The terminology as such does not make essential discriminations which stem from a matrilineal way of thinking; it is almost neutral with regard to lineality and could presumably be utilized in a system of patrilineal thinking, in which case one's mother's patrilateral brothers would be the 'real *ishwakam*' and one's father's patrilateral brothers the 'real *iya*'.

Nevertheless, Uduk try to explain the logic of the terminology with reference to their ideology of matrilineal descent. *Ikam*, 'brothers', are said to be such because they have one mother, and share the same blood. If you ask, 'In that case why do you call your father's brother's son *akam*; isn't he of different blood?' —the reply is likely to be an analogy: 'Ah, but your father and his brother had the same mother and were of one blood; and therefore their children call each other brothers.'

There appears to have been one fairly recent change in the northern Uduk terminology, apparently disturbing a former symmetry. In the southern Uduk dialect, the term *nam*, 'sister's son' as a reciprocal for *shwakam*, 'mother's brother', does not occur. *Shwakam* is used as a self-reciprocal between mother's brother and sister's son. The word *nam* is undoubtedly a new introduction among the northern Uduk, and almost certainly has a Nilotic derivation (compare, for example, the Nuer *nar*, Shilluk *na*, 'mother's brother'; if the Uduk *nam* is cognate with this cluster of words, an interesting transformation appears to have taken place). The very important word *wak̲*, matrilineal birth-group, is also absent from the southern Uduk dialect, and it is tempting to see a connection between these two new usages and the development of a new pattern of asymmetrical authority relations within an increasingly formal theory of matrilineal descent as the northern Uduk established themselves in their new homeland. I shall return to this point in the final chapter.

Before concluding this discussion of the way in which terms of relationship are understood and used, I would like to raise the matter of how these terms are sometimes used in contexts where the idea of physical connection, or connection through affinity and paternity, is not in question. That is to say, where terms of 'kinship' are applied to people who are not thought of as kin in the ordinary, or literal sense. In English we speak of trade union brotherhood without at all implying common parentage. Uduk terms of 'kinship' are sometimes used analogously: they are lifted out of the context of supposed physical relationship and applied elsewhere.[8] The literal physical aspect of kinship that they imply in a straightforward discussion of kinship and marriage, is left behind, but they carry the moral and affective aspect of brotherhood, or in-lawship or whatever, with them. A relationship that otherwise would have no name is being called, by analogy, brotherhood; and ironically, because of the absence of the tensions of real brotherhood, brotherhood between former strangers can be contemplated as even closer to the ideal. It is possible to approach the ambiguity

[8] Compare Bloch, 1971.

of Uduk brotherhood in this way; real brothers with whom one has common blood are those one most frequently finds irksome and it is recognized that brothers are always fighting. But patrilateral 'brothers', who are brothers because of their analogous relationship to the common blood of their fathers, may demonstrate the mutual loyalty and ideal affection that are so difficult to attain in the circumstances of the closest brotherhood of substance.

There are other and much more clearly evident usages which can be understood as the analogous application of terms connoting substantive relationship to non-substantive relations, with the consequence of creating both personal moral ties and wider political allegiances. A good deal of the language of wider political sympathies and associations is lifted from that of substantive kinship and affinity. From one point of view, these usages are mere metaphors, but from another their imperative character in political and moral terms is greater than that of the ordinary kin relations after which they are named. In the course of history, a brotherhood of two birth-groups which began as such a metaphor, may become a new reality.

A particular example, not weighty in itself, will illustrate how the language of relationship can be used in these two senses: that is the notion of a friend, *amugu* (plural *imugu*). The word is used in two contexts: the first a 'kinship' context, where the *imugu* are linked through a pair of marriages; and the second is a 'non-kinship' context, where *imugu* are linked through having shared an experience in youth together, usually an adventure in which they have been hunting, or fishing, fighting or courting together. In the 'kinship' sense, two people (of either sex) are real *imugu* when they are each married to one of a pair of full siblings. Thus two men married to a pair of sisters, two women married to a pair of brothers, or the spouses of a brother and sister, are *amugu* to each other. Between these *imugu* there is a relationship of the classic 'joking' type; verbal witticisms of an abusive kind are permitted and enjoyed by all; and between a man and woman there may be serious practical joking.[9] What seems clear is that people in the position of *imugu* in this sense

[9] For example, a woman with the help of friends may kidnap a man and strip him; this kind of horseplay incurs a specific debt, *amure*, which has eventually to be paid off.

have not actually shared any experience together, but find themselves linked by marriage to the same birth-group; they share in-laws, in fact, which appears to be the root of the idea of their connection. The second sense of *amugu*, and my friends insisted on a distinction between the two meanings of the term, refers essentially to young people who have grown up together, and formed friendships among themselves as a result. Pairs of friends call each other by a single 'friendship name', which refers to their joint experience in the past. The friends may or may not be related through kinship or affinity. These nick-names, known as *gway maŋkin*, are used for addressing people, but not for referring to them. There are two networks, one linking men and one linking women, which scarcely overlap. Only rarely do these friendship names occur between a man and a woman. The names arise through two friends, usually in youth, doing something special together; and from then on addressing each other by a term which refers to their joint experience. For men, this experience often turns out to be hunting, catching, and eating an animal together. Sharing of meat or other food occurs frequently as a theme among the women's friendship names as well, for it is consistent with the strong emphasis in Uduk thought placed upon commensality as a basis for social incorporation. These names tend to link a person with others of roughly his own age, and the friendships thus born often last throughout life, although there is no formal age-grouping system.

Each individual may acquire an unlimited number of these friendship names.[10] One man recalled thirty-six of his friendship names without difficulty. By each of these he is known to just one of his contemporaries, whom he calls by the same name. Thus two men meet: one greets the other with the exclamation 'Mobinto!' He is greeted in reply, 'Mobinto!' This name indi-cates that they once shared the foreleg of an animal together. Men's friendship names usually carry the prefix *Mo-*, which is explicitly derived from *mugu*, 'friend', and so the name Mobinto could be translated 'friend of the foreleg (*bi*) of the animal (*to*)'. Other examples are Mo'kabocka, 'friend through eating *bocka*' (a type of rat); Mo'cenycish, 'friend of the ears of the gazelle',

---

[10] My article 'Ephemeral Names: the Uduk case' (1978) includes some details of friendship names.

Bwanto, 'stomach of the animal', Moish, 'friend through sleep-ing' (probably in the bush, on some escapade). It is curious that particular parts of an animal are usually mentioned as linking the pair of friends, and not the whole creature; this suggests that in each case a number of other people were sharing the animal as well, possibly several friendships being made out of its various parts.

Women's friendship names do not usually carry the prefix *Mo-*, although they may do so. The names refer less often to eating meat, but frequently to eating other foods, which is consistent with the practical division of activity between men and women. For one woman, I collected fourteen such names without difficulty, and from another, thirteen. Women tend to lose contact more easily than men with their childhood friends, as they become scattered in many hamlets through marriage; and they do not make as much use of their names in everyday conversation as do men. Examples of women's friendship names are: 'Dam, 'cooking-paddle' (from eating porridge off the same paddle while cooking); Moshwapu, 'friend of eating sesame'; Ishkat 'sleeping friend'; Binto, 'foreleg of animal' (from eating the foreleg of a pig together). In one or two cases, a pair of complementary nicknames is used instead of the same friendship name: for example, two women jokingly call each other *Washan pem* and *Nyaram pem* respectively ('My boy-friend', 'My girl-friend').

These friendship names, which are in frequent use, are obviously less names of people than of relationships. One advantage in communication is that if you hear a shout from one end of the village 'Mobinto'—you know not only who is being called, but who is calling! There is no 'named' and 'namer'; the name is equally given and accepted on both sides and expresses a relation which is usually symmetrical in terms of age and sex. If one of the name-partners dies, the name drops out of usage. The individuality of these names lies in their use between particular pairs of friends; as words, they may recur, and quite often do, but between different couples. It may happen that one man uses the same friendship name with two separate friends, but recalling in each case a different experience.

What the two uses of *imugu* have in common is that two people who began their lives quite unrelated by the natural circumstances of their birth, are brought together by events to share a common situation. It may be in the physically substantive sense of having established a marital relationship with persons of the same blood; or it may be independent of kinship in this sense, having come about through sharing experience, especially through hunting and eating. There is a powerful analogy between mating with the same blood, and killing and eating the same animal, and it is difficult to be doctrinaire as to which is the primary, and which the metaphorical usage. Uduk however say that real *imugu* are those married to siblings, although they admit that the sociable friendship established by the manifold *imugu* ties of childhood and youth are of far more consequence in everyday social life.

Parallel powerful analogy with kinship pervades political language. When a claim of close alliance is being made, the emotively compelling language of kinship may be used—'We are all of one blood, we are brothers', or 'We have married each other's women', or 'We all have the same father's people'; and in a cooler tone the reasonable language of common shared experience will add, 'We have all fought together, lived in one place, dug the ground and drunk beer together.'

6

A HOLD ON TERRITORY

You will be a real brother
to me perhaps . . . There will
be a pathway between us.

Birth-groups among the Uduk exist 'on the ground', though in a highly fluid and sometimes ambiguous way. The first part of this chapter describes something of the ebb and flow of birth-group communities, of the way in which natural descent is interwoven with historically-made ties of co-operation and friendship, to the point where the one may become emblematic of the other. On the tiny scale of the hamlet, the Uduk community is a temporary accretion of fragments seen for a period as a provisional unity. The hamlets of northern Pam 'Be provide most of the substantial illustration.

On a larger scale, the hamlets of the Uduk are grouped on a regional basis, into what we may call territorial clusters. These clusters, as I mentioned briefly in the first Chapter and will explain further below, used to be geographically quite separate, each grouped around its own hill for reasons of defence. Each hill community contained many birth-groups, between which there were links of mutual aid and intermarriage. Sometimes one birth-group would be able to offer protection to many others. But with conditions of greater security, the various birth-groups of each cluster have moved apart, and now live widely dispersed around the hills to which they still nevertheless acknowledge political and ritual ties. The Beni Mayu people, or the Pam 'Be people, are still supposed to fight together, to hunt together, and all are still buried with their heads towards their own particular hill. The second part of this chapter discusses the way in which these territorial clusters have been formed in northern Pam 'Be, on the basis of relationships of protection and blood-friendship, themselves closely analogous to and often congruent with the bonds of affinity, paternity, and personal friendship I have already described.

Matriliny is not the only principle of association conceived of by the Uduk; it is specifically a principle of natural connection, but it is complemented in the social world by all sorts of other links. It is thought of as a natural basis for the grouping of people, whereas other forms of connection, including paternity, are forged through history. Men and women are thus continually renewing the fabric of society by initiating and maintaining ties with those outside their own naturally given grouping. But the primary idiom for representing close ties, even if historically and arbitrarily created, remains the language of natural connection, the language of blood and brotherhood; people often wish to speak of 'historical' associations as though they were 'naturally' based. Sometimes this use of analogy and metaphor which lifts the core of moral significance from its physical vehicle of blood and brotherhood to give substance to political association creates a new reality. For the Uduk, the language of real physical substance is the language of connection by matrilineal birth. But a stranger may become a brother, or a sister; and what began historically as an amalgam of people accidentally thrown together, may become a community spoken of as linked by blood and swearing to common descent. Even if a girl waif, the *çiŋkina/* of history, marries into a protective birth-group, her own matrilineal descendants are likely to be called *abas*, blood friends, and may become 'one' with their patrons.

I have already suggested that this masking effect of the language of natural connection leaves one with the impression that local birth-groups are 'real' groupings of known matrilineal kinsmen, when in fact they may embrace two or three assimilated fragments, whose different origin is almost forgotten; even when they appear to be homogeneous, the genealogical links between two or three families may well have passed beyond memory. The same process, of the application of the language and imagery of physical cohesion to what in other contexts is known to be a heterogeneous amalgam, even a ragbag of refugees and runaways, goes on at all levels. This ambiguity of language is a part of political relations. There is an idiom in which one can speak of cohesion, incorporation and natural community, and this may be variously applied; it may be used in a straightforward, literal way of groups which are matrilineally connected, and it may be used of others about which the speaker may have private reservations; or it may be used in a consciously analogical manner, of the whole Uduk people, for example. On the other hand, there is the language of division, of discrimination and opposition, where natural community may be denied, and attention drawn to the artificial, historically-formed, relationships which signify different origins, former political patronage, and so forth. There is a dynamic principle in Uduk history; people who were once apart can be brought together, through the formation of specific bonds in the first instance, which may through the continuous practice of living, working and eating together produce a community which can be spoken of, at least metaphorically, as a natural grouping. Later it may come to be regarded truly as a natural grouping. Without a basis of common co-operation and sharing, however, the group may fragment; and the divisive language of natural difference will be used to prize the fragments further apart.

FROM PROTECTION TO BLOOD-FRIENDSHIP

Just as the essence of the patrilateral link is seen as the giving of life, and nourishment, by the people of one birth-group to members of another, which results eventually in a mutual tie between them, so it is with other links between birth-groups. Where one group has given protection to members of another in time of famine, war or flight, through taking in *çiŋkina/*, or where the rescue of a girl from death has prevented a line from dying out; or where protection was given to those fleeing from witchcraft accusations, who otherwise would have been killed; or where one group indirectly saved the life of another, by rescuing its runaway cattle; or where reconciliation has been achieved by sacrifice after hostilities, then the respective birth-groups regard themselves as being in a relationship of *abas*, literally 'blood', but more suitably translated 'blood-alliance', or better 'blood-friendship'. This relationship involves mutual aid and reciprocal defence. It is supposed to be a symmetrical relation, even where it was initiated through political protection, where one party took charge of (*buthi me'd*, literally 'held in the hand') another. Even in a case where one party is known to have been protecting or in charge of another, it is bad taste to point this out and very indelicate to make such enquiries.

Public reference to a past history of such patronage can be a serious insult, and may provoke violence.

In the relation of *abas*, the symbolism of common substance is extended to embrace both birth-groups. 'Kinship' terms may be applied without regard to the different origin of the two groups; they become 'brothers' and 'sisters'. Cattle may be herded together, the people will be supposed to defend each other in war, occasionally cultivate together, and help each other out in time of food shortage. There are different degrees of intensity of this relationship; in some cases it is so close that intermarriage is not supposed to take place. Where it is close, often between local birth-groups who live near each other, people deny the difference between them and insist on using one birth-group name.

Although the same word, *abas*, is used to refer to the physical blood which circulates in the body and in the matrilineal birth-group and also to the blood-friendship between birth-groups, Uduk use the words in such a way that from the context it is perfectly clear which meaning is intended. It is only rarely that a person has to refer to the physical blood-connection he has with his own matrilineal kin—and they are never referred to collectively as *abas*, or *abas pem*—'my blood'—in the way that allied birth-groups are. This usage is common and crops up in almost any political and historical discussion. I asked early in my stay why it was possible for Lake men of Waka'cesh to marry Bitko women, as the two birth-groups were *abas* and one was not supposed to marry blood relatives? The answer Danga gave me, after short consideration, was that the Lake were certainly *abas* with the Bitko birth-group, but only with their men, and not with their women! It was a restatement of the political association between the two groups, as opposed to their natural distinction. Sometimes, when the physical blood of the matriline is referred to, it is called *abas gana*, 'real blood'. I was often puzzled by the apparent ambiguity of these ideas, and particularly on one occasion when Danga told me that a boy is *abas* with his father. I had understood (correctly) that in conception, a child received blood from its mother only. But Danga was meaning to point out the continuity of interest and the life-long bond between a father and his son, in contrast to the lack of common interest and long-term obligation of a husband and wife; and he was using the term *abas* in its sense of a moral and political bond rather than its biological sense:

Danga: And moreover, the man [your father] then looks upon you as though you were *abas* with your father's people.

W.J.: What?

Danga: The man looks upon you, you, this person from your mother, as though you were *abas* together with your father's people. You are someone from a distant place: he goes, and marries from there, and you are from there. That man, because he is your father, because he gave birth to you from this woman, the woman is not *abas* with him, but you are. You who are their child, you are the one who belongs to them [i.e. your father's people]. But the woman is not theirs. The woman stays in her place apart. And you who are the child, you are the one who is theirs. The woman is not theirs. No: just the children are theirs.

When one birth-group is said to be *abas* to another, they call them *abas bana*, 'our blood-friends', with the same implication of a long-term mutually-interested bond. These bonds are thought of as historically created, in particular circumstances, whereas matrilineal blood-connection is taken for granted as the continuing background to such events.

A Lake man, Tente, described to me the way in which his people had become linked to the Bitko:

'Long, long ago, our people joined together [*gam me'd*, literally to join hands] with the Bitko, long, long ago.

'The Bitko knew that their women were plentiful; and they acted very wrongly. Some Bitko acted very wrongly, they did a terrible thing. They killed the women. They were killing the women . . . because of hunger. They killed the women: *ta'b*, throw in the water, *ta'b*, throw in the water, *ta'b*, throw in the water. And the treatment of women became worse; they were attacked and chased away, chased to other villages. They attacked and killed them all the time, killing them so that they would have been finished off altogether.

'Our people long ago were the Lake. They saw what was happening, *ay*! They captured two young women. Captured two young women, and took them away to prevent their discovery. They looked after them and reared them. That is how some seeds survived to grow until now. At that time, if those Lake people had been of ill will and had not taken the women under their protection [*bu'th me'd*, literally to seize in the hand], then the Bitko people would not be living now.

They would have disappeared. The name would be absent for ever.'

In discussion Tente pointed out that the Bitko had not killed their menfolk, for they were needed to cultivate. The women were said to have been killed just before the harvest. The *abas* link between the two birth-groups, according to this story, derives from the nourishment of the two rescued girls. At other times in history, the Bitko are said to have helped the Lake, and so their relationship of blood-friendship is in theory a symmetrical one, as it certainly is in practice.

A story explaining the *abas* link between two other birth-groups of northern Pam'Be, the Woshalethdhe/ and the Kunthuk, goes as follows. Long ago, a Woshalethdhe/ man, Bwoha, was very ill, and went to Pijaulu (upstream) to see if a change of environment would help. He died there, but there were none of his relatives to bury him. So Pakke, a woman of the Kunthuk, and her people buried him, and sacrificed their own cattle and goats for him, at his funeral. So there is now an *abas* blood-friendship between the two birth-groups.

Several standardized legends exist to account for the origin of some of the smaller birth-groups in a 'protected' relationship to others. For example, there is one of a gourd floating down a river, which when rescued and opened was found to contain people, who are today linked by *abas* to their rescuers. I have heard this story of different birth-groups. Here is one version, from the Yabus, given me by Sheikh Puna:

'A great gourd was carried down by a swollen river. A great water, a real flood. It brought that person from the direction of the highland there. When the gourd was opened, this great gourd, they found a man. The man was called Bittona. They found him together with another person, who was a woman. That is why they became called the River People ['Kwasi Yudu].'[1]

Abas blood-friendships are still formed today, and the following account by Nyethko, of the Woshalethdhe/ people of Pam'Be, described how this happened recently after the rescue of some of their cattle lost by Eyan:

[1] This is the southern Uduk dialect version of *'kwani yide/*, 'people of the river', or of the water.

'The cattle were stolen by thieves from Yabus there, they were led away at night. The Keral people.[2] Then they led them on and on. . . . Until the cattle acted of their own accord, and went and entered among those of Manas.

'And then Eyan came, not knowing where he might find them. Until he saw the cattle being looked after by Manas. From that point, Eyan called Manas "My brother". "You are very good indeed to take and protect these animals for me while I didn't even know your face. Very good, indeed. For such a thing as this, yes, you will be my real brother perhaps. From here, you kept and protected my animals for me and brought them home to me. It was as if I had died.[3] Really, this is very good. I know what we must do: you and all your mothers, you must bring your mothers to me, to my doorway, so that perhaps I can give you the blood of an animal. Because you are the one who looked after me first, by saving my cattle.

' "You saved my people from disaster; for it was like death indeed. It was as though my house were destroyed by fire, as though I had died.

' "It is", he said, "very good to recognize the things which *arum* [spirit] places before you. Yes, we will be real blood-friends [*abas*]. You will come to my doorway: I will kill a beast for you at my doorway.

' "Bring your mother, and your sisters; and then we will bring our mothers' brothers. It must certainly be so: there will be a pathway between us, for the cattle saw the path of the blood-connection, through being given back to me. While I was sitting there as though I were someone else.[4] I had never seen you once before." '

In this account, the *abas* link is to be explicitly confirmed in the act of blood sacrifice,[5] which joins the two previously un-connected birth-groups. This act is paralleled by stories of the reconciliation of hostile, fighting birth-groups in the past, through the sacrifice of cattle. The opposed parties are said to have dipped their fingers in the sacrificial blood, and then to have greeted each other in the normal manner, by snapping fingers. The relationship thus established is sometimes termed

[2] The nomadic people referred to are possibly wandering Hadendowa of whom the Uduk are afraid. 'Keral' may be a corruption of the name Karrar, common in the eastern Sudan.

[3] Nyethko means that the condition of being without cattle was almost as though he had died.

[4] That is to say that there was no previous relationship.

[5] Cattle are sacrificed only on occasions of major importance among the Uduk, as they are in short supply. Most sacrifices are of goats or smaller animals.

simply *abas*, and sometimes more specifically *abas 'per*, 'red blood', which recalls not only the colour of the sacrificial blood but the context of tension, hostility, and perhaps loss of life from which the relationship has been born, for redness often signifies heat and danger.

The bond of the blood-friendship is not limited to the Uduk people in the southern Funj; it is widely understood, across the various language barriers, and many *abas* links exist between individual Uduk birth-groups and particular descent groups among the Meban, Ganza, and other neighbouring peoples. In a more general sense, the unity of Uduk together with Jum Jum, Hill Burun, Meban, Ganza, Shita and Komo, in opposition to Ingessana, Dinka, Nuer, Galla, Berta, and northern Sudanese, is expressed by saying that the former group are all *abas*, 'blood-friends' to each other, for they all intermarry. This is interestingly the converse of the ordinary literal sense of blood-relationship within the birth-group, which by definition is properly an exogamous group.

I have suggested that the two uses of the idea of relationship through blood are used quite distinctly. This is true, but at the same time the apparent ambiguity can be made use of; it can be covertly suggested that what is called a great birth-group by some is a collection of miscellaneous down-and-outs who have been taken charge of, even *bought* in some cases, who have become *abas* and now use the birth-group name of their protectors when they are not—by natural blood—really members of it at all. Sheikh Puna, whose account of the mythical origins of the Lake at the time of human appearance on earth I have quoted in an earlier chapter, continued his account of the Lake in these terms. These words followed on immediately from the passage already quoted (above, p. 114):

'But all the people who are called Lake, nowadays, huh! They are not Lake. Because of the blood-friendship arising from killing, through some people being witches and harming [the Lake people] in dreams at night, they say. At night. Then people get angry, and kill [the witch] with a spear, and he dies. Then the [Lake] people settle it by discussion. They take an animal and sacrifice it. They give animals freely[6] to become blood-friends. Those people who are

---

[6] The implication is that no return was expected; the transfer of cattle seems to have had the character of blood-compensation which is not practised today. This

given animals, are blood allies. They then give birth to children . . . and that is why they are called Lake, Lake.'

Sheikh Puna gave further details on the processes of making blood-friends in a description of how the first Lake woman collected and even bought people (with cows) as followers:

'And the people who were protected by her, who are now called Lake, Lake, live just over there [indicating]. They are living near here. One of them, he came here yesterday. The people who were given protection, were chased out of the places where they used to live, the places from which they originated. People took charge of them, protected them, brought them along. And it was the same with people who were starving, long ago. That woman, that woman: she is known as the Lake woman. They say she said, "Bring me that one"; she would take him and buy [*yol*] him for cows, they say. That is why they [i.e. modern descendants of those protected] are finally called Lake.'

I was at first tempted to label the *abas* link, which is often formed in the first place between a stronger and a weaker partner, as clientship; but this term would not be appropriate, as there is no necessary subordination in the relationship, and obligations ideally become the same on both sides. Where there is a real initial element of protection, the imbalance is often corrected, and even reversed, with time; and the protected party may well reciprocate at a later date, thus guaranteeing a symmetrical relationship. Even where one birth-group has afforded protection to several others in the past, and become the focus of a defensive fan of bilateral alliances, there is no formal political domination or ranking, though leadership might stem in time of crisis from the central birth-group. But such arrangements are not permanent. In the areas with which I am familiar (Pam'Be, Beni Mayu, and Chali), the birth-groups which were supposedly dominant in the past through their protection of others (for example, Pa'dwosh, Pa Ṭe, and Ça'ba) are no longer represented in strength, and certainly not politically pre-eminent.

The *abas* links between birth-groups are often described in terms which entail mutuality and the friendship of equals. For

tale suggests that the payment, and acceptance, of cattle after deaths leaves the second party in a subordinate position to the first.

example, a link may be said simply to have come about through the two parties having long lived together in the same place (*'kwani 'ko e muŋkun*, or *'koyi mon tal'de/*). The speaker may hold his two forefingers together, parallel, to illustrate the relationship. In further explanation, he may say that the two birth-groups have herded their cows together, at one time exchanged cows or children or cultivated the same lands together for years; they have eaten and drunk beer together, and have built their homes in the same place. Another common explanation is that they have fought the same battles together; they have *gam me'd*, that is joined hands, on the battlefield, and they still *nyakka bwa* (use their 'bows together'), or *uni tan inyak bwa* ('they are comrades-in-arms', literally 'fellow bow-fighters'). Some birth-groups have picked up, in the course of migration, a series of *abas* links in different parts of the country, both inside and outside Uduk territory. The significant history of each birth-group, in fact, could be represented in analysis as the Uduk represent it in their own traditions, by the story of its acquisition of blood-friendships with others. The story of the initial formation of a blood-friendship may not of course be told in the same way by different people; one informant may even reverse the protector-refugee relation between two groups as it has been mentioned by another informant. This may be interested misrepresentation, or it may be innocent selection from a rich and complex history between the two groups in which the relation has indeed taken both forms. But the persistence of 'patronage' will always be denied, and transformed by language into mutuality, if not by circumstance.

There is no doubt about the meaning of *buthi me'd*, to 'hold in the hand', 'protect' or 'take charge of'. The term is used of political control, conquest of territory and its domination, as well as of private patronage. Chiefs, for example, are said to be 'caught and held in the hand' of the Government. The implication is that they are Government servants and far from gaining power or responsibility as a result, are seen as having lost something of their freedom and independence as persons. This sort of domination is resisted and evaded within Uduk society, and when a stronger party aids a weaker party the aggressive political language of domination and subordination, of gathering dependants, supporters and followers for the sake of building up power, is hushed. Such things are mentioned only in discreet whispers and if spoken aloud are insults which can lead to bloodshed. As far as possible, the language of political association is a defensive language; and to a remarkable degree, the political relations of Uduk society are defensive relations. Most of the language used in sociological English for the discussion of politics is 'aggressive', stemming from classic utilitarian notions of the struggle for power, and this makes it difficult to describe the defensive structural relations of a society like that of the Uduk. Great efforts are made to speak publicly of any community of Uduk as a community of equals, and the symbolic language of natural community, of blood and common body, *buŋgwar*, is a way of achieving this; the positive moral qualities of natural kinship, which find little foothold in their proper context anyway, can flourish in the image of the various defensive mutual ties of friendship which articulate political society. It would be dishonourable and provocative to hint at power-seeking, patronage and difference of status, as it would be indiscreet to point out debts owing or feuds unsettled. These matters are on the whole kept secret, and according to tradition —and practice in at least one case I know of—a young man learns of them in detail only at the death-bed of his mother's brother, or more likely his father.

The ideal legend for public telling, and for contemplation, about the beginnings of an *abas* blood-friendship is of the kind mentioned to me by Buḵko, of two birth-groups who vowed their allegiance through exchanging (*wan*) and bringing up each other's children. Such a mutual pledge would certainly be satisfactory to look back on, and a proper source of friendship— a very different matter from the rather shameful story of the Lake buying (*yol*, bartering or trading) clients for cattle.

BIRTH-GROUPS 'ON THE GROUND'

In May 1968 some information was collected, with the help of two assistants who had a bicycle between them, on the hamlets of the whole Uduk *omodiya*. A count of huts was made, and the main birth-groups of each hamlet were noted. This information, summarized in Figure 7 and Appendix 2, should be treated very carefully for several reasons. First, there are of course members

DOMINANT BIRTH-GROUPS OF HAMLETS

AREA

BIRTH-GROUP	Chali	Pam'be	Bigin	Yilejada	Beni Mayu	Puduom	Gwami	Borpa	Gindi	Bellila	Belatoma	TOTAL
					Tombak Valley →					*Ahmar Valley — Yabus Valley —*		
ANZA											3	3
BAGGARA		3			8							11
BERSANG											5	5
BIGIN			1						1	9		11
BITKO		3			1							4
BONYAŊGADHE		1								1		2
BORPA										1		1
BUNTHA				2				8	1			11
BUNYAN										1		1
BWANTHUK						2			3			5
CA'BA		9									5	14
CARKUM				1	2	3			2	6		14
CEGA											8	8
DURU										2		2
GUNYAM				1								1
GURUMURU						1						1
GWAMI [Bisho]											1	1
GWAMI [Tombak]							14					14
GWAMI UCAŊ		3										3
GWARA				2								2
GWARA ma KOŊA					1							1
GWARA MASHUWA	6	1										7
GWARA NYAMA			1									1
GWARA TOŊON										5		5
KOMA (ARU)	3									1	2	6
KOP											11	11
KORO					2							2
'KOSAYINKALA					5							5
KUM'BA'TH										10		10
KUM PI										2		2
KUNTHUK		1			1					9	3	14
KWAMAS		3										3
LAKE	15	4	2		1	1		2	3	10	17	55
LAPE			1									1
MEBAN											3	3
MALINKENY									1			1
MURINYE		1								2		3
PA'DWOSH		1									5	6
PAN'THAMU	1											1

DOMINANT BIRTH-GROUPS OF HAMLETS—*Continued*
AREA

BIRTH-GROUP	Chali	Pam'be	Bigin	Yilejada	Beni Mayu	Puduom	Gwami	Borpa	Gindi	Bellila	Belatoma	TOTAL
				Tombak Valley						*Ahmar Valley* / *Yabus Valley*		
PAN'THUS		1										1
PUR											9	9
RUTHU										4		4
'THOPA (Combuse)										3		3
ULU				1					4			5
WATHKE					2							2
WOSHALETHDHE/		3									7	10
WUGA		2					1				1	4
YAKON		1						1				2
YID											12	12
YIDE											2	2
No information	1	4							1	4	5	15
	26	41	5	9	21	7	15	11	16	70	99	320

Figure 7 (data collected by Stephen Missa and Joshua Abdalla, May 1968)

of foreign birth-groups living in a hamlet anyway—growing boys and in-marrying women, as well as assorted adult men with their families who have their own particular links with the hamlet. Second, informants were often unwilling to name their own real birth-group, or that of others, because it would draw attention to differences which are better hidden, especially from strangers. I had not expected this feeling, for I had approached the whole matter with the textbook idea of a 'matrilineal clan' in my mind, and could not understand why people should wish to be so secretive about their 'clan' membership. It was once reported back to me, after I had been enquiring about differences of *wak* and why 'clansmen' did not all live together, that a complaint had been made that I was trying to divide people and break them apart. For one birth-group may discreetly be sheltering another; and when I was later on more intimate terms, people would sometimes tell me, in explanation of other matters, that certain particular members of a hamlet, who used the name of the main birth-group of that hamlet, were not *really* such and such. The implication was that they had been protected and fostered. After all, eyebrows would be raised in Britain if a sociologist were to request information on genetic fatherhood or blood-groups. Thus, many small accreting fragments may be concealed in the list of birth-groups and hamlets in Figure 7, hiding under umbrella names which may be those of protecting hosts and allies. A third difficulty over the interpretation of this material is that there is often more than one name for a birth-group. For example, the Murinye may call themselves Baggara or Bunyan, though not, I believe, *vice versa* (see the text quoted below on page 197.) Finally, in the southern region of the Yabus valley, and even occasionally among the northern Uduk, informants may give the name of their father's birth-group, when asked for their own. This may mean that community solidarity is being emphasized, at the expense of strict accuracy on 'physical origins'. But it is also consistent with the greater emphasis placed upon the patrilateral link among the southern Uduk; indeed, the circumstantial evidence, as I shall show later, is that the fully-fledged matrilineal thinking and practice of the northern Uduk is not shared in the south. The list of birth-groups as it stands does not include the extreme southern Uduk hamlets, in the hilly Jebel Bisho region, outside the Chali *omodiya*, where this evidence is strongest.

In spite of these reservations, the list does provide a useful picture; for example, the predominance of the Lake birth-group is clear—it was named as the local birth-group in 55 of the 320 hamlets. No other birth-group was named in more than 14 hamlets, and none was spread so widely throughout Uduk territory. This appears to confirm oral traditions of the historical precedence of the Lake, and their central position in the making of the people as a whole. Relatively few other birth-groups appear to be represented both in the southern and northern valleys—only six in fact, with fairly small populations (Ca'ba, Koma or Aru, Kunthuk, Pa'dwosh, Woshale<u>th</u>dhe/ and Wuga, all of whom reckon to have come from the south). It is safe to assume that these birth-groups constitute in some sense a core to the historical development of the Uduk. A surprising number of the other birth-groups are named after foreign tribal groups or places outside Uduk country. There are at least eighteen in this list alone (and I know of others which for some reason do not appear—for example, Jerok). Of these, four are found only in the Yabus valley, fourteen in the northern valleys, and one is found in both regions. In the northern valleys we find for example Ulu (from which people returned at the beginning of the century, as they did from Jerok); Carkum (Jebel Surkum to the north); Wathke; Baggara and Bunyan (both plausibly derived from escapees of the *jihadiya* garrison at Surkum from 1885, with a Baggara officer—see Triulzi, 1975, p. 63). There is a surprising total of at least seven birth-groups named after the Meban (known to the Uduk as Gwara), or various distinct clans of the Meban (Gwara Mashuwa, etc.) Their distribution indicates the particularly close connection the Uduk, especially in the north, have had with the Meban, mainly through protection and intermarriage. Finally, we may note that a fairly large number of birth-groups are found only in one region or the other. Nine in the present list are exclusive to the Yabus, and twenty-eight to the northerly valleys (of which eight are found only in the Ahmar valley). Since many of these bear 'foreign'-derived names of peoples and places the Uduk encountered after their migration to the northerly valleys, it is evident that such small birth-groups have sprung into being through the vicissitudes of the last century or so. Many are probably re-formed communities of persons returning from refuge or slavery after the various disturbances of the last century, and others are probably groups which have accreted around links of protection and alliance with new neighbours. This evidence alone suggests that the society of the northern Uduk has undergone considerable reconstruction since their arrival in the Ahmar and Tombak valleys.

The birth-group is ideally a unity. But even in 'normal' historical times the practice of actually living in communities on the ground inevitably leads to friction, which combined with population growth results in splitting and fragmentation of groups. The natural growth of the birth-group is met by division caused by the social and political difficulties of co-operation. Members of the same birth-group are estranged and each goes his or her separate way. Bukko gave a description of this matrilineal growth and fragmentation after commenting critically on a birth-group in which a division had occurred, because of a homicide within the group, though the links of co-operation had not yet been fully broken:

'Did you have different mothers? Different mothers from the beginning? There is no difference.

'We are born: one is born from the mother, another is born from the mother, they go and separate on the ground. This one, born from the mother, goes and gives birth with her vagina. Another vagina [i.e. another sister] gives birth, and her children split off with angry words, saying, "This is my line ['*pen*] here, this is my line here." That's how it is.'

It can happen that branches of a birth-group between which there is little intimate co-operation today, and between which marriage can take place, were previously one group observing common residence and common exogamy, even within living memory. The large birth-groups may be composed of several local branches each practising common residence and exogamy; though there are plenty of small, named birth-groups which in themselves constitute exogamous units. There is no rigid means of distinguishing between birth-groups which observe all the proper conventions of intimate matrilineal relationship—co-operation in the fields, sharing of crops, food, and animals, sharing of responsibilities for debt, common residence, and the prohibition of sex and marriage within the group; those which observe some of these conventions, keeping up appearances but no longer behaving as matrilineal kin ought; and those which have fallen into separate communities, no longer taking care of each other's debts and responsibilities, and between which sex and marriage are tolerated. There is a continuum between these various stages, representing to some extent a developing trend, for demographic growth is quite likely to lead to the splitting of a tenuously cohering birth-group into two smaller and more compact groups.

But besides splitting up, matrilineal kin may come together; individuals from one remote branch of a birth-group or a closely allied birth-group can be assimilated. Even in small matrilineal communities, exact genealogies are not remembered further back than three or four generations, and even in a compact hamlet the only genealogies known are short lines going back to three or four named women whose sisters are said to have been lost in the bush, and whose own parents' names are forgotten. The descendants of the women whose names are remembered however will insist with great vehemence that these women were 'all sisters' (*i'bwaham*). But since the use of the term *'bwaham* extends throughout the birth-group anyway, at least to the limits of exogamy, thus including female parallel cousins as well as 'real sisters', this does not assist any critical enquiry into the social or biological history of the birth-group.

It is convenient to speak, as I have been doing, of the *local* birth-group as that group which actually lives together, observes joint responsibilities for building a cattle-herd and sharing debts and assets, and, crucially for the purposes of this discussion, regards itself as an exogamous unit. A person is bound to his local birth-group by common substance, by working duties and a right to share in the fruits of its common labour, including its cattle herd. He may expect the local birth-group to get him out of debt and to avenge his death if necessary, in the spirit of an eye for an eye, for this is the group which pursues blood feuds and does not accept compensation in the form of animals or anything else. A man should be killed for a man, and a woman for a woman, from the local birth-group of the killer (no other relative is suitable) and the vengeance should be carried out in the same manner as the original homicide.

Rivalries, tensions and quarrels develop within the local birth-group as within any community sharing joint interests. It is in practice a very fragile association, in spite of its ideal solidarity. Its common interests are not very substantial—each member of a local birth-group has strong ties binding him to persons and groups outside it. The community often breaks up after quarrels, although the sanction of the anger of *arum* is invoked by those who are trying to keep it together.

The problem of holding the local birth-group together, and overcoming the hostilities which arise within it and may cause a split, dominates the everyday politics of Uduk hamlets.

COMMUNITIES OF NORTHERN PAM'BE

I have already drawn heavily for my description of Uduk society on the communities I know well in northern Pam'Be, the three hamlet clusters usually known as Pany Caran, Waka'cesh and

Kalagorko. All these communities are Kum 'Be, Pam'Be people, although Kalagorko is at present situated just inside the modern administrative boundaries of Beni Mayu. Figure 5 shows the eighteen hamlets of these three clusters as they were in the rainy season of 1968, and the main birth-group of each. Eight main birth-groups are found in the three clusters. Some demographic details, genealogies, and so forth for these communities may be found in the Appendices.

It is generally agreed that the first Uduk to settle in northern Pam'Be were the Pa'dwosh. They are variously referred to as the fathers, or the protectors, of all the other people who now live there, and who trace blood-friendships with them, directly or indirectly. These relationships were established in the dim past. I assume that some date back to the period of earliest Uduk settlement on the Tombak, perhaps two centuries ago, and others to the disturbances of the late nineteenth century. The whole area was evacuated in the 1890s, as described in an earlier chapter, and after a period of some years at Jebel Ulu, the people of northern Pam'Be claim to have returned more or less to the area previously occupied. Further links of protection and aid may have been formed at this time. An old lady described to me how the Pa'dwosh were the 'fathers' of everybody in Pam'Be, for they had protected (*buthi me'd*) everyone else in a time of great hunger. People were lost out in the bush, she said, and the Pa'dwosh were the only ones growing grain. They said, 'Come, and we will look after you, you will eat things, for hunger has struck you'. The Pa'dwosh people had enormous grain stores, she said, sweeping her arm around the hut we were sitting in. Their stores, and those of the people of Janna (of the Pa Ṯe: another protecting group of Pam'Be) were full of grain; and all the other people flocked to their villages for they were suffering from hunger, and dying. Today, both the Pa'dwosh and the Pa Ṯe seem to be disappearing; there were only two old men of the Pa'dwosh left in the district, but they were repeatedly pointed out to me as the 'fathers' of everybody else. Informants will press the point home by picking out the relevant links from their genealogical history; one person's mother's father was a Pa'dwosh, and another's mother had a paternal grandfather who was a Pa'dwosh, and therefore, it always followed, all are one people, one body, *buŋgwar*. Women used this language of 'kinship' very often, whereas men more frequently used direct political terminology.

The birth-groups which claim to have been resident in northern Pam'Be from long ago are those of Waka'cesh and Kalagorko: the Bitko, Lake, Koro, and Wuga. The Bitko claim a local origin, but the others preserve traditions of having originally come from the south; the Wuga from 'Pur' (on the Daga river) and the Koro and Lake from Jebel Bisho. The four are now closely linked by overlapping blood-friendship. The Wuga and Koro claim to be *abas* from long ago, and the Bitko c aim to be *abas* with the Wuga, through having fought together with them and suffered many deaths in the same place. The Lake have been *abas* from ancient times with both the Wuga and Koro. The Lake and Bitko have each helped the other in the past and are symmetrically *abas*; I have already quoted one story of how the Lake rescued Bitko girls and thus the birth-group was saved from annihilation (above, pp. 172–3). There are also separate accounts of the Bitko having protected the Koro and vice versa; and the Bitko have more recently, in the last generation, protected the Lake again. The four birth-groups thus form a tightly-knit unit. 'Kinship' terms are applied without discrimination through the Lake, Bitko, and Koro (though this is not extended to the Wuga). However, it is only the Koro and the Lake who traditionally do not intermarry. There are plenty of marriages between the others. But recently a case I have already referred to of a young Lake man marrying a 'mother's sister' of the Koro took place, and this was accepted though not really approved of. There is a certain rivalry between the Bitko cluster of these four birth-groups (sometimes referred to collectively as Bitko) and the cluster of Pany Caran. There is also rivalry between the Bitko cluster and the people of southern Pam'Be, although some of these are very close matrilineal relatives. I shall explain something of the past history of the Bitko and Lake birth-groups of Waka'cesh before considering these wider relations.

The Bitko are a small and united birth-group: they all live at present in Waka'cesh, and there are no Bitko anywhere else at all—that is, no male Bitko who have built houses elsewhere, though there are of course women married into other hamlets. But this has not always been the happy position. I was told that

the Bitko had always lived in Pam'Be, either on the north or the
south side of the Tombak, but they were once persecuted.
People—the implication is other Uduk people—were chasing
them in order to kill them. They broke into three groups, and
each fled in a different direction. Each group found protection
with others: one in Bellila, one I believe near Chali, and one
with the Koro people. Eventually, when the danger was over,
all three groups reunited, and have lived ever since with the
Koro, with whom they are now blood-friends and brothers.

The Bitko story is rather generalized, and undatable, but
similar events have happened to the Lake local birth-group, and
their story has more circumstantial detail. They are moreover
at a different stage of the cycle; they were dispersed far and wide
in the 1930s, they are not yet reunited and the people in
Waka'cesh represent only a fragment of the whole local birth-
group—that is, of the group who formerly lived together, and
who still retain ties of mutual aid and observe joint exogamy.
These Lake settled in Pam'Be after migrating from Jebel Bisho
long ago, and after living on both the north and south sides of
the river, there was a fight, which probably started over girls
according to my informant, between them and the collected
people of Ca'ba, Kwamas and Murinye of southern Pam'Be.
The Lake were driven to Chali, where they were taken under
the protection of the Bwan'de and others. I assume that this
happened in the last century. However, there was an epidemic
in the 1930s in the Chali area, I believe of smallpox: the Lake
from Pam'Be were suspected of being responsible for it and had
to flee. One woman went to Deim, a *Bunyan* (Berta-Arab)
village near Kurmuk, and her sons still live there; one man and
his sister went to the Yabus, to their father's people, where they
still are; and two brothers came with their sisters to northern
Pam'Be, where they were protected by the Bitko and the Koro,
with whom they were already blood-friends. There are other
scattered fragments of the birth-group, but I am not sure of the
date of their separation: there is a small community of the
birth-group in Bellila with whom close ties are maintained;
there is a woman who went in obscure circumstances to Jum
Jum country and married there (some of her children returned
to Waka'cesh); and there is a substantial group of Lake still in
southern Pam'Be who are said to be closely related to the

Waka'cesh Lake. Some tension exists between these two groups, and I understand that there was a homicide in the past which resulted in the split. Today, the two groups often herd their cattle together, but buy them separately; and although there is no inter-marriage, their common identity is sometimes disclaimed. The southern group are known as Laken Golga/, but the northern group are reluctant to accept this name.

One of the senior men of the Waka'cesh Lake, Ha'da, told me the story of their flight from Chali because of the smallpox in about 1937, two or three years before the 'Italian anger', the disturbances of the Second World War. It was one of the most solemn and deeply important matters I had been told about. Ha'da's account went, in part, as follows:

'When I was in Chali, the smallpox struck people, and people gossiped. We were three, I and my sisters. I myself, Ha'da, Kunke, Thamke, we were about to be killed by people with spears. We were three. So I made my sisters go away. Because the smallpox was striking people still, I said "Go. Leave me, and then I alone will be killed in the bush there, I will be killed. I will be killed in the bush there, I will be killed. For otherwise, you will be killed in the bush too, you will be killed, yes."

' "And I," I thought to myself, "if I am left behind, I will go and live in the bush. If my sisters are going to die, I will go and live in the bush, and I will become an antelope or something, I don't know."

'For I was intending to attack the others too. It was my father's people. They were about to kill us off,[7] because they were stricken by smallpox. The smallpox struck people here very severely, and they told us that we had brought the smallpox.'

The situation was particularly shocking as it was Ha'da's own father's people who were leading the accusations; and although Uduk expect to put up with a good deal of criticism and even this kind of accusation from their own matrilineal kin, there should be generosity and affection and understanding between a person and his father's kin. It should be possible to rely on them for protection even when one is accused of evil; so Ha'da's dilemma was compounded by the hostility of those he should have been able to go to for help, and as a result he found

[7] Many homicides among the Uduk are the consequence of witchcraft suspicion and accusation.

himself actually planning to attack them himself. But he and
his sisters were led away from Chali by people from Pam'Be—
and other members of his community went their own ways:

'And then, some people came. People came from Pam'Be, they came
to lead me away; because they had heard the word that I was about
to be killed, with my sisters too. Then we—people led us away. And
a great pig like this, that belonged to my mother, I would have taken
it home.

'I have told this story with unhappiness. This story lies heavily in
me [literally, these words are very bad in my stomach].
. . . .
'And from that time, I have always been unhappy because of my
father's people. Right up to now. For my father's people were about
to kill me for nothing because of the smallpox. But why? The smallpox was not understood by us. We didn't know anything about the
smallpox, anything at all.'

Birth-groups should ideally live together, though experience
teaches people how difficult this can be. The Waka'cesh Lake
hope that in time the various scattered fragments which compose their closest relatives, including two women and part of
their families who live right outside Uduk country altogether,
will come together again. Ha'da talked more than once of
bringing back his sister from the Bunyan country near Kurmuk.
Divisions and distance between matrilineal kin, refusals of
practical assistance which follow from living miles apart, can
cause ill will which may make people sick.

It is remarkable how well contact is maintained between the
separate fragments of the Waka'cesh Lake; when the women
visit, they carry baskets of grain on their heads, even over the
twenty-five miles to the Yabus. Individuals from the Bellila
group sometimes come to live in Pam'Be, and efforts are made
to get the brother in Yabus to join in the affairs of the birth-
group—to contribute to debt-payments for example. Great
pressure was put on him to make such contributions when the
rainstones of a former creditor were causing storm damage in
Waka'cesh. He was reluctant, even though the debt arose from
his own treatment when sick as a boy, and the resentment that
was felt was known to be dangerous for the group as a whole.
Gossip suggested that sooner or later, if this went on, someone
would fall ill.

The ideal state, of peaceful and co-operative living within the birth-group, has the blessing of *arum*, the powers of spirit. If members of a local birth-group do not live in peace and quiet, they may stir up trouble for themselves from the ground *arum*, the spirits of the dead, and in particular the spirits of those of their own number who have recently died. Violent sickness may result. The truth of such a situation is revealed usually by one of the older men of the birth-group, who practises as one of the many divining specialists in Uduk hamlets; or it may be revealed to anyone in a dream. A gathering of all members of the local birth-group can then be arranged, at which things are talked over and a ceremony held for reconciliation, followed later by a special beer and sacrifice for the *arum*. The ceremony can only take place when everyone assembles; and this is only possible when everyone is willing to make peace, which is by definition difficult to arrange.

A case of this kind happened soon after my arrival in Waka'cesh. A Lake woman, who we would say seemed subject to epileptic fits, had a seizure one evening and rolled over into the fire, around which she and her children were sleeping in the open space in front of her hut. She was badly burned on her back. A diviner from a nearby hamlet, close blood-friends with the Lake birth-group, after consulting the fire oracle[8] said that she had been struck by *arum*. This was because there had been anger in the local Lake birth-group; a 'sister' who was married and living in Chali, some six miles away, had been annoyed that the hamlet in Waka'cesh had killed a large pig of hers (for a Gurunya ceremony, for the saving of children's lives—this is described in the next chapter), and was also angry that people never came to visit her and her children. So that night Ha'da, who practised as a man of *arum*, sprayed water from his mouth onto the bodies of the people, cooling them for the while; and later, though I missed the occasion, a special *asu arum* (beer for the *arum*) was held, with a blood sacrifice.

The dangers of quarrelling and rifts in a birth-group are particularly clear when the group is widely scattered as the

[8] One of the commonest forms of divination used today by Uduk specialists is to hold a lighted ebony switch over a gourd of water; it burns erratically, and also makes patterns of smoke and ash in the water, from which types of affliction and debt can be diagnosed.

Waka'cesh Lake are; but they are also present when the group is living together. Indeed the very processes of working together and sharing the product can lead to tensions. Brothers often find cause for complaint.

Rivalry and hostility between brothers of a birth-group is often connected with the tendency of a man to favour his sons at the expense of other children of the hamlet—and to lend them and give them food, seeds, animals and rainstones which otherwise would be available for members of the birth-group. Each man tries to bind his own sons more closely to him, by using resources which are strictly not entirely his to give away. I know of one case in Yabus where the mere resentment of a Lake man's very large young family, who were consuming what seemed to be vast quantities of the community's food, led his brothers to secede and leave him on his own, with his (Wuga) wife and family. Fortunately the man's six sons (full brothers) were growing up and soon were able to help him in the fields. These sons are still together in their 'father's place', most having married, and their sisters' sons are joining them to form a substantial hamlet, which may in time become regarded as a separate local birth-group of the Wuga.

There are often simmerings of discontent within a local birth-group over the disposal of joint resources. Sometimes they reach the court, as did the case of Ya'ka of Pany Caran (Wuga birth-group), who sold a cow belonging to his maternal grandmother without the permission of his relatives in the hamlet. He sold it to the Omda, through a merchant in Chali. The price agreed was £8.000 (Sudanese). The merchant gave Ya'ka £4.000 (Sudanese), promising the rest later. Meanwhile Ya'ka's relatives found out that he had sold the cow. Two of his brothers were furious, saying that it was the only cow of their grandmother. They went to the Omda's court in Chali. The Omda's failure to pay the full price came to light. He flung the extra £4.000 (Sudanese) at them, but they said they didn't want the money, they wanted the cow. (This was out of the question—I believe the cow had already been used for a further transaction). The case went to Kurmuk, where the arguments of Ya'ka's brothers prevailed, and he was given a six month sentence (by a local magistrate from Keili, familiar with Uduk custom.) He emerged from prison about February 1966, when his now forgiving relatives rallied round to help him build a new house, although he could not provide them with any beer and there was only a little food for the work-party. Blame was transferred to the merchant and the Omda.

Resentment and friction between brothers of a birth-group can easily arise over work in the fields. Appeal cannot be made to any court over a man's laziness as a cultivator; but sickness in the birth-group may be diagnosed as caused by the wrath of the dead at grumblings and grudges between matrilineal kin over work. Such a diagnosis was made when a young woman of Pan Gathe, married into Pany Caran, was taken ill. She was coming home from the river meadows in the rainy season when suddenly the tall grass 'came over her'. It may have been a whirlwind, or she may have fainted; at any rate she was frightened and ill when she arrived home. After some local diviners had consulted the fire oracle, it was announced that she was struck by *arum a'cesh*, the ground *arum*, and it was understood that a particular spirit was responsible—that of her recently dead sister. Her birth-group 'brothers' in Pan Gathe had recently been quarrelling over cultivation in the fields. Some of them were being lazy and arriving late, and the quarrel had almost reached the point of fighting. A ceremony of blood sacrifice was held the following day. The girl's mother was sent for, and all the available members of her local birth-group. A confirmatory diagnosis was made, and the diviner told me that her body 'appeared in the water, covered in blood', after he had studied the patterns made by burning ebony sticks over his calabash of water. All the matrilineal kin who had been gathered sprayed the patient with water from their mouths. Then the three men of *arum* present (only one was of the girl's birth-group), with preliminaries common to most healing ceremonies, consecrated a chicken and sacrificed a goat. The man of *arum* and all the affected kinsmen touched their fingers in the blood and on to the bodies of the girl and her mother. One of the men of *arum* then 'stretched' the patient's limbs, a common rite for realigning and resettling the body. The sacrificial blood would free the girl from further disturbance, and the whole affair no doubt made for quieter relations among the girl's 'brothers'.

At any given time, there are rifts within many local birth-groups.

Some are in the process of splitting up, and although the bond of joint exogamy still holds, there may be two or three residentially separate sections of a local birth-group who find it increasingly difficult to extract proper support from each other. The process of fragmentation is usually deplored by everyone; it appears as if the unfortunate squabbles and hostilities of human life in practice are always cutting across the naturally given and divinely ordained continuities of relationship through women, breaking up communities which, if the world were properly ordered, ought to be living together in peace.

A number of reasons are recognized for the fragmentation of birth-groups. I have already mentioned that the Uduk consider the commonest historical reason for the breaking up of these groups is the repeated raiding and scattering they have experienced, especially the devastation of their country at the turn of the century. Returning ex-slaves and refugees, who had lost contact with their relatives, founded new local birth-groups, under the protection of their fathers' people or other allies. In present-day life, it is known that quarrels within and between birth-groups can lead to fragmentation. There are extreme circumstances, where fighting within a birth-group has led to a death—which cannot be avenged in the normal way—and a permanent split is then likely. Individuals may be chased out of a community, or may flee, because of witchcraft suspicion. If they are women, they may bear offspring elsewhere who do not return to their mother's brothers. If the fugitive is a man, he may be joined by a sympathetic sister, and in either case, a new local birth-group may start from that point. Even if the reason for the original break is not so extreme, people are not keen to discuss it, and merely remark that the so-and-sos are just 'living with their father's people, their mother married into that area, and her children stayed with her'. This situation is not uncommon, but it can usually be presumed that there is some very good reason why the children did not return to their own people. Women suspected of witchcraft may find it difficult even to find a home with their own people, and flee where they are safest, right outside Uduk country.

But the communities of northern Pam'Be illustrate the way in which birth-groups may support each other, cohere, and even assimilate one another, as well as fragmenting. The close association between the birth-groups of the Bitko cluster has been mentioned; and the fact that within each birth-group of the cluster there are distinct genealogical lines which end in two or three 'grandmothers' who were 'certainly sisters, real sisters', although the details of their parentage is forgotten. Within some of the birth-groups there are hidden divisions, which are rarely spoken of; the criteria of common matrilineal descent, although clear in theory, may be blurred in practice. There is a part of the Wuga known as *she o'da cish* ('near the fire of the gazelle'). According to legend a woman appeared from the bush and was welcomed to join the Wuga people around the fire on which they were roasting a gazelle. But I never learned, in spite of discreet enquiry, which particular people were indicated. Part of the Woshalethdhe/ of Pany Caran, who themselves came from Chali to be protected by the Pa'dwosh, were said to be of Gwara Delwin origin (a Meban clan) though this is only spoken of in confidence, for these people were protected by the Woshalethdhe/ and are usually known by their name. For all purposes they are fully a part of the Woshalethdhe/. To assert, even by the use of a birth-group name, common matrilineal descent is to assert the reality which exists in practice of living and working together. Differences of origin, where small fragments have been assimilated, may fade out of memory; the lack of concern with precise genealogy facilitates this amnesia. The distinction between what is real blood connection, the blood of matrilineal descent, and what is blood-friendship between non-kin, here becomes difficult to define. The possibility of ambiguity is certainly there: of the slipping over from the moral bond of blood-friendship to the assertion of physical unity. Such a shift in meaning is potential among the Bitko cluster of birth-groups, for example, where the ambiguity already exists in that the whole cluster can be called 'Bitko' and is based on intimate and overlapping ties of blood-alliance. To be indebted for the saving of the blood of your line to another is almost like having been born, or at least reborn, from that line, and thus sharing a common source of life. People in this relation, especially where the saving of life-blood has been reciprocated, are mutually indebted as they owe each other their birth, or rebirth; and although the ascription of a new physical unity in terms of the English language 'descent' does not quite match the situation it is perfectly reasonable to conceive the new physical unity as a 'birth-group of common—or mutually dependent—origin'. The notion of a 'birth-group' rather than a descent-group accommodates more easily the process whereby fragmented matrilineal groups may by mutual aid, envisaged as the saving of life, come to regard themselves as a single *wak̲*, or a community of related physical origin and continuity, whose amity is jealously watched by the spirits of the dead.

TERRITORIES AND THEIR DEFENCE

The Kum 'Be or people of Pam'Be, Ngau explained, were 'a whole together' (*dhana kuluny*) and distinct from the Kun Jale (the people of Chali) and the Kum 'Penawayu (the people of Beni Mayu), who each constituted separately 'a whole together'. These groupings of people are territorially based; each has at its heart a mountain, which formerly provided its main defence— Jebels Chali, 'Be or Tombak, and Beni Mayu, which still stand proudly up from the widening plains and are seen as landmarks for miles around. These mountains are respected; the spirits of the dead live beneath them, and the people of each territory are buried with their heads towards their proper mountain The territorial divisions still correspond to large-scale hunting units. When people of more than one territory take part in a hunt, they operate as separate groups, and conflicts often develop between them. A person always takes the side of his territorial unit, unless in circumstances which were formerly very unusual, his father happened to belong to the other side. The grouping of people into territorial units appears to be similar over the whole of Uduk country.

The territorial units are essentially defence groupings. Each may have a core, a particular birth-group which protected others who sought refuge in their territory—or rather around their mountain. The birth-groups of each territory are linked together with a fine network of *abas* ties. These blood-friendships are not exclusively within the territorial unit, but inevitably, because of past conditions of insecurity and political threat, not only from outsiders but from other Uduk, they tend to be very closely knit within the unit. People's sense of political identity, of belonging to a particular territory, is very strong. If you ask a person for his country (*bampa*), his people (*'kwani*) or his 'tribe', using the Arabic *gabila*, he will almost certainly give you his territory—he is from Pam'Be, or Beni Mayu. The allegiance is not of the individual so much as of his birth-group; even if you as an individual have a father in Beni Mayu, as some of the younger Koro men have, and to whom therefore you owe filial obligation in battle, that is your individual problem; for the Koro as a whole are Kum 'Be, people of Pam'Be. Their past history of association with Pam'Be is engraved in the mesh of *abas* ties they have with other birth-groups in Pam'Be.

When political conditions were very different from the colonial peace of the mid-twentieth century, self-defence based on territorial units was vital for the Uduk. There is evidence that defence and survival required that the people of each mountain should live near the mountain, or possibly even on it, and build close together. Each mountain community would be separated by wide distances from the next, and there would not be much contact between them. In times of real threat, it was even necessary for the community to build a stockade and live within it. There are several traditions of stockaded settlements which appear to refer to the mid-nineteenth century. Ngau told me of the evidence of a stockade destroyed by fire long ago which he had seen in Bellila, on the south bank of the Ahmar. It appears to have been one or two miles in diameter, and the ground is still discoloured along the line of the former defences, as can be seen, Ngau said, when the grass cover is freshly burned at the end of the dry season. The Kum'bath birth-group were the owners (*cil*) of the enclosure (*cur*), and doubtless those under their protection would also live in it. Crops were probably cultivated inside the stockade, which must have been piled high with logs, branches, thorns, and possibly earth. It must have been an enormous construction for the signs still to be visible after about a century. Ngau emphasized that the stockade was built before the time of Ibrahim Mahmoud and the disturbances from the Ethiopian border kingdoms. People sheltered in it from the Turuk (qualified as 'the real Turuk') who came wanting to take away children. People refused, and then the Turuk burnt the stockade and nearly everyone was killed. Those who survived were those who covered themselves with the blood of others (presumably to appear dead). The story probably relates to mid-nineteenth-century slaving activities. A stockade is also said to have existed near Chali, to the east of the modern village, where Uduk used to shelter from the Galla, though I could not be sure what period it dates from. Ngau considered that there were probably many stockaded settlements in the past.

At Jebel 'Be, or Tombak, the birth-groups around which others clustered seem to have been Pa Te, Pa'dwosh, Ca'ba and Murinye. Deke, an old lady of the Murinye, or Baggara or Bunyan as she called them, told me graphically of the part she considered her own people—she speaks of them in the first person singular—to have played in the gathering of others to the mountain of 'Be. I asked her who came to the area first:

'It was I. I am the one who gathered people together, I alone. I alone, from all this area up to Borpa . . .

'Which is my mountain? The mountain known as Jebel 'Be, Jebel 'Be. Because I came and settled on it. What place did I come from? I come from that road there [pointing north]. I alone. Didn't I gather all these people together, all of them? People [now] come from there, they come and dispute the land with me. I am challenged by people over this homeland . . .

'I gathered the people together here, when this place was just grassland. Was anyone living here? I gathered people together, I alone. The great Murinye; we were called by people the great Murinye . . .

'I settled here [after some previous wanderings]. People came, came, and filled up round the sides, and behind me there. And I built a stockade. I built a stockade to surround the huts, to encircle them completely. I lived in the middle of the stockade like that, for I was a Bunyan . . .

'People came and joined with us [*gam me'd*], they came and found me, while they were living in that village of Te that is spoken of. I was fathered by them . . .

'The Pa'dwosh came up the mountain to me. They became my relatives [*buŋgwar*, body] . . . They said, "Where can I settle? The place is full of Bunyan." Heh! I filled the place completely. The Bunyan filled the place completely, they encircled that mountain. I alone, alone; I, the Murinye . . .

'I took people under my protection [*butha 'kwani me'd*]. You can't count the people I protected; I took them in *rap̣, rap̣, rap̣*, as far as over there . . .'

A more common version of the history of southern Pam'Be is

that the Pa Ṭe, whose origin is the Ganza country to the south of Udukland, were the first to arrive there; under a leader called Janna, who lived before the late nineteenth-century troubles, they protected many refugees running from fighting in other places (mainly in the south). All these people are now known as *kum 'Be* (the people of 'Be) but the 'real Kum 'Be' are the Pa Ṭe. The famous Uduk leader of the turn of the century, Abu Magoud, who is credited with having gone to ask for help from the Turuk against the ravages of the border kingdoms, and to have been instrumental in persuading them to send the official patrol of 1904, was of this group, of whom very few now survive.

Since the days of great insecurity when people lived in nucleated settlements huddled near isolated mountains, sometimes inside stockades, the tight territorial units which were created by the requirements of defence have loosened. The formerly cohesive communities of each mountain began to break up; and now small hamlets are scattered continuously from one mountain to the next along the river valleys. The ties of mutual defence have loosened too. Buḵko deplored the way in which birth-groups which formerly clustered together, as at Beni Mayu, were now spreading out and losing their unity:

'Everyone was together [*gam me'd*] in the past. They now have pointless divisions . . . '

'People are living divided up now, when they were not divided up before. The people of this birth-group, this is the homeland they lived in, here, together with those people of the red soil. My mother's brothers lived here. They lived here always, mixed together with those people of the red soil. You split yourselves up now, but did people split up in the past? Nonsense. Why do they call villages so many different names? This village is known by one name: just 'Penawayu [Beni Mayu]. Why must you divide up the village [*pa*]? Was any village divided up like that in the past? . . . Those people, those that you divide up like that now, are [so-called] 'Penawayu people,[9] but where are the real people of 'Penawayu? There is Goḵko alone, by himself . . .[10] That's his mountain, their mountain.'

[9] Buḵko is referring to the people of Pam Bwawash, who have moved a couple of miles west from the hill of Beni Mayu, where they used to be with his people.

[10] This old man is one of the few surviving members of the formerly important Pa'dwosh birth-group in the area.

He continued to criticize the modern loosening of ties within the territory of Beni Mayu, addressing the younger generation in general:

'You have recently divided up this village. Those Lake you speak of: why do you exclude them? Whoever excluded the Lake in the past? They are our Lake. Heh! Why do you mark off the Lake, split up the village *shwar, shwar*?[11]—causing them to leave angrily, and keep themselves in their own birth-group, separately? Are we not still in charge of [and he names one of the Lake of Beni Mayu]?'

Not only have the territorial units begun to crumble residentially through a dispersion of small hamlet communities which formerly would have been together; but the tie between fathers and sons, on which a good deal of the cohesion of territorial defence formerly depended, has been eroded. In the past when a call to arms might come at any time, sons used to live with their fathers until a mature age, according to the memory of old men. This did not contradict the unity of territorial units, for on the whole, again according to tradition and memory, marriage used to take place within those units. A person's own people, and his father's people, belonged to the same mountain, and the divided loyalty implicit in Uduk thinking about a man's immediate obligation to his birth-group and long-term political tie to his father did not become a real conflict. Territorial endogamy ruled out the more bizarre forms that this personal dilemma might take, and in a structural sense provided a basis for the political cohesion of territorial communities. Informants agree generally that boys now leave their fathers' homes earlier than they used to, and that this is a consequence of greater security. Today they sometimes leave for their mother's brothers' hamlets before puberty. Bukko, for example, insisted that in his day (the early part of this century) young men married while still in their father's hamlets:

'They lived and married among their fathers. They would go [to their mother's brothers] later, when they had given birth to children. When they had given birth to children, and then they would bring their children with them. I myself married while among them [i.e. his fathers]. I married while among them, and carried Ŋapko in my

---

[11] An ideophonic expression suggesting repeated separation.

arms [his son]. I went later to their place [i.e. his mother's brothers] in the red soil there, to those people of mine in the red soil.'

He further explained that a young man might go as a visitor to his mother's brothers, to cultivate there, but return to cultivate with his fathers, where he was based.

Territorial defence units have weakened since the establishment of relative peace in Uduk country. Their geographical boundaries have been blurred—people of one unit have even spilled over into what was strictly the territory of another. Marriage has increasingly taken p'ace across the boundaries of territorial units, and consequently created a more diffuse pattern of political allegiance, in some individual cases producing a profoundly divided set of loyalties. Young men no longer live close to their fathers, but move out to the widening diaspora of matrilineally-based hamlets.

But the old territories are by no means forgotten, and still command loyalties when occasion arises. Large-scale fighting is not a frequent occurrence these days; and when it happens, it often breaks out in the hunt when territorial teams of men are already mobilized and armed. Ngau gave me an account of such a fight, which arose over a minor incident at a hunt. He claimed that the people of 'Be and Chali usually ally themselves against the people of Beni Mayu. A man from Beni Mayu shot at a Chali man (of the Woshale<u>th</u>dhe/ birth-group) by mistake, thinking he was a Meban. (Meban and Uduk often join in each other's hunts; but I have no idea what provocation lay behind this attack.) The fight probably took place in the 1930s:

'And the Kum 'Be ally with the Kun Jale. Didn't you know that? Against the Kum 'Penawayu. For example, take that fight at the hunting ground there [near the Meban country]. The Kum 'Be didn't they all join together? Joined with the Chali people too . . . The Chali people, do we want to leave them aside?'

'Those Beni Mayu people fought with the Woshale<u>th</u>dhe/ first. They pressed them back, pressed them to the brown soil ['*kop*] of Dhele.[12] And that fellow Dhanapije/, who's now dead, shot at Baŋa at about that distance [indicating], *jig*![13]

'Baŋa took out an arrow immediately, and put that great arrow

[12] A place, I believe towards Meban country, near Jebel 'Be.
[13] The sound of an arrow missing its target.

right in his shoulder, *daaw*![14] The great shaft was stuck in him, shining white.

'Quickly, everyone joined in. All the Kum 'Be came flocking, *tuc̣*. They were dodging about and colliding into each other, *diŋdiŋ*. Could anything be done about it?

'There was my cross-cousin Ḳujul; some people shot him with arrows from the side, but he split them up and dealt with them on his own, very severely.

'And then a lot more people turned up, when the fight was nearly over. They came flocking in with their bodies, *tuc̣*. All those people of Pam 'Be, coming to help the Woshalethdhe/ in one mass. Was one left out? They said, "Haa! You have chased away the Woshalethdhe/ people and pushed them to *'kopa Dhele*. And now what's your answer [i.e. now that we have arrived]?"

'Then [the Beni Mayu people] were dealt with by the others. They dealt with Dhalma/ in the lower leg, *daaw*. It was Leḳo. He shot his brother Dhalma/, right in the lower leg with an arrow, *daaw*!'

Two of the younger listeners to this story were surprised that the Kuseje, a local birth-group of Beni Mayu, should have been fighting against the Wosalethdhe/, for these two birth-groups are blood-friends. But evidently the ties of each to their respective territories prevailed. This fight was not reported to the Government, for the chief of Pam'Be, Karim, was himself involved, in fact he was leading the fight (*cil ma nyor*, 'owner of the anger'). He was a Woshalethdhe/ of Pam'Be, of the same birth-group as the well-known chief of Chali at the time, Gubertalla (sometimes called Babu).

I asked Ngau, in relation to the fight he had described, whether those young men of Pam'Be who had fathers in Beni Mayu would have supported the people of Beni Mayu? He replied that in the past, there were no children of Beni Mayu living in Pam'Be. The people of Beni Mayu used to marry among themselves. The people of Chali and Pam'Be, however, he said have long intermarried—thus explaining the reason why they are supposed to fight on the same side, at least against Beni Mayu. Recently, however, and only in the last generation or two, the men of Beni Mayu have begun to marry the women of Pam'Be, and there are children of Beni Mayu among the Kum 'Be.

[14] The sound of an arrow hitting a body.

The traditional territories of Uduk country have been made the basis for modern administration, more or less. Each was in the 1960s in theory under the charge of one or two Government-appointed sheikhs who collected taxes, reported breaches of the law, and received tiny salaries. But these weak sheikhs and their affairs were not the main concern of Uduk village politics; they were not the big men of the villages and there was no competition for their jobs. They could not carry out Government policy with any ease. Village politics, feuds, and dispute settlements went on in the traditional manner, on the whole, and the key relationships remained what they have been for a long time: relationships through birth-groups, and between them, the bonds of blood-friendship, paternal ties, and territorial defensive alliances.

7

THE GURUNYA BIRD AND THE
SURVIVAL OF THE WEAKEST

'Gurunya babies are different
from ordinary babies.'
Why?
'All the other children have died;
that is why we make him a Gurunya,
for then he will live.'

A stranger will begin to wonder, when he lives in a northern
Uduk community, what can be the meaning of the word
gurunya/. He may notice, for example, that there are several
children who seem to be called Gurunya, and this will puzzle
him, for he will have been told that everybody has a distinct
name, quite different from everyone else's. He may ask about a
lullaby he hears, and be told that it is the Gurunya song. He
may hear of a bird called Gurunya in myths, as in the tale
which introduces this book. He may find a major feast and
ceremony being prepared, and be told that he must bring along
a contribution, as it is a 'Gurunya beer'. A mother may bring a
crying baby to his door, demanding a sweet or titbit for the
child, because he is a Gurunya, and will die if he cries too
much. He may wonder why the mother and child are not wearing beads, and look dark and naked by comparison with everyone else; and he will be told that Gurunyas do not wear beads,
or red ochre, for they must 'sit black'. The presence of those
involved in the Gurunya cult is quite conspicuous in Uduk
hamlets. As he learns more, the stranger will realize that people
are drawing upon a very wide range of experience for parallels
and analogies to make him understand the idea of the Gurunya;
and the more he discovers about the Gurunya the more he will
perceive of the history and society of the *'kwanim pa*.

The fundamental idea and aim of the rites he will not find
alien, for they centre upon a universal problem: that of the
creation and preservation of human life and the fabric of the

community against what at times may appear frightful odds. The wastage of life, especially among the young, through illness and death, and the destruction of society through famine, war, and the loss of home and kin, are not peculiar to the experience of the Uduk. But they have acquired special meaning among the Uduk, and find particular symbolic expression. The Gurunya rites and practices, for example, are specifically concerned to ensure the survival of a child born to a woman who has already lost a number of children in infancy.

It is true that this notion, that through special treatment children can be saved from the death which has overtaken their predecessors, finds widespread expression in eastern Africa. Among the Akamba of Kenya, for example, such a child may be given a name which will denigrate the child, and deflect the interest of the spirits which took his elder siblings, such as 'hyena' (John Mbiti, personal communication). Among the Dinka, Godfrey Lienhardt has noted a similar practice and pointed out the element of exorcism involved (1961, p. 149). There is a special class of children among the Mandari. Möjut is used as their personal name, and they wear their hair long, as a sign of mourning; Mandari say, 'This child is born after great sorrows', and 'Creator sees and spares it' (Buxton, 1973, pp. 249–50). Among the northern Sudanese Arabic-speaking peoples, the name Awad is given to a child who follows the deaths of others; and he may go around the neighbours' houses, begging for gifts. Among the south-eastern Nuba studied by James Faris, there is an organized society of *chimtinin*, those who went through special protective rites in childhood, in the same circumstances, and who retain throughout their lives special privileges in relation to the rest of the community (Faris, 1970). *Chimtinin* literally means 'supported by God' (*chimto*, timber supports, *tinin*, God). To the east of the White Nile, there is a comparable cult among the Ingessana, where the children are known as *mwanya*, used also as a personal name. In Ethiopia, Tsehai Berhane Selassie tells me that a *gudifäča* child born after losses to an Amhara woman is passed through a newly-made hole in the wall and usually given to an Oromo foster-mother.

I have mentioned in the first chapter of this book the Arabic use of *'attuq* or *'atiq*, literally freed slave, which in the Gulf region at least can be applied to one saved or spared by God from death.

Among close neighbours of the Uduk, the Meban have a cult where the special children are known as *jieng*, a word which appears to have the meaning of slave, or foundling; and the Jum Jum have a corresponding cult, termed *kiengol*, which bears a comparable meaning, and from which the Uduk cult is immediately derived. The Uduk term which would correspond to the last two terms is *çinkina/*; but beyond this, the cult and the children involved are *gurunya/*, after the blue-black glossy starling.

The cult is found under this name only among the northern Uduk, the *'kwanim pa*. Although it seems to have taken root and flourished among them only fairly recently, it has older analogues. This was revealed when I was making enquiries in the Yabus valley, among the southern Uduk, and was assured that they certainly had 'gurunyas' as well as the northerners. But although they used the name of this highly successful cult, they were referring to an older practice, which seems to have been superseded in the north and yet persists in the south. In the Yabus valley, the infants were called by what was stated to be an old name—*banjaha*, the southern dialect equivalent of *bambala*, meaning 'under the eaves' and implying that they were foundlings protected by a household without actually belonging to it. Such an infant would be smeared with *jiso* (black oil), pigs' and dogs' dirt, and old beads were collected from the ground to make into a little wristlet for him to wear. But these practices did not have the status of a major cult.

THE GURUNYA IDEA

The Gurunya cult proper, practised by the northern Uduk, is only one of their many complexes of symbolic ritual. I have chosen to describe it in some detail here, although I am not dealing primarily with religion and ritual, as it constitutes in some respects a synthesis of many of the images I have discussed in connection with Uduk history and legend, and should be understood in this context.

The cult is primarily in the hands of women, who organize it and who pass on the special knowledge connected with it. The children who are created Gurunyas may be either boys or girls, and it may be either a boy or a girl who acts as a baby-minder to the Gurunya baby, just as for any other child. The minder of a Gurunya also becomes involved in the ceremonies held for the baby. But the adults who run the cult are without exception women, although male diviners may be called in to assist the Gurunya specialists at certain points. All adults regard the cult as a whole as the business of women, and its ceremonies as occasions for the children. The great procession which passes round the hamlets of a neighbourhood, singing and soliciting greetings and presents from every household, is composed of women and children only. From what I can gather, among the Jum Jum or Wathke people to the north, from whom the Uduk received the Gurunya cult, it is also the business of women. But among the Meban, it is merely one of the responsibilities of male religious leaders to look after the specially protected *jieng* children; and the same appears to be the case among the Mandari, where the corresponding *möjut* children, dedicated to Creator, are themselves all male.[1] The significance of the Gurunya rites being a women's specialism among the northern Uduk lies in their central notion of the human community springing from the fertility of women. The female line provides a link of substance with the past, and the future depends upon the continuing child-bearing capacity of women. The whole community is dependent upon the success of a mother in bearing and raising a family of children; and the whole community is therefore involved, by implication, in the aims of the Gurunya rite, which are devoted to the survival of this little group. The particular aim of protecting the fruitfulness of the female line is revealed in the case where a woman who already had four healthy male children, then had a girl, who was promptly made into a Gurunya, to ensure her survival. Thus, although the Gurunya business is a special concern of women, it is not simply a 'feminist' movement, for it is practised for the benefit of the whole community. Men will say, 'We know nothing about the Gurunya business, that is an affair of the women'; but they will come along to the Gurunya festivals, greet the Gurunyas when the procession calls at their house, contribute a substantial gift to the feast, and bring along a small token gift to lay at the

[1] See Buxton, 1973, p. 249.

beer-pot. In the other major healing and religious cults of the Uduk, by contrast, male practitioners are dominant and women are scarcely in evidence.

This leads on to the second major distinctive characteristic of the Gurunya cult; it is a charge, and a responsibility, upon the whole community. The Gurunya specialist, as distinct from diviners and men of *arum*, does not receive a substantial fee for her services, only a few bangles and beads, perhaps, from the presents brought along to the final feast. She is acting, in a sense, on behalf of all, and not merely on behalf of the 'patient', the mother whose child has been created a Gurunya. The Gurunya cult spreads in snowball fashion. If your next child is selected as a Gurunya, through informal discussion between women friends and relatives or the suggestion of a Gurunya specialist, you yourself, your child and the youngster who acts as baby-minder all belong to the large community of those 'saved' by the cult. Any adult woman of this community may eventually become knowledgeable in cult matters, and start to practise as a specialist. No formal initiation is required; you gradually learn what has to be done, and why, through helping more experienced women, for many hands are needed at a big Gurunya ceremony, and women discuss Gurunya matters among themselves quite frequently. In the other cults, it is often a particular spirit, controlled by a certain individual, which creates illness around him, and which he himself is the best person to cure. This personal element is not so marked among the Gurunya specialists; although it is always known, and remembered, that it was so-and-so who created this or that woman's child a Gurunya, there is no question of the specialist's powers as such being responsible for illness and death, and there is a feeling that the woman sponsor is acting not on behalf of special personal powers, but on behalf of the community as a whole, its women in general, and the Gurunya community of those who have suffered and been saved in particular.

However, in narrower terms of the patterning of rituals and symbolic activities, there are very close parallels between the Gurunya cult and other rituals. The connection with the diviners' cult (*ŋari*) is particularly close. Both have entered Uduk society from the Jum Jum, and each has a comparable set of rites (of which I give some account below). The parallel with the rites of passage through which ordinary children pass is also very marked; and it is not difficult to point out recurrent themes in the various complexes of rain ritual, field ritual, and so forth which proliferate in Uduk society. But the Gurunya cult, which is practised with great enthusiasm by the women, is spreading fast; its ceremonies are among the most lavish and spectacular that may be witnessed in an Uduk community; and its imagery touches a very deep chord.

Let me say something first of the way in which Gurunya people are represented as individuals, and how they are set apart from others, conceptually and in their everyday treatment. I should make it clear that when I speak of a Gurunya, I mean the child who actually carries this name; and when I speak of Gurunya people, I am referring to all those who become involved when a child is created a Gurunya: the baby, the mother, and the young baby-minder. The state of being Gurunya people will last several years, until the infant Gurunya has gone through his final ceremony, marking his attainment of normal childhood. Before this is achieved, no community can forget that it harbours Gurunya people in its midst.

There is, first, the use of 'Gurunya' as a personal name. It refers, literally, to a glossy blue-black starling. Its use is conspicuous because, with very few exceptions, names among the Uduk are not recurrent, but unique, freshly minted for each new individual. Occasionally coincidences occur, but these are infrequent, and thus there can be no confusion of one person with another. The name 'Gurunya' is the only one which exists before the individual who is to bear it is born, and the only one which labels a fixed category of people, which is replenished as they pass out of it.[2] There are, it is true, those names which fall into a general class of 'dirty names' (*gwaya thus*) such as Gure (literally faeces), Kalkuthar (pig-sty), and 'Cila'th (charcoal). Names of this kind, which refer directly or indirectly to dirty, polluting, or very black substances, are given to children with the deliberate aim of 'self-denigration'; when jealousy is feared from neighbours, when critical gossip has been overheard or passed on, or when suffering has been attributed to human ill will or the harmful attentions of spirit powers, these names by degrading their holders may divert any harmful consequences.

[2] See the exposition of modes of naming in Lévi-Strauss, 1962.

The use of Gurunya as a name is similar; for the quality of the *gurunya/* bird which is always emphasized when it is discussed is its very dark colour. *Tan 'thi, ca'b ki dhis dhis*, people say; it is dark, very, very deep blue-black. The colour words *'thi* and the more intense *dhis dhis* normally include a range of 'blues' as well as what we would call grey or black, or dark in general, and the glossy starling's appearance is dark, shot with blue-green. The significance of individuals' names is not always known beyond a small circle of relatives and neighbours, but the significance of the name Gurunya is plain to all. There are a few other names by which a Gurunya child might alternatively be known, which are themselves derived from associations with the *gurunya/* bird; for example, Nya/a, which represents the cry of the *gurunya/* bird, and Waya, which is a phrase from the Gurunya song (see below).

When speaking to adults, or about them, it is quite common to use a teknonym, especially when one is being respectful. Thus it happens that the parents of a Gurunya child may often be called Co Gurunya (Father of Gurunya) or Ko Gurunya (Mother of Gurunya) respectively; and moreover, the baby-minder may sometimes be addressed or referred to in this way, as an honorary parent of the Gurunya, especially in later life. Because of these usages, there are reminders all around one of the existence of a Gurunya in the community. Usually, when a Gurunya has passed through the complete set of rites, and reaches maturity and adulthood, he or she is known by an ordinary personal name, and the use of 'Gurunya' drops. But even when he is grown up, someone may comment, casually, that he (or she) used to be a Gurunya child; but that 'people looked after him so well, that now he has grown up strong and healthy, and has children of his own'.

Gurunya people, during the first few years before the final ceremony, are of distinctive appearance. Since ordinary people wear beads and sometimes a little red ochre as a cosmetic, it is striking that the Gurunya mother, baby-minder, and baby do not. They may use plain sesame oil as a cosmetic, giving a shining black appearance. The Gurunya child's head will not be shaved, as most people's are; and he wears around his neck a black thread, perhaps a cowrie shell, and perhaps also the hair shaved off his head at the last ceremony he passed through.

Moreover, Gurunya children are given very special treatment. They are associated with birds, naturally enough since the *gurunya/* is a bird, and bird imagery recurs in various forms. Gurunya children are often given eggs, sometimes raw eggs to suck, and they are given bits of chicken when it is available. Other children spend happy afternoons arranging traps for small birds, in order to give them to the Gurunya. Any special snack or delicious titbit will be saved and given to the Gurunya; and small gifts of food, especially, will be solicited from anyone who is preparing a meal. If the child cries, every effort is made to comfort him; he is cuddled, given titbits, and women sing the Gurunya song for him. Quite often I had Gurunya mothers bringing their squalling children to me: 'Haven't you got a sweet or something for the Gurunya—he's crying?' It is feared that if he cries too much, and gets worked into a frenzy, he will die. He is a particularly vulnerable child. If he shows any sign of serious discomfort, the mother will take him along to a Gurunya specialist, if possible his own sponsor. She may kill a chicken for the child, who will then wear the wing-feathers around his wrist. If he is really sick, diagnosis and healing of the normal kind will be carried out by diviners or people of *arum*, though perhaps with greater urgency than usual.

On everyday occasions, as well as ritual ones, Gurunya children are 'greeted' (the normal term for greeting, *the me'd*, is used) with a little wood ash taken from the domestic hearth. You scoop up a little of this white ash, and touch it onto the crown of the child's head. This is not done for anyone besides Gurunyas, although this white ash (*piny*) has many other uses. Some of these other uses have a clearly protective aspect: for example, if you have had a bad dream (signifying, for the Uduk, the presence of witchcraft or other evil), you will smear a little of the ash from the hearth on each temple before going out in the morning. It is also the ash taken from her father's hearth by a girl who wishes to conceive.

The way in which Gurunyas are spoken of makes even more explicit than does their appearance and treatment the gulf between them and the normal social community. Thus for example, they are said to be dogs. I have been told that they are like dogs because they come from families which die like dogs, for dogs are dying all the time and have no proper relatives to help them; and I have heard of an even clearer association. When the Gurunya baby is small, it may be given dog's milk to drink, and the mother may share her own food with the dogs. Dogs are very close to human society, even to the extent that a newly-acquired puppy, not yet weaned but taken from its mother, may even suckle at a women's breast together with her own child. Dogs are today dependent on the human community, although originally in myth, it was the dog who helped people. It is perhaps the marginal, and dependent, position of the dog that Maya, a leading Gurunya specialist, had in mind when she replied to my question about the Gurunya being a dog: 'Yes. We give dogs' milk to Gurunyas. You take out food and put it in the bowl, and the dogs come and eat it. So if a dog gives birth, the child can drink its milk. This is before the *tora gap* (the first main Gurunya ceremony). The child is given dog's milk because he is a dog at the same time. He is just a dog. The child is a human being but drinks dog's milk, together with that of his mother.'

Beyond these specific associations with the animal world, the Gurunya is spoken of in more general terms as a *çiŋkina/*: a waif, a foundling, without kin and without any hope of survival on his own. This is a fundamental image, in terms of which others are explained. Thus, dogs are *çiŋkina/*; and in answer to the question as to why a Gurunya is a dog, one is often told that it is because he is a *çiŋkina/*. The term refers particularly, as I have explained earlier, to persons of history and legend who were lost in the bush, without kin, food, or clothes, and who were taken in and looked after by others. It is also used for those who were enslaved in history, those who today leave their homes and work as domestic servants, and in general for anyone who is pitiable, poor and miserable, and in need of adoption. If you ask why a baby Gurunya is a *çiŋkina/*, you are told that it is because he has lost his brothers and sisters; he has no kin. The mother, similarly, is a *çiŋkina/* because she has lost all her children, she has no child in her hand, she is alone. In addition to the idea of loneliness is the idea that such a person cannot survive by himself or herself, but must be rescued and succoured by others, as were those ancestors who were rescued from the bush in the old days.

Maya, a woman of middle years who herself had been the mother of a Gurunya baby, was recognized as the most knowledgeable person on Gurunya matters in northern Pam′Be. She had been made a Gurunya mother by Merke, and Merke had been the protégé of Helke, and Helke herself had been the protégé of a Jum Jum woman. There were at least two other Gurunya specialists in our small neighbourhood, Oiyga and Thaduse, who had been brought into the cult by Merke. Maya explained Gurunya matters to me, continually coming back to the idea of *çiŋkina*/. The ultimate explanation was usually in terms of *arum,* here in the sense of 'creative spirit'; one woman said, 'A Gurunya is called by *arum* a thing, and not a real person [*wathim paŋ gana*]. He is called by *arum* a *çiŋkina*/.' The word *to,* translated here as 'thing', can also mean animal; in this context the point is that a Gurunya is a non-person, a creature not worthy to belong to the community of *′kwanim pa.* Maya explained, in answer to my question as to why a Gurunya was a *çiŋkina*/:

'Yes: because that group is always dying. This woman who is made a *çiŋkina*/, does not find any children. They always die and she sits empty-handed. Alone by herself.

She conceives; the child dies. Again she conceives, and the child dies. The last one is made a Gurunya, because people are frightened; they say, this woman has no children. Let us go and try to do something. They try it. Now, he lives and is feeding at the breast. He will sit on the ground, and then crawl about. He is kept as a Gurunya until he can walk. Then people will grind beer for the final ceremony. The child will grow. You who made him a Gurunya, you will go to his house and watch over him until he grows up.'

When a woman has no children, or when they die, it is a serious matter for her whole community; the local birth-group will die out if its womenfolk fail to bear and to bring up children, especially daughters. The aim of the Gurunya rites could not be clearer: they are concerned with the saving of life, and not merely that of individual women's children, but of the whole community.

THE GURUNYA RITES

(1) *Birth*

It is usually decided when a woman is still pregnant, by informal discussion between her, her friends and a local Gurunya specialist, that her baby should be made a Gurunya. The specialist then ties a piece of black thread or strip of cloth around the woman's neck. When the child is born, one or more Gurunya specialists may be present, and they put a black strip of cloth around the baby's neck before the navel cord is cut. I believe it is cut in a special manner but could not establish how. They then remove all the mother's beads. The ears of the baby are pierced and little metal rings are inserted, sometimes at the top of the ear, and a slit is made in the nose, all 'to make the child a Gurunya'. I believe the slit is made so that the child is no longer a whole or perfect creature. He is greeted with white ash. Cowrie shells may also be hung around the baby's neck.

All these features differentiate a Gurunya birth from a normal birth, according to my informants. I have not been present personally at the birth of a Gurunya, nor at the rite which follows shortly after. The following account is therefore based on what I have been told.

(2) 'Taking out the baby' (*kal a'ci ka pije*)

When the end of the cord has dried up and fallen off, there is a ceremony, as with normal children, to bring the baby outside the hut. The mother has not left the hut since the birth (except at night-time), and a small hole has been made in the hut wall behind the bed, where she has been in the habit of washing herself since the delivery. The dirty water, carrying with it the remains of the blood of birth, runs out down a special little channel which leads from the hole in the hut wall to the bush. These preparations are the same for Gurunyas and ordinary babies. The normal rite for taking a baby out consists of carrying him through the front door of the hut, where he is given a little attention by a man of *arum* and then anointed with red ochre. But the Gurunya baby does not come out by the front door. A special hole is made in the hut wall, I gather different from the hole already made for the mother's ablutions; and the Gurunya baby is passed out through this hole, with a string around its neck, 'like a dog'. It does not appear to matter where the hole is made: some say to the left, some say to the right of the door. To the accompaniment of dancing and singing of the Gurunya song, and blowing of the gourd flutes which are reserved for

Gurunya rites, the child is carried round the hut once, anti-clockwise, and put down on 'a dirty place near the edge of the village' for a while; then he is carried round the village and laid at the door of each hut, where he is given some little presents such as a cob of maize. He is then brought to his mother's hut again and laid on his stomach outside it. His head is shaved, except for a tuft on the soft spot, and the hair is attached to a string and put around his neck. (Ordinary babies may be shaved, but they do not wear their hair in this way: it is thrown into the bush.) A chicken will be 'dedicated' to him, and its toe cut to mark the dedication. The people of *arum* may sacrifice a chicken for him, as for ordinary babies, but unlike them he will wear the wing feathers around his wrist. There should be beer prepared for this ceremony, though ordinary children rarely have it at this time. The Gurunya baby is *not* anointed with red ochre, as other children often are, but he may be given a touch of plain oil.

Two important themes dominate this rite, which partially introduces the baby to the social world. One is the idea of his being 'led' carefully into it: after having a black thread hung on his neck even before the navel cord was cut, he is now led 'like a dog' out of a special small exit from the hut in which he was born, on a string. This image recalls the old days, when the Uduk often had to shelter inside stockades for self-defence; some had the personal experience of being herded into stockades like animals, during the period of slave-raiding at the end of the last century; and this memory has not been lost. In one account I have quoted (p. 56) the old man Jahalla remembers how he escaped from such an enclosure and managed to get his little brother out as well by leading him on a string through a hole in the stockade. The same image of surviving and escaping to freedom by making a hole in an enclosure, recurred in the memories of Losko, also referring to his experiences of this period. He described how the Bunyan besieged the Uduk who were sheltering in caves and on the flat top of Jebel Bisho, to the south of the Yabus, how eventually they were obliged to make a dash for it, and how some managed to escape by opening a way through the stockade the Bunyan had built at the foot of the mountain (see above, p. 57).

The other important theme, which is developed through the

whole series of rites, is that of the child being a charge upon the whole community. Everyone should contribute to his 'rescue', or 'adoption'. At this stage, he is laid at the door of each hut in the hamlet of his birth, and a token present is made by each household. He has not entered the community from his mother's house, as normal children do; but from the 'outside'; this is clear from the way in which he is brought to the householders of the village from 'a dirty place near the edge of the village'. They have shown their willingness to look after him, as a group; but he still wears his hair around his neck, and the chicken feathers around his wrist; it will be some time before he is fully 'adopted'.

(3) 'Showing the banks' (*tora gap*)

Some weeks or months later, beer is made and the child, mother and baby-minder go through an important rite, 'showing the banks', at which they are escorted across the river to the other bank and back. This rite, which I have observed once in its entirety, corresponds in name and structure to a preliminary initiation rite practised by some but not all of the diviners' societies. In terms of the whole set of Gurunya rites, this one signifies essentially the entry into the prolonged black period. It also marks the fact that from now on, the Gurunya people are able to cross the river and generally move about more freely than they were able to do previously. From the time of the birth until this rite, their movement was very restricted and they were certainly not allowed to cross the river. They were in an extremely vulnerable state, and the anointing with black, the sacrifices and so forth of this rite provide a degree of protection.

BRIEF DESCRIPTION OF THE RITE

(i) Early in the morning, before I had arrived, the three mothers whose children were being 'shown the banks' on this occasion were escorted to the river by their sponsors. They had taken with them a certain type of grass (*leheny*) from the roof of the beer hut, which was the hut of one of the mothers. This grass was thrown into the river. Then they all rushed across the river and back, and bathed themselves. The mothers may be led to and from the river with ropes around their necks. The babies and baby-minding children may or may not join in; if not, they are washed back in the village. If they do join in, women may climb up trees with the babies on their backs as they return to the village.

(ii) Guests who arrive in the village to drink beer from the early morning pot which is put outside, greet the Gurunya people by putting white ash on their heads; and all bring a small gift, of beads or bangles or food, to lay beside the beer-pot.

(iii) The heads of all the Gurunya people are shaved, and the hair put aside.

(iv) Sacrifice: chickens are killed by the Gurunya sponsor by twisting off their heads, and holding the bodies firmly between her thighs as she sits on the ground until they are still. A goat may be killed by a man, usually a diviner, who is called in to help by cutting its throat.

(v) A large meal has been prepared as at all big rites: but this one is distinguished by the fact that dirty pots are used, and the Gurunya people are supposed to eat at the *edge* of the village, where the bush encroaches.

(vi) Before the beer hut is opened for the guests to come in and drink, the Gurunya children eat a little of the beer mixture first, and are persuaded to give a little to their mothers as well.

(vii) The Gurunya people are finally, in the late afternoon, assembled for anointing with *jiso*, a mixture of charcoal and oil which has been specially prepared, and to be adorned with new blackened cotton necklets, perhaps with a cowrie shell or two attached, and blackened cotton belts. The baby's shaved hair is again made into a ball and attached to his necklet.

It is after this rite of 'showing the banks', and anointing with black oil, but before the final ceremony, that Gurunyas are 'sitting black'. This is the state in which one is particularly conscious of the presence of Gurunya children in the village; and it may last several years, although it can be concluded after a few months. It is during this period that the children are given so much special attention, talked about so much by the women, and watched so carefully. The Gurunya song is sung to the children during this time, to comfort and cheer them; it goes as follows, and may be sung as a part-song by several people. It will be noticed that *çiŋkina/* is interchangeable with *gurunya/*:

Gurunya/ wayaa pu/ waa	Gurunya pluck me a fig
Yanti Yanti yee	Yanti Yanti, oh
Gurunya/ wayaa pu/ waa	Gurunya pluck me a fig
Yanti Yanti yee	Yanti Yanti, oh
Gurunya/ Gurunya/ yee	Gurunya, Gurunya, oh
Gurunya/ wayaa pu/ waa	Gurunya pluck me a fig
Çiŋkina/ wayaa pu/ waa	*Çiŋkina/*, pluck me a fig
Ḳal a'di pa Gaja	Take him to Gaja
Ci ako aGaja	Give him milk at Gaja's
Yanti Gurunya/ yoo	Yanti Gurunya ooh
Gurunya/ wayaa pu/ waa	Gurunya pluck me a fig

Yanti appears to refer to a type of grass found near Wadega, the centre of the Jum Jum area from where the cult came. Gaja is a senior Gurunya specialist; the name of any woman expert may be substituted here. The plea 'Gurunya, pluck me a fig' recalls the way in which the *gurunya/* bird, the glossy blue-black starling, often perches in wild fig trees, eating the fruit, and the way in which children may go and play under fig trees, and try to get down the figs. The situation recurs in the myth of women's discovery of men in the bush, which appears at the beginning of this book.

A few notes should be made here on those elements of this rite that are peculiar to the Gurunya, rather than the diviners', version of 'showing the banks': the leading of the mothers by ropes is said to be like dogs or cattle, and is reminiscent of leading the baby himself out of the hut of birth on a string. An older echo, and not a comparison explicitly made by my informants, is that of the yoke used in transporting slaves. The leading of Gurunya mothers by string or rope around their necks recalls painfully pictures such as those of Cailliaud and Trémeaux of the yoking of slaves in this region in the early nineteenth century.[3] The climbing of trees in the bushland underscores vividly the bird-nature of the Gurunyas; the image appears to be that of the Gurunya sponsors leading back into the village bird-like creatures of the wild, who might escape altogether if left alone. The *tableau* of the Gurunya song and of Woman's original discovery of Man as a bird-creature up a tree is also recalled. The bringing of gifts to 'buy (*yol*) the beer' is

[3] See for example, Plate no. 48 in Trémeaux, 1852; and Plates I, II and III in Cailliaud, 1826.

otherwise unknown in ceremony or ritual—beer is always given freely. It signifies the fact that a Gurunya family are not in a position to *give*—they are *çiŋkina/* and the community as a whole is responsible for them. The way in which the chickens are killed is peculiar to Gurunya rites, and is explained in terms of the fact that the Gurunya must be kept calm and quiet; if the chickens were allowed to flap around on the ground in the usual way, the Gurunya too might get agitated and begin to cry.

Further to those aspects of the Gurunya connected with its wildness, its animality, its blackness and helplessness, is its dirtiness during this middle period. The parallels between the rites of the diviners' societies and those of the Gurunya cult have been mentioned, and in the following explanation, Rusko, who knew a good deal of diviners' lore, makes the parallel explicit in his discussion of the 'raw', immature and dirty quality of both diviner and Gurunya:

'Now things which are still raw: for a child who is a Gurunya, you will give him things which are still raw like that, for he is a *çiŋkina/*. It is a wretched thing [*tonthus*] which is called Gurunya, for he was just saved because he was about to die. That is why *arum* kept him alive. And then, if food is being cooked on the fire, you will go and find a broken gourd from the waste-heap for people to keep and to serve him food on it. Then he eats, eats, eats because he is a *çiŋkina/* as they say, rescued from death. While he would otherwise have died. *Arum* will keep him alive they say because of eating dirty things [*to nyo/ga*]. It is the same as the *ŋari* [diviners'] practice. In *ŋari* rites, you do the same, and dog-dirt will be taken from the ground to mix with food for you, and you eat.'

Maya and Rusko both introduce the concept of *arum*: the power, both creative and destructive, without which life is not possible, and yet on which life is dependent. Ultimately, the efforts of people to save the Gurunya, or a *çiŋkina/* of history, will be futile without *arum*. The healing ability of diviners and people of *arum* stems from their control of a particular power of *arum*. But the ability of the Gurunya specialists to save life does not depend on the control of any specific *arum*; they plead on behalf of the community as a whole to *arum* in its most general form. There is no special 'spirit of Gurunya'; I never heard a phrase remotely approaching such a connotation. The general idea of *arum* constitutes a remote point of reference compared to the very specific images drawn from historical and immediate social experience upon which the Gurunya rites are constructed.

(4) 'Head-shaving' (*'thi 'kup*)

The final rite, the beer ceremony for 'head-shaving', may take place any time up to several years after entry into the black period. I have been present on two occasions at this ceremony. The rite should take place when the child can walk, and when all the special treatment accorded him seems to have moulded him into a viable person, strong enough to fend for himself in the ordinary social world, no longer needing special protection. This final rite, confirming the success of the whole project, corresponds in name and structure to head-shaving rites which conclude periods of convalescence, when the relatives of the sick hand over the final fees to the specialist who cured him. It does not correspond directly to the final diviners' initiation rites, and so indicates that the path of the Gurunya has now diverged from that of the diviner, who remains marginal to ordinary humanity for the rest of his life, but the Gurunya has become adopted into the ordinary social world. All head-shaving rites are character-ized by the final anointing of the person who has emerged from convalescence, 'blackness' and abnormality, with red ochre. Analogous too is the *ƙal a'ci pa* for a first-born, conducted from his mother's to his father's home in a procession. The Gurunya procession winds around the hamlets; but the father in each case is adorned as a woman to receive his child.

BRIEF DESCRIPTION OF THE RITE

(i) Early in the morning, the Gurunya people, maybe led by a diviner, go to the river to bathe: 'Their dirtiness is extreme.' The Gurunya people are still black, and if wearing any cloth it will be dark blue or blackened.

(ii) After the Gurunya has been given priority, and then the children in general, guests start drinking the beer which has been brought outside, each bringing a small gift as before, 'to buy the beer'.

(iii) The women start singing and dancing the Gurunya song, with the accompaniment of the gourd flutes, and the singing party moves off, a long procession of women and children, to

visit all the houses in several neighbouring hamlets. At each
house they pause, singing and dancing outside, working up to a
climax of shouts and ululation. Then the occupant of the house
comes out, greets the principals and as many others as possible
with ash (*piny*) from the hearth, and then gives them a substantial present, which is usually food (grain, sesame, chickens
etc.) and goes towards the feast later that day. If the occupant
is absent, the party enters the hut uninvited and takes a little
ash from the hearth as a greeting, and also collects a little grain,
sesame etc. as the involuntary contribution of that household to
the feast. The singing party may visit several dozen huts in
nearby hamlets soliciting gifts and forcibly taking them from
empty huts. During the procession, the Gurunya's mother may,
as before, be led on a rope. The procession may continue the
rounds, collecting gifts and swelling in numbers as more women
and children join in, for the best part of the middle of the day.
(iv) On return, there will be animal sacrifice, as before; though
more animals will be killed, some of them having been collected
during the procession. Children, who are present at this
ceremony in large numbers, may be given a pig or other meat to
take and roast and eat all by themselves (I have not seen this in
any other ritual context).
(v) The heads of the Gurunya people, and the father of the baby,
are shaved. All old black necklets and belts are removed and the
Gurunya people are again thoroughly washed. Then they are
all, with the father, dressed up in beads, bangles and a profusion
of other ornaments, some of which have been given as presents
by guests. They are then covered in a rich, thick layer of red
ochre and oil. The father's beads are in women's style.
(vi) The Gurunya people are ceremonially fed, and then the
general meal takes place. They are ceremonially fed a little beer,
and the general beer-drinking proceeds inside the hut, giving
priority to children.
(vii) In the late afternoon, a chicken is taken—the same chicken
that was dedicated to the Gurunya when he was first brought
out after birth, whose toe was cut to make a little blood at that
time. This chicken 'leads the hair into the bush', that is it
accompanies the person taking the shaved hair of the Gurunya
people, and I believe their black necklets, to be thrown away in
the bush. The chicken is brought back, not to be killed but to

'remain alive' and give birth to many more chickens, which will be used in sacrifice and dedication to other Gurunyas.

This is a very general account of the ceremony; the order may not be quite as described, since the same women performing the ritual actions have to get the water and firewood, and do the cooking. The sponsor will receive a very small token payment for her services: perhaps a few bangles. As in other *'thi 'kup* ceremonies involving a kind of thanksgiving to *arum*, a pot of beer is set aside for *arum*.

THEMES OF THE RITES

The whole sequence of rites represents a development; none is complete on its own, and none is merely a static charade. The rites do more than merely represent the non-human, marginal character of Gurunyas. Taken as a whole, they clearly constitute the whole process of first saving, and then bringing into society, the helpless and vulnerable child, through a period of several years. The total time involved may be, I would judge, between two and five years. Each rite forms part of the whole process, and creates a change in the state of the Gurunya. If particular symbolic themes are followed through the whole set of rites, the developmental sequence can be clearly seen.

For example, we may consider the treatment of the child's hair, in relation to the passage of time and the changing state of the Gurunya. Shaving of the head as such can hardly be said to have any particular meaning, but becomes significant when one considers what is done with the hair, since that varies in the different cases. In both the bringing-out rite, and the rite for showing the banks, the Gurunya's hair is shaved off and then hung around his neck. He carries this discarded hair about with him for the first few years of his life; until at the final rite, it is thrown away together with his latest clippings as something impure, in the bush. The chicken dedicated at birth to the Gurunya 'leads his hair into the bush' at the end of the black period and concludes this theme: throwing away of this hair marks the final emergence from the marginal black period.

Normally, everyone likes to keep their hair very short, or completely shaved off. But when you have been ill, and sitting black after being treated by a specialist, you do not cut your hair. It grows longer and longer, a conspicuous sign of the fact that you have not yet paid off the doctors. It is said that Gurunyas are not in debt to anyone, but since the 'payments' at the final rite are made by the whole community, it might be said that the community as a group was acknowledging its obligation to *arum* for having spared the life of the child. As long as the child carries its hair around with it, its life hangs in the balance, like that of a sick person.

The physical restrictions placed on the Gurunya baby are another developing theme of the rites. The black thread is put around his neck before the physical connection with the mother is broken; he is guided carefully through the narrow hole in the wall of the hut; he and his mother are not allowed to go beyond the river until after the 'showing of the banks'; and even afterwards, as long as the black period lasts, they may not cross the river in the late afternoon when the sun is red. Only after the final 'head-shaving' and anointing with red ochre, are they free of this, to move independently.

Similar restrictions of movement, especially crossing of the river, apply to persons in various types of ritually marginal state. For example, pregnant women, and diviners, avoid crossing the river late in the afternoon (although diviners can spit medicine on the river, which will make it safe for them). Sick people are not usually supposed to go far from their home villages. One reason is that dangerous spirits inhabit water-holes and rivers. The increasing freedom of movement of a Gurunya marks the progressive relaxation of protective care over him, as he gains strength and independence.

If the question of colour symbolism is considered, the outstanding fact is that the Gurunya is 'sitting black' (*'ça'b ki 'thi*) for an extended period. There are many other occasions when Uduk people are sitting black; most of them are times of illness, or during the central, transitional period of rites of passage. All babies and mothers are sitting black immediately after the birth; but the Gurunya, his mother, and his nurse have to go through a prolonged and more intense black period. The idea of blackness here is clearly to be interpreted as a state of transition or 'liminality',[4] and in this context of the structuring of rites of

---

[4] For an extended discussion of these notions, see for example the work of V. W. Turner, especially his books of 1967 and 1969.

passage and the rites of sickness, black is opposed to red; the sequence of development is from extreme vulnerability into a protective, deep black period, until the danger is past, the child has survived, his emergence can be marked by red ochre, and he can face 'red' things.

The opposition between black and red states is central to understanding the Gurunya rituals. The Gurunya baby does not come out of the hut after birth to be anointed with red ochre, as ordinary babies are. He gets just plain oil; later he gets *jiso*, the charcoal mixture, and only when he is several years old does he wear red ochre and beads for the first time. Now similar themes run through other sets of Uduk ritual. In most rites of passage, the intermediate transitional period, typically characterized here as elsewhere in terms of ambivalence, vulnerability to ritual danger, and exclusion from society, is signified by 'sitting black'. The conclusion of the transitional period is usually marked by red ochre. Thus for example at a first marriage, as I have described, after the initial elopement and discovery of the couple, they are separated and each covered with the charcoal mixture in their own villages; when, after some time has passed, they are reunited, they are covered with red ochre. During a mourning period, close relatives of the deceased anoint themselves with the charcoal mixture and sit black until the final death ceremony, which ends the mourning, when they use red ochre again. A bone may even be dug up from the grave at this time and anointed with red ochre. Initiation rites into some of the diviners' societies involve a passage through a black period and then final anointing with red ochre.

There is a special expression for one mode of 'self-denigration', which clearly contains an element of exorcism. *Mmotuk 'ba'th*, to *tuk* the illness, designates the practice of countering an illness by sitting black. The word is also used when one takes off beads and sits black in order to mourn a relative. It does not apply, however, to any black period associated with a normal rite of passage. It appears to apply to abnormal situations in which a dangerous presence must be kept at bay. Thus, I was told by William Danga that in an epidemic, a man of *arum* may give instructions for everyone to take off his beads and decorations and sit black, *mmotuk 'ba'th*, to *tuk* the illness. They may put pig dung or dog dirt on their bodies. He explained that this was

'To treat your body like a *çiŋkina*/. You are not a human being, you are just a thing, a worthless object. And you will sit black, to *tuk* the illness, until people recover from the illness which has struck them. The people of *arum* then put the country right (*nyoŋ*) with a sacrifice, and people look out the flutes for dancing, and put on their beads, and the country is in a good condition at last'.

This actually happened; there was a series of unexplained deaths in the southern part of Pam'Be in 1969. Everyone there 'went black', and many people on the northern bank of the river did the same, of their own accord. Ha'da, a man of *arum*, gathered the people of the hamlets of his neighbourhood on the north side, and sacrificed a chicken, *mmotuk 'ba'th*. The sickness did not spread to the north side.

The notion of exorcism, of ridding a person of something alien which has taken a hold, is paralleled in another interesting use of the term *tuk*. If a girl is seized in the bush and forced to make love with a young man she doesn't want at all, she will go home and take off all her beads and go black, *mmotuka washan jan mo* (to *tuk* that young man). He will then leave her alone. There is no special treatment or sacrifice associated with this; but the very simplicity of the action clarifies the idea of *tuk*. There are the elements then of separation and avoidance, of the exclusion of an alien influence; of protection from danger; and of purification from the contamination, or pollution, of death, illness, and sex.

A comparable situation arises after the killing of a wild animal. For example if someone kills an ostrich in a hunt, he stays black and avoids people (*ga*/ '*kwani*). He takes the feathers and the head, and one leg (either leg) to his father's people, and sleeps at their village. In the morning they shave his head and put on *jiso* (sesame oil and charcoal). Later, a beer party is held, his head is shaved, sacrifices are made (perhaps of a goat) and he is anointed with red ochre. Everything in the way of food is carefully reintroduced to him for otherwise he will go mad. If these things are not done, he will die, of the *arum* of the ostrich. There is a similar, and more serious, treatment if one kills a leopard, or a man; and a rather different set of rites for protection against the *arum* of the elephant. Indeed the killing of wild animals in general can be dangerous as the *arum* of the animals may return to affect the hunter.

In addition to the standard rites of passage, through which people pass in the normal course of life, there are particular occasions on which the 'protective cover' of sitting black is sought. One of the commonest is illness; in the ordinary treatment of many illnesses, where the state of sickness is at least partly due to an alien spiritual presence, and the aim of the treatment is to rid the patient of the undesirable contact with this presence, the patient removes his beads and stays more or less at home, sitting black. He may or may not be anointed with plain oil, or with *jiso*, but will certainly not use red ochre, and will not wander far from home. Other situations of protection against 'spiritual' powers, requiring the use of black oil, include the treatment of people who have suffered from the action of the rain and the storm, sent by the rainstones of others; the owners of the rainstones who are responsible anoint the victims with black oil in order that the stones should not send any further damage. Black, burnt sesame is even thrown into a rainstorm to protect the village from its worst effects.

It is said that in the old days, people who were sick would even make a black mixture from pig's dung, and smear it on their bodies. Here is a paraphrased account of the practice:

Long ago when there was no medicine here [*dawa*, Arabic], when people were ill they would take pig dung, heat it on the fire, then mix it with oil and rub it on their bodies. This is a type of *jiso* and it would make them deep black.

Arum would see these nasty black bodies with pig dung on, and curse them [*wak uni*] and leave them alone. When *arum* left their bodies alone they would recover from their sickness.

People would also wear a piece of dom palm fibre round their necks, like a dog, so that *arum* would despite them and leave them.

W.J.: Like a Gurunya?

Answer (emphatic): Yes.

And I have been told, though have not observed, that pig dung and dog dirt are smeared on the bodies of Gurunyas.

The idea of restrictions, of leading people carefully from one state into another, are clear in the rites of passage I have mentioned, and in the rituals for illness. The ideas of protection, of exorcism, are there in the self-denigrating mode of naming children and the singing of self-deprecating songs; the idea of purification is there in the rites for illness; all these find parallels and echoes in the Gurunya rites. Indeed most of these elements are vividly present in the idea of the Gurunya, a creature which must be led carefully into the world of the living, and of human society, and saved from the alien powers of illness and death which would otherwise claim it.

The most important themes of the Gurunya rites, however, cannot be deduced from a consideration of such elemental stuff of symbolism as the use of hair, patterning of movement, or colour contrasts. They relate to the larger moral notions of the responsibility of women for the continued regeneration of society, for the birth and growth to maturity of children, especially girl children; and the need for the whole community to support the women in this matter and make contributions to the welfare of the weakest infants, and to help by communal 'adoption' the families least able to help themselves. The prominence given to children at all the Gurunya rites, the way in which they are given special priority at the beer pot, special shares of meat and so on, reflects this dominant concern. The Gurunya ceremonies sometimes seem like children's festivals.

THE FIRST WOMAN AND THE GURUNYA BIRD

I have already quoted two versions of the well-known story of the beginnings of society, when women lived in the village and grew sorghum and men lived like wild creatures out in the bush, until they were discovered and brought in by women.[5] The parallel with the image of the *çiŋkina/* of history has been traced; and the fundamental affinity of this vignette with Uduk matrilineal thinking has been suggested. In the version quoted as a prologue to this study, Woman calls specifically to the creature in the tree, *Gurunya/ waya pu wa!*—Gurunya, pluck me a fig. This special call does not appear in all versions I have heard, but as an explicit link between this story and the rites which I have described, it makes an extended interpretation possible. The story of the beginnings of mating and village life is almost

[5] See the Prologue; and Chapter II, pp. 79–80. I might mention here that I have collected a tale from the Komo which, although it only mentions the story of men and women finding each other, does tell of the first mating between the moon, a male, in the hut of the sun, a female. The sun had fire in her hut, and the moon was begging it from her. This Komo tale can be seen as a cosmic analogy with the Uduk tale, which is of more human and immediately historical and circumstantial import. I hope to deal more fully with comparisons of this kind elsewhere.

certainly older than the Gurunya cult as it is now practised, and
the symbolism of this tale lies behind the Gurunya rites. The
story is even, probably, the direct source of the dominant
symbol of the *gurunya/* bird for the cult.

Three main questions have to be considered if this claim is to
stand. The first concerns the position of the bird in the story:
why should this bird appear in the way it does in this particular
story, and be mistaken for the first Man? The opening of the
tale portrays a familiar enough scene. Birds, especially starlings,
do perch in fig trees and their pecking knocks down the fruit.
Children are in the habit of looking under fig trees in the hope
of finding figs knocked down by the starlings. Adults often gather
and eat fruits and seeds for refreshment when walking through
the woodland, and figs are among the most delicious. Fruits and
seeds naturally often come from trees; and trees, moreover,
appear in other tales. The Birapinya tree, for instance, was a
means of everlasting movement between earth and sky, in the
days before its destruction and the beginning of death. Trees,
as a focus of shade and rest, are often meeting places and the
focus of social life in this predominantly outdoor society; and
thus, the fig tree as a meeting place for Woman and Man is
fitting, as well as being the source of new fruitfulness in Woman.
In present Uduk thought about spiritual help in healing,
fertility, and so forth, the bush and wild plants and creatures are
often a potent source of new medicines and the possibility of
renewed life; and so it is fitting that Man, a new source of life,
should be taken for a wild creature—especially one that casts
down fruit. Why the *gurunya/* bird? It may be the very deep
blue-blackness of the bird, the quality that Uduk always
emphasize when it is mentioned, that makes it so appropriate.
'Blue' and 'black' are not distinguished in Uduk, except in
intensity, and when asked what is so special about the *gurunya/*
bird, people will usually say *ça'b ki 'thi, dhis dhis* (it is dark, very
deep blue-black). The intense *dhis dhis* suggests more than hue;
it suggests the rich glossy shine of the bird's plumage—or the
rich glossy shine of the black charcoal and oil mixture used by
people in the intermediate, transitional stage of rites of passage.
This shiny blue-blackness seems to sum up, for Uduk, the
character of the bird; and it may well be the primary symbolism of blackness in the context of rites of passage that

makes the *gurunya*/ the appropriate bird to signal the first discovered Man, out in the forest, before he is brought into the
village and before he mates. His maleness is not properly realized, until he is brought in by Woman—it is potential only. In
ways that could be further elaborated, he is analogous to a
person 'sitting black', not yet fully married, not yet fully
initiated to a specialist cult, or not yet fully readjusted to social
life after a long illness or bereavement. The *çiŋkina*/ of history,
lost people brought into the village, are associated with blackness
too—especially with the *'cume* ant, which can survive periods of
starvation in the bush. The alternation of black and red, as
marking the stages of life and rites of transition and incorporation is certainly long-established among the Uduk, and the bird
of the story, because of its colour, has a clear relationship to this
scheme.

The second question concerns the reasons why the *gurunya*/
bird, given its position in this story, should be selected as the
dominant symbol for a cult devoted to the saving of children's
lives, a cult brought in by the Uduk from the Jum Jum. As I
have mentioned, there does not seem to be a comparable
identification among the Jum Jum, or the Meban, where the
children are known simply by the equivalent of *çiŋkina*/. The
constellation of imagery around the *gurunya*/ bird seems to be
peculiar to the Uduk—the northern Uduk specifically—and
seems to have been built up by the Uduk women specialists of
the cult. The children to be saved are doubly marginal to
normal society—they are marginal in the sense that their
initial entry into society and the receiving of a personal name
are long delayed, for their relationship with the earlier world,
the dim transitional world preceding human existence, is prolonged beyond that of others; and they are marginal in the
sense of their being *çiŋkina*/, helpless and dependent, on being
brought into the community through the general help and
support of all its members, especially the women, just as *çiŋkina*/
were adopted by the community in the old days. The *gurunya*/
bird is fitting as an emblem for these infants, by virtue of those
qualities I have discussed. These children must 'sit black', for a
prolonged time; and beyond this formal marking of their marginal position, they are like the *gurunya*/ because their animal-
ness, their non-human quality, yields to their human personality

when they are brought in to the village, just as the original wild creature turned out to be a person and was brought in. The bringing in of these infants, just like the bringing in of the first Man creature, is the responsibility of women. It is not difficult to see the suitability of the *gurunya/* bird, given the background of this myth, as an emblem for the foundling children.

But a third question still has to be dealt with. What were the particular circumstances in which the Uduk, specifically the northern Uduk, took over this cult and elaborated it in the way I have indicated? What made the elaborations so apt for the Uduk, when they had not been particularly thought of by the Jum Jum or the Meban—even though rites concerned with these children appear to have been in the hands of women among the former? Why was the cult among the Uduk newly put into a relationship with the older story of Woman's discovery of Man? The adoption of the cult seems to have taken place in circumstances of a newly-constructed matrilineal social world among the northern Uduk. I shall explain in the final chapter the evidence which supports the theory that the matrilineal system of thought and organization which I have described in this book is a new creation among the northern Uduk: here I simply point out that the imagery of the Gurunya rites, and its connections with history and myth, may have something to do not only with the history of dispersal and loss which the Uduk share with many of their neighbours, but also with the making of their matrilineal society, unique for the region, which took place within the communities of the *'kwanim pa* after their migration northwards to their present home. Northern Uduk, as mentioned above, are prepared to make into a Gurunya a girl child who follows four boys—something that would not be found among their neighbours! The notion of saving not merely a child, but a matriline, is often implicit in remarks about the Gurunya practices. The saved Gurunya, in the abstract, is even spoken of as a female. Maya said, in an explanation following the quotation at the head of this chapter, 'The mother stays without a child in her arms; this one dies, that one dies, so they make her child a Gurunya. If you give birth to a child, it immediately dies. But a Gurunya will grow up to become the mother of family . . .' This might appear to be at odds with the maleness of the mythical *gurunya/*, but there is no contradiction

when we remember the potential fertility which is the gift both
of that original male, and of the present-day Gurunya child, to
the first Woman and to the community respectively. The conditions under which the promise of fertility is crucial have
merely changed.

GURUNYA AS A CENTRAL SOCIAL RITE

We are familiar with societies in which there are central,
dominant rituals which define the political and social order,
symbolize its principles and articulate the relations of men and
divinity. In the Nile Basin, we immediately recall the installa-
tion rites of the Shilluk king, or the lineage and age-set rituals
of southern Nilotic peoples, or the religious sacrifices of the
Dinka. We remember also the harvest rituals of the Pueblo
Indians, and the yearly festivals of the Eskimo. The Uduk have no
sort of central political authority, and certainly no institution of
kingship around which rites might cluster to represent the essential principles of their social being, and their historical continuity, to themselves. Their rites seem miscellaneous. There
are agricultural rites which follow a yearly cycle; there are rites
of passage, of which I have given brief hints in this study; and
there are a variety of competing healing-cults, most brought in
from the Jum Jum and the Meban. But the older Uduk rites of
the fields, and also (though to a lesser degree) the rites of
passage, are declining—marriage rites in particular are far less
elaborate than they used to be. The healing cults, founded by
prophetic leaders especially from the Meban, flourish, but like
mission Christianity and Islam where they are known, appear
to sit lightly on Uduk foundations. Foreign ritual practices,
based upon the Nilotic theology of a sky god, are carried out but
in a rather casual manner. The older Uduk theology is based
on an earthly presence of spiritual power, *arum*. But the cult
which appears to be flourishing most successfully at present, and
to constitute one of the most colourful and elaborate festivals of
northern Uduk villages, is the Gurunya cult. Although owing
something to the Jum Jum, it does not rest upon a foreign
theology; the symbolic echoes are immediately recognizable, and
the newly-established matrilineal orientation of the northern
Uduk has opened the way for the enthusiastic embracing and

propagation of this cult. Many of the pre-existing themes of myth, of other rites concerning illness, transition, and protection from death, have been drawn into the practice and the exegesis of the Gurunya cult. It is a synthesis of a wide range of elements from pre-existing rites and imagery. But more than that, I have suggested that the Gurunya cult has drawn on images from legend and remembered history. It touches not only upon a far-fetched myth which no one regards as literally true, but also upon incidents and echoes of past happenings which everyone knows to be true in the everyday sense. The Gurunya rites are a dramatic representation of the historical knowledge of the Uduk. They represent symbolically a play upon the political history of the people; the northern Uduk *were* fragmented, they *did* emerge from an amalgam of adoptees, they *have* been able to reconstitute their communities of *'kwanim pa* from scattered individuals—from *çiŋkina/*. And it is true to state, as the Gurunya rites do in symbolic fashion, that it is largely through the preservation of biological continuities through women that the people have survived disaster. Since the loss of stable long-term transactions between social groups upon which the sophisticated economic and political structures of public life are built among the Uduk (as among ourselves), the survival of the community of *'kwanim pa* has been possible only through the natural fertility of women. The Gurunya rites constitute, and display dramatically, the making of a *wathim pa*, a complete moral and social personality. The drama is closely analogous to the historical making of the *'kwanim pa*, the northern Uduk people.

It is generally agreed that something of the essential and distinctive character of Shilluk society is contained in the royal rites of succession, which enshrine Shilluk conceptions of mankind, God and history. The Uduk Gurunya rites are not as large and spectacular, nor as firmly established. They belong to the hamlet, or group of hamlets, and not to a large polity. Nevertheless, they are emblematic of the distinctive 'totality', in the Maussian sense, of Uduk society. The Uduk social world is not defined upon the basis of central institutions of kingship or priesthood, nor even by politically important lines of descent or clanship. It is defined rather by the ease with which outsiders may be brought in and fragmented groups assimilated. At heart, a principle of democratic inclusiveness, a facility for quietly absorbing people at the margins, gives the society of the *'kwanim pa* its basic constitution. This contrasts with the formulae of exclusive descent, or of restricted rights to citizenship and central political office, found in so many other societies of the region. The Gurunya cult, by bringing in bereaved children who are nobody's kinsmen in particular, highlights this principle of inclusiveness, and some of the institutional and moral features of Uduk life which give it substance. And although we may not get a complete and fully reasoned historical account of themselves from the Uduk, we can discover, in the Gurunya rites, a richly drawn play or picture, a collective 'work of art', which tells us just as much.

8

A HISTORICAL VIEW OF THE UDUK

The distinctiveness of tribal peoples is often explained, by the wise old men of village Africa as well as by the scholar, on the model of a branching tree. A common ancestral stem divides, as a result of peoples from a common homeland parting and going their separate ways, each taking their own inheritance of language and culture. The variety of Nilotic peoples, for example, is often seen in this way. Such branching migrations may well have played a very real, if not the only, part in the history of Nilotic differentiation. But in the case of the Uduk, it would be unhelpful to see their culture simply as a branch, or twig, of the Koman stem. They have assimilated as much from 'foreign' neighbours as they have inherited from the Koman past. This is true, to varying degrees, on the level of population history, on the level of language, myth and tradition, and on the level of social and cultural institutions. Their present culture must be seen therefore against the background of their political history. The capacity to synthesize, to assimilate and reconstruct, has been a major factor in their survival, and in their cultural divergence from the other Koman peoples. The Koman peoples anyway have probably never, and certainly not in the last few centuries, exercised the kind of spreading cultural dominance that we know has been exercised by the Nilotes or by the Oromo, or by the Arabic or Amharic civilizations, and which is evoked by the metaphor of the branching tree. The Koman peoples might be better compared to a seed-bed of culture, well composted by the falling leaves of many mature trees.

Uduk experience of recent history, as we have demonstrated, has been of a world and a people fragmented. Consequently, traditions and memories of the past, not for the first time either, have themselves been broken up and partially lost. But from this jumble of fragmentary knowledge, an experience of discontinuity itself further broken up as a collective tradition by the very conditions of that experience, a new synthesis has been made. From shared images of the past and shared contact with 'foreign' worlds, a common sympathy has made possible a newly integrated world of feeling and of rationally justified action, of which I have described something in this book.

The present-day world of the Uduk can be received on its own terms, as yet another exotic way of life and of thought. Such institutions as matrilineal descent, such values as the impropriety of trade, even obviously imported myths like the tale of the Birapinya tree or imported rites like those of the Gurunya cult, can all be accepted as a living tradition; a tradition founded on a set of 'collective representations' informing present experience and guiding present action, constituting a social reality without reference to anything outside itself. Like a language, it could be argued that such component cultural elements form a systematic 'world-view' with its own internal coherence and self-justifying rationale, to be approached as yet another problem in 'cultural translation'. The Gurunya cult for example could be treated as a self-defining symbolic whole, representing the world as it is or as it might be, but without reference to what it is known to have been. Attitudes to production and exchange could be rationalized as 'maintaining the social structure', or as 'reinforcing ethnic boundaries', in a quite non-historical sense. Even the explicit views of the past which the Uduk hold, such as the Birapinya tale or the stories of running in the bush 'like antelopes' because of slave-raiders, could be treated in essence as an arbitrary and self-sustaining system of representations, as though the past existed merely as a projection of the present, shaped by present-oriented vision alone. To such an interpretation, it would not matter what really happened in the past. It would not even matter that the very self-appellation of the northern Uduk, *'kwanim pa*, incorporates a Nilotic loan-word for the notion of the homeland.

But to take such an idealistic and relative view would be to overlook the most important aspect of Uduk statements about the past, about work and exchange, and about their myths and images of *çiŋkina/*, *gurunya/* and the overcoming of historical disaster through the natural fertility of women and the remaking of the homeland. These things are *toŋ gana*: true matters. Sometimes personal memory can provide particular evidence for their truth, though more often and more importantly collective tradition avows their general truth. This avowal is not merely relative to the Uduk condition. It is not imprisoned by language or culture, though expressed in a richly local idiom. On the basis of that fundamental moral sympathy which crosses arbitrary linguistic and cultural barriers we can apprehend directly Uduk judgements on slavery, bridewealth, commerce and so forth, judgements built in to so many of their social and cultural institutions, and translate them into the terms of our own political and social discourse. Direct moral intuition can confirm at a deep level the truth of some Uduk 'collective representations'. But on another level, perhaps a more superficial one, with our scholarly techniques of historical and comparative research, we can confirm the relevance, and even prove in our sense the truth, of some Uduk insights into the past.

We can go beyond a merely intuitive acceptance of the validity of Uduk views of the genesis and survival of their own society, and behind those symbolic analogies of what happened in the past which occupy their present lives so centrally. In the rational spirit of our own tradition of historical enquiry we can examine the genesis of modern Uduk society, drawing on external evidence not available to them, or available only partially. We can then see how far there may be a correspondence between the symbolically represented truths apprehended by the Uduk themselves and the truths of past conditions and development of the society as it might be analysed by the professional historian or ethnographer. Perhaps a link may be forged between the 'analytical' understanding of the comparative scholar and the 'synthetic' understanding or personal knowledge of the Uduk villager, as we find it expressed in a collective 'work of art' such as the Gurunya cult. Perhaps these modes of understanding are not exclusive or contradictory; perhaps they may converge. For both seek to record what truly happened in the past, in human terms, and to draw out its significance for the present.

In this concluding chapter I review some of the historical and comparative ethnographic evidence which sheds light on the conditions under which we can say Uduk society, and in particular the society of the northern Uduk, has developed. I shall consider mainly those features of Uduk society which have been described, especially their matrilineal form of organization and associated ways of thinking about kinship, economics and history. The Gurunya cult is itself one synthesis of various elements the Uduk see as having gone into the making of their society; we are in a position to sketch in some evidence on the making of the Uduk which might be used to build a different account, of the ethnographic history type. Any ethnographer, of whatever school or period, would wonder at the apparent anomaly of a 'pocket of matriliny' on the ethnographic map; we may at least guess at connections between this puzzle and the historical conditions under which the present structural bias of northern Uduk society has emerged. The evidence does suggest that on the basis of cultural assumptions and funda-mental institutions common to the Koman peoples, and in the circumstances of the fragmentary northward migration and uncertain resettlement of the forerunners of the northern Uduk, a whole social world has been restructured by the people who now know themselves as *'kwanim pa*. An implicit principle of matriliny has become intellectually and morally dominant in these conditions, and has become entrenched through its rele-vance to practical organization. Before considering this argu-ment in more detail, it is necessary to review some of the present differences between the northern and the southern Uduk. This comparison throws into relief the distinctiveness of the northern Uduk, the *'kwanim pa*, when put alongside both the southern Uduk and their immediate neighbours, the Komo, Ganza, and Shita.

NORTHERN AND SOUTHERN UDUK

I have said something, in the opening chapter of this book, of the differences between the Uduk of the Tombak and Ahmar valleys (numbering at least some seven thousand) and those to their south, in the Yabus valley and the hills to the south of the Yabus (numbering two and a half to three thousand). There is a marked contrast in the dialects of the northern and southern areas; the differences of pronunciation together with a number of vocabulary differences sometimes make it difficult for a northerner at first to understand the southern dialect. I have also mentioned differences in social organization—the southern-ers tend to live more often with their father's people than the northerners, and nearly always identify themselves in relation to their father's people. They occasionally practise, and as often as not for the fun of the escapade, reciprocal elopement—*ri'c mash*, or 'revenge marriage'. Hamlets are smaller and more scattered in the south, and the people have been more disturbed than the northerners by the recent troubles of the southern Sudan, having had in some cases to leave their homes for a period during the 1960s because of Nuer incursions. However, northern settlements are more securely established, and the region is more densely settled. I have also indicated the strong local tradition and confirmatory evidence that the northern Uduk have come from the south; indeed that the Uduk-speaking people as a whole have almost certainly come from the Daga valley, where they still claim relatives.

The distinctiveness of the northern Uduk deserves further consideration. Built into their very language there are contrasts with the southerners, which bear closely on their social history. I have pointed out that the northern Uduk lack an ordinary ethnic name for themselves, of the same order as their terms for other peoples, or the terms others use of them. They call themselves simply *'kwanim pa*, people of the homeland, the homestead, as against not only foreigners, but also the refugees and kinless *çiŋkina/* of the bush, and in distinction also from animals and spirits. The southern dialect of Uduk possesses the phrase *'kwanim pa* too, but it is used only in its sense of 'human beings' and is not used as an ethnic self-designation. The southerners call themselves, in the ethnic sense, K̲amus. This is also the term used of them by their close neighbours, the Komo and the Ganza; these neighbours extend its use to the northern Uduk too, when they have cause to refer to them, though the Ganza may also call them Tam. The expression K̲amus does not have an ordinary-language meaning, as far as I know, but is simply a proper name. The northerners have a birth-group I have written Kwamas, which is almost certainly derived from K̲amus, but northerners would laugh and reject the name K̲amus for themselves as a whole. The southern Uduk call the northern country Bwa'cesh, the 'centre of the earth', and call the northerners Bun'cesh, those of Bwa'cesh. This may refer indirectly to the fact that the main body of Uduk speakers have migrated to the northern valleys; or it may refer merely to the open and low-lying plains and wide valleys of the north, as against the more mountainous country of the south. The majority of the Uduk-speaking population, then, those who have migrated farthest from their former relatives and neighbours to the south, and have settled in what is probably quite new country for the Koman peoples, have no term for themselves but *'kwanim pa*, with all the moral burden that this expression carries, and of which I have given some account.

I have emphasized at some length the importance of the concept *wak̲*, the matrilineal birth-group, in the preceding chapters. This word is peculiar to the northern dialect of Uduk. It is absent from the southern dialect, and although quite a few southerners know it from conversation with the northerners, I do not believe they understand all it can mean. For there is not even a synonym in the southern dialect. Southerners use the word *mos*, which people familiar with both dialects may say is the equivalent of *wak̲*. But *mos*, as used of groups among the southern Uduk such as the Lake, the Pa'dwosh, and so on, is ambiguous in terms of lineality. When a person is asked the name of his *mos*, he is likely to name the group of his father, rather than that of his mother. The word *mos* does not mean a matrilineal descent group, but a named collectivity to which you may attach yourself by one of various means. A person can even be described as belonging to two *mos*, or at least as being related to two *mos*, one through his father and one through his mother. Thus a typical series of questions and answers would be on the following lines, between myself and a southern Uduk:

> What is your *mos*?
> I am Cega.
> What is your mother's *mos*?
> She is Bersaŋ.
> But are you not also Bersaŋ?
> Yes, I am Bersaŋ by the vagina, and Cega by the penis.

This ambiguity is not present in the northern Uduk use of the word *wak̲*. The southern Uduk however are aware of the difference between the custom of the northern Uduk, and that of their southern neighbours the Ganza, where affiliation to a 'clan' is patrilineal. They say that the Ganza live according to the penis, and the Uduk according to the vagina. The ambiguities of southern Uduk usage do not indicate a system of 'double descent', but rather a flexible situation in which an individual's affiliation to a named group depends on circumstances of his family history rather than on dogmatic descent rules. Affiliation to either side may be emphasized according to individual cases. The scope for adjustment is very wide, even crossing ethnic boundaries; a young woman explained to me that she was not Ganza but Uduk, for her mother was Anza (a Ganza 'clan') *only from her fathers*. That is, the girl was classifying herself according to the Uduk matrilineal rule, although her mother would be fully Ganza according to the Ganza patrilineal rule. It is very interesting that the word *mos* is shared also by the Komo of Yabus Bridge and the more southerly Komo of the Gerre valley in Ethiopia, where it is an abstract noun referring to the various named *patrilineal* clans. The Ganza also seem to use this word, though my informants were bilingual in (southern) Uduk and Ganza, and I am not sure of its meaning for them. In the use of this word, which connotes patrilineal descent among the Komo and is ambiguous among the southern Uduk, the intimate connections between these peoples separate them from the northern Uduk, who do not use the term.

Another word peculiar to the northern Uduk dialect is that for 'sister's child', *nam* (male speaking). In the southern dialect, the word *shwakam* doubles as a self-reciprocal between 'mother's brother' and 'sister's child', just as the term *iya* (father's brother or brother's child) is a self-reciprocal in both dialects. Among the northern Uduk, it would appear that an earlier use of *shwakam* as a self-reciprocal, shared with the southern Uduk, was replaced by a new differentiation, *shwakam* being retained for the mother's brother, but a new term, *nam*, being applied by him to the sister's child (see the comment on p. 163). There is a strong circumstantial possibility that this differentiation came about through a restructuring of relationships, particularly the establishment of new matrilineal lines of authority.

The distinctiveness of the northern Uduk is particularly striking when the close ties and resemblances are recalled between the southern Uduk and their Komo, Kwama, Shita, and Ganza neighbours. Outward culture between the ethnic groups in the hills and valleys south of the Yabus is scarcely distinguishable, and although Ganza is linguistically very distant from the Uduk-Komo grouping, many individuals in the region speak more than one language. I have travelled through Ganza villages, speaking to people there in Uduk, without realizing that they were 'not Uduk' (or rather, not Kamus). There are no rigid territorial boundaries between the language communities, and in recent generations there has been plenty of intermarriage. Many individuals would find themselves ambiguously placed, if ethnic boundaries were to be sharply drawn.

There is at least one Ganza 'clan' which as a whole unit is in an ambiguous position; most of the members of this 'clan', the Anza, are bilingual with Uduk, and there has been in recent times a good deal of intermarriage with the Uduk. Some of the Anza are said to be Kum Bishi (that is, people of Bisho, or the 'Uduk' group of Lake) because the Lake are their fathers, as a result of some Anza women having married Lake men. The southern Uduk say that a person born by the penis from the Anza is Anza himself, and that the Anza follow the general Ganza custom of living with their fathers. They practise exchange marriage. But whereas in the past they belonged exclusively to the Ganza, because there was enmity between the Ganza and the Uduk, more recently their affiliation has changed because they have allied themselves with the Uduk (*gam me'd*, literally 'joined hands with'), and are therefore 'real Uduk'. One reason for the blurring of boundaries was hinted at by an informant who said that of course the Anza spoke Uduk, for nowadays, because of the Government, everybody had joined together and people were no longer enemies.

Political as well as cultural and kinship ties thus bind the southern Uduk closely to their neighbours in the region south of the Yabus. The northern Uduk on the other hand, although they recognize in general their affinity with the other Koman peoples, especially the Komo and the Shita, no longer live in direct touch with any other Koman people at all. They live as neighbours of quite foreign peoples—whose languages are remote from theirs, who trade, herd cattle, pay bridewealth, and so forth—peoples such as the markedly Nilotic Meban, Jum Jum, and Hill Burun, and the Berta and Arabic-speakers to their east. Economic and political forces have drawn the Uduk towards people to their north, with whom they have now reached a reasonably friendly accommodation. They have lived, and still live, on the fringes of wealth, power, and state-formation; they used to pay tribute to the Funj kingdom of Sennar, and have felt the impact of nineteenth-century history and the growth of the Sudanese state to a greater extent than their fellow-Komans to the south, who still preserve a degree of traditional independence and political innocence. It is this confrontation with more powerful and wealthy peoples, perhaps, which has helped shape those moral and political values which by acknowledging and transcending the memory of failure and enslavement give northern Uduk society its character today. It is that context in which we can better understand the loss of the ordinary ethnic term, Ḵamus, by which they are still known to their former neighbours, and the adoption of a new self-designation embodying a foreign language-element, the Nilotic *pa*, for the very concept of home: *'kwanim pa*.

THE KOMAN BACKGROUND: EXCHANGE-MARRIAGE

One of the central institutions of the Koman peoples as a whole is that of exchange marriage, and some consideration of its working is necessary to appreciate the circumstances from which northern Uduk society has sprung. The system of exchange marriage varies in detail from place to place, but right across the range of Koman-speaking peoples it occupies a crucial and distinctive position.[1] The language of marriage, and of affinity, reflects cognate usage between different Koman groups, even where lexical similarity is slight. In Uduk, the word *mash* can be translated simply marriage, affair, or sexual intercourse, and the word *mase/* means brother-in-law. In Komo, which is closely related, *mash* refers either to exchange marriage as such, or to the girl one exchanges for a wife. In the linguistically much more distant Gumuz language, *mashi* or *misa* is the term for brother-in-law.

The essential principle of Koman exchange marriage is that an exact balance should be preserved between the marrying parties. A newly contracted or projected marriage should be reciprocated, so that ideally a sister of the bridegroom should be made available for marriage to the brother of the bride. In all

[1] I have described something of Koman exchange marriage in a recent article; see James, 1976.

its variations, this exchange secures to the husband rights over his children which are not automatic if there is no exchange. Without an exchange, the children may grow up with their mother's people, rather than their father's. Furthermore, in spite of the variations of this kind in personal circumstance, among all the Koman peoples except the Uduk, a person belongs to the named 'clan' of his father.

The Gumuz, who live in the valley of the Blue Nile in both the Sudan and Ethiopia, are the most numerous of the Koman peoples (I would estimate between 30,000 and 50,000). Although they and the Uduk-Komo-Shita bloc of peoples are in the main ignorant of one another's existence, the cultural similarity is very striking. Of all the Koman peoples, the Gumuz have today the most elaborate and internally coherent system of exchange marriage.

The exchanges take place ideally between patrilineal clans or lineages and they are normally arranged by elders, who have considerable authority over the younger men and women. If a marriage takes the form of an elopement and there is no subsequent exchange, it is described as 'stealing' and could provoke violent retaliation. The matter may be put right a few years later when an exchange girl is found, or even in the next generation, when a daughter of the 'stolen' woman may be paid back to replace her mother. Then the daughter may be used in an exchange, as her mother should have been.

Elaborate arrangements may be made for borrowing and lending girls for exchange within the lineage or between closely linked lineages. When you borrow a girl to exchange for a wife, you should eventually give your own daughter (whose birth is made possible by the exchange) back to the donor or his son as a replacement; your daughter can then herself be exchanged. There are thus sets of debts linking people over the generations, both between lineages and within lineages. Once an exchange-marriage link is made it is fairly durable in itself; if one wife dies, a replacement may be found (and even a second replacement if the first replacement dies). Small girls, promised in exchange, may go to live with their future husband's people and be brought up there in anticipation of their eventual marriage. It is common for a widow to be inherited by one of her husband's brothers. Fathers exercise a fairly strict control over the marriage of their daughters, allocating them to one or another son or nephew, or even exchanging them for a second wife for themselves.

Everyone among the Gumuz is caught up in this network of exchanges; there is no alternative mode of marriage contract. In a sample of over 370 marriages surveyed in a village in Ethiopia in 1975 only two could be described as bridewealth marriages, and both were highly exceptional. One old man's father had bought his bride out of slavery years ago, paying for her with goats and salt, and one young man had recently paid a large cash sum to the mother of his wife. That was because the mother had refused to allow any of her in-laws to use her daughter as an exchange. (Some years earlier the in-laws had killed a son of hers.) She insisted on keeping the money as compensation to herself. Marriage arrangements among the Gumuz are major political matters, both causing hostilities and being a means of peacemaking.

The Komo are of particular interest because their marriage system is now changing. Past disturbances and present government pressure have scattered the patrilineal clans of the Komo, and the authority of the elders is much weaker than it is among the Gumuz. The position of women, particularly the younger women, is more independent. The majority of Komo marriages are still exchange marriages, but a growing proportion of them are accomplished by bridewealth payment.

Komo informants believe that sister-exchange has been practised from very early in their history. If you ask them why they like to make these exchanges, they are likely to reply: 'Are we not all the children of exchanged girls? So we must ourselves exchange.' As among the Gumuz, a man is expected not to marry into his own (patrilineal) clan or into the clan of his mother. The result is that exchanges are not repeated generation after generation between the same groups of people or the same clans. For each clan a new fan of marriage links is made in each new generation. The Komo allow polygamy (that is, a particular man may be married to more than one wife at a time), but a woman may be the wife of only one man until that marriage is dissolved.

When the Komo speak of their wives and sisters or their *mash* (the girl they exchange for a wife), they are not thinking of women as commodities. For them the marriage system turns on the positive value of women, who are central to its functioning. A woman's work complements that of her menfolk, and when a girl marries, her father and brothers will miss her at this practical level. Conversely, when a new wife joins a hamlet, it is as a working woman that she will be judged by the community as a whole. Beyond these everyday considerations a woman is precious as a potential mother of children. Her honourable position, in her own community or her husband's, flows from this, and as a potential mother she sees herself as the pivot of the exchange-marriage arrangements.

The Komo think of a woman as the source from which the local community, and the society as a whole, will be replenished and grow. They regard the physical bonds between a child and his mother as being stronger than those between the child and his father, and like the Uduk they see the natural continuity of society as passing from mother to daughter. A sister's potential for childbearing is regarded as belonging 'naturally' to this female line. Marriage arrangements, however, cut across this 'natural' line of descent, and exchange marriage in particular results in the transfer of a sister's potential offspring from the guardianship of her own people to that of her husband's people. If an exchange-marriage contract breaks down, the rights to a sister's children may revert to the 'natural' line, primarily to her brother. Clans or *mos* among the Komo, the named groups in terms of which history and politics are discussed, are based not on this idea of 'natural' descent through women but on patrilineal links from father to son. They are regarded as having been built up through repeated sister-exchange marriages.

The Komo, at least those with whom I am familiar in Ethiopia, are beginning to give up exchange marriage, under various pressures. It seems likely that, as in the case of the Uduk, although there is official encouragement for them to pay bridewealth at marriage, they will not abandon their similar fundamental attitudes to matters of personal relations, exchange, and money. Their society is likely to come to resemble that of the Uduk under these pressures.

Although the northern Uduk say that they have never practised exchange marriage, the circumstantial evidence strongly suggests that their forebears did. Even if they did not, the fundamental notions which they have in common with the other Koman peoples, especially the Komo, place the actual social practices of the Uduk very close indeed to Koman practices, based as they are on the key institution of sister-exchange. The sister-exchange of the other Koman peoples, and the present marriage and social system of the northern Uduk, could certainly be seen as logical variations on a single set of basic principles, even if no chronological and developmental connection can be proved at present.

There are two main features of exchange marriage as it is practised by the neighbours of the Uduk, particularly the Komo and the Ganza, which we should particularly note. The first is that for the Komo, at least, there is an important notion of the natural continuity of humanity through women, and that when an exchange marriage contract breaks down or is not properly fulfilled, the children revert to the 'body' (*is*) of their mothers' people, rather than their fathers'. This local group, which ideally lives and works together, is the unit within which a young man may expect to find a girl to exchange for his wife. If girls are brought up in their mothers' community because their mothers' marriage was not a properly completed exchange, they may be exchanged in marriage by the young men of the group: that is, the young men are exchanging girls who are their cross-cousins. It may be imagined that in a local group, in which a large number of women have not been exchanged in the proper manner for one reason or another, a large number of girls and boys will be brought up there, in the groups or 'body' of their mothers' people rather than of their father's; and so *de facto* there exists a 'matrifocal' group on the ground. Modern communities among the Komo and Ganza, and I think very possibly among the Kwama, Shita, and Mao as well, are based mainly on a number of men living with their sons; but with a few sisters' sons too, as a result of the non-contracting of exchange marriages in the previous generation.

Dwash, a young Ganza man who was fluent in Uduk, gave me the following account:

'Look, in the place where we come from, women are not married on one side alone. If you marry a Ganza woman, for the Ganza women it is just exchange, exchange [*oke, oke, oke*]. If one has no exchange-partner, she will be taken home again. . . .

'If [a girl] has no brother, no brother at all, the father will exchange her to marry. She will not be left to be married asymmetrically [*kup 'de*/, literally one-sidedly]. It is the Bisho people [i.e. Uduk] who marry just on one side. But the Ganza, the Ganza don't marry only on one side. When the Ganza marry, if a woman's husband dies, she will be brought another man and given to him. That's how it is. If a girl should die, another will be brought and put in her place. And if a son dies, his father will then marry the girl who was his daughter-in-law. He won't remain without doing anything.'

An account by Ukka, a Ganza woman also fluent in Uduk, emphasizes similar points, although given on a different occasion. Ukka suggests that sometimes, 'bridewealth' may be acceptable instead of an exchange of women; it seems to consist of goats, in addition to the small presents made anyway by each party to an exchange among the Ganza, but does not result in the transfer of rights over the children to the father:

'Someone will court a girl and flirt with her, and if she is then married, the people of the village from which she is married will come and seize another girl, to equalize. That is revenge marriage.

'At the marriage, she brews the marriage beer, and those people will bring hoes and spears, and money, and put them at the foot of the centre-pole. And the other one too, she brews beer, and she also installs her marriage partner at home, taking money in the same way. It is put at the foot of the centre-pole. Hoes, and spears, and bangles, and so on.

'That is how they deal with women: they take them and marry them in that way. But marriage among you Uduk [Kamus: the Ganza word for the Uduk, especially southern Uduk] is one-sided. Only a few marry "in revenge".

'We here [Ganza] always marry women "in revenge". If some girl should marry on one side, without an exchange-partner, she will be seized [by her people] in order to claim money, bangles, and goats. If these are not forthcoming, she will be led back by her people. Led back home. A woman who has no exchange-partner will remain in a lopsided situation if no partner is provided. When children are born, those children born of an exchange marriage will stay with their father. Those children will stay with their father like that. But those borne by you, on one side only without an exchange, will be taken home [i.e. by their mother's brothers].'

I have mentioned that the southern Uduk on occasion reciprocate a marriage, or rather an elopement. Sheikh Puna

Marinyje, of the southern Uduk, who knew the Ganza well, told me—and he was referring only to the southern Uduk: 'It used to be done thus by the [southern] Uduk, in the same way as the Ganza. But nowadays they have left it, because the custom of exchanging is very bad. People may die when an exchange is carried out now; for the problems of exchange marriage are fought over sometimes.'

Puna's mother agreed warmly on the evils of exchange marriage, and expanded on the problem of finding sons to match daughters, and the unequal zest of exchanged women for grinding and cooking. As in any contractual agreement, there is always an element of tension in the exchange arrangement, and it may break out into open hostility. Among the Shita and Komo there have been recent cases of fighting leading to deaths over exchange-marriage disputes; and among all the Koman peoples, marriage is spoken of in terms of losing a sister, rather than gaining a wife. It is therefore interesting that the Uduk term for what in general I have called 'exchange marriage' is *ri'c mash*: literally, 'revenge marriage'. Among those Uduk in the southern community of the Yabus valley and Jebel Bisho where revenge marriage occasionally occurs, it does not take the form of prearranged betrothals and agreements between the elders on either side; it literally takes the form of elopement followed by counter-elopement—approaching what we would call 'kidnapping' at times. The Uduk term fully signals the hostility potentially present in the more formal exchange agreements of the Komo and the Ganza. When revenge marriages occur among the southern Uduk they are rarely stable; it is very unusual, although not unknown, for children to be brought up in the village of their fathers among the southern Uduk because of the successful 'exchange' marriage of their parents. As boys in this position grow up they seek a girl from among their (paternal) cross-cousins to exchange for a wife. Sheikh Puna explained this situation and explained further the tradition of the southern Uduk having practised the exchange system properly in the past:

'Long ago, people lived with their fathers. Some live with their fathers now until they are grown up, and remain with their fathers until they become old. They live with their fathers like that from the time when [their mothers] were exchanged in marriage, long ago. There are plenty of them, some with their sisters as well. In the past, you married by exchanging your cross-cousins, but this practice has now disappeared.

'And other people live permanently in their mothers' brothers' hamlets. The women of today are feared because of their behaviour in connection with exchange marriage. It is said: "Ay, this exchange business is very bad, for the women who are exchanged, just go home. They go home. When one sees the other going home, she goes home."

'And you, if you see that your friend is beating your sister, if your sister is beaten by him on the head, *tuup̣!*—if you hear that your sister has been hit, you will beat that sister who is your wife right on the head too, *tuup̣!* Just to equalize. You see, the old practice was like that. If you keep [your wife] properly, that man will also keep his properly. If your sister is lazy, and doesn't do the grinding, that marriage will break up. . . . They will say: "*Caah!* This sister of yours is kept for no reason at all here. She doesn't make us anything to eat." She is led home, and the marriage breaks up.

'The [southern] Uduk, from the time of exchange-marriage, lived like that: in the old days, they lived in the place of their fathers. They didn't leave. That's how the Ganza live now. Just as, from the time when Marinyje died, we have been living. As if we had been born in an exchange marriage.'

Puna's last remark refers to the fact that he and his brothers are living where their father used to live, and not with their mother's people.

Even though 'revenge marriage' is not always practised among the southern Uduk, indeed it is unusual, cases do occur and may lead to trouble. In 1967 a fight took place in the Belatoma area which was eventually dealt with by the court in Kurmuk, which arose from disputes over an exchange marriage. The situation was as follows: a young man Adam, of the Bersaŋ birth-group but living with his father's people (who were Lake), on the north bank of the Yabus, married a girl from the Gwara people who were living on the south bank. Adam had no living sister from his own mother, and the brothers of his girl wanted to marry Nona in exchange, Adam's mother's sister's daughter. However, Nona's mother wanted her own son Marko to use Nona in exchange for a wife. Adam kept the girl for a couple of days, and then her brothers, angry because they could not marry Nona in exchange, came and took their sister away. Marko, who wanted to marry the same girl, then ran off with her; and her full brother Yuli came and married Nona. When Adam heard that Marko had married his girl, he and his mother were very angry and went to find her, and brought her home with them. When Nona's mother heard of this she of course took her away from Yuli. The girl in question, Yuli's sister, had meanwhile decided that she loved Adam and not Marko, and she and Adam went off together. Her brothers then came and fought Adam's father's people, who were Lake, using throwing sticks. They also traced the couple, found them in the bush and beat up Adam, who was badly hurt on the shin. A number of fines were eventually imposed, and the local sheikhs agreed that Adam should keep his girl, and Yuli should have Nona.

This case presents several interesting features: for example, the rivalry between the two sisters, each trying to do the best for her own son; the fact that Adam's own people were not involved in the fight, but only his father's people with whom he was living; the girl's own preference, which seems to have been decisive, although Marko was older than Adam and had a full sister. Marko, whom I did not meet, was said to be ugly, with some teeth missing at the top. Women are said by the southern Uduk to cause most of the problems of marriage exchange; and Uduk women appear to assert themselves rather more than their Ganza counterparts, whose marriage is more of a community arrangement, and less a personal whim.

Further cases, relating to a single hamlet community, are given in Appendix 4.

In many southern Uduk villages today, there are no examples of exchange marriages at all; and in others, only one or two. When it does occur, it is not usually taken very seriously; and sometimes positively as a joke. Those exchanges which do occur are not expected to last.

I would like to quote part of the explanation offered me by Sheikh Puna as to why the Uduk in general do not wish to pay, or to receive, bridewealth. I had asked him, in particular, why those people who are giving up sister-exchange marriage, do not accept bridewealth as an alternative security.

'People say they fear that practice because of debt. They are afraid of the talk of debt. They say, "Some time in the future, if she dies, they will come and claim repayment from here, saying that women are useless, and only active women should be exchanged for money."

'That practice of exchange marriage has been dropped. Women were given for bridewealth at one time. Divorced women were given for £1.500 [Sudanese], and girls, for £4.000 [Sudanese]. They were paid for thus, and then some time later people gave back the money. Some others were married "in revenge" nevertheless; and one group of people would obtain money, then the other group would collect money to balance it, and the money was given on top of the exchange of women.

'People saw how things were going, and later returned the money back. They gave it back, in those cases where bridewealth money had been paid. Bridewealth money was paid at that time, all over this area. But people have paid the money back.

'Now, people live and marry freely. Nothing more is said of money. They marry freely. A few still think of sister-exchange. But they say that the sister-exchange business of today is no good. It's half-hearted. Very bad. In the past, it was all right. Today it's very bad.'

Rights over women, therefore, may be exchangeable for rights over other women; but not for anything less valuable. Sheikh Puna's mother made the following comments to me, in which she used the ordinary word for buying and selling (*yol*), an action which has no positive moral content and which only takes place between unrelated people: 'Yes, they were acting according to the word of the authorities. They told us that we should leave revenge marriage. The authorities told us that we should buy [wives] but then the Uduks refused to buy-and-sell. A few here and there bought women to marry, as you do in your country . . .'

The old lady's moral repugnance at the idea of buying people was matched by her realistic opinion that it doesn't work anyway. Her views echo the standard cry of Uduk people when asked why they don't want bridewealth: 'Are we to sell our girl as if she were a goat or something?'

The principle of natural continuity through the female line, which the Uduk share at least with the Komo, gives women such value that their loss cannot with honour be compensated by anything else. They cannot be used as the objects of what might be called *yol* in Uduk, that is commercial transaction. If their loss is to be compensated at all, it must be through the substitution of another woman. This is what might be designated *wan* in Uduk, or *wada* in Komo with all the connotations of mutuality between equals that it carries. If the northern Uduk ever gave up a practice akin to the exchange system of the other Koman peoples, they have refused to replace that exchange system with bridewealth payment, on the same reasoning that the exchange system itself is frequently defended. A woman, said a Gumuz friend in Ethiopia who had never heard of the Uduk, is not a packet of soap to be bought in the market-place: and that is why we exchange them, one for another. With the likely abandonment of exchange marriage among the ancestors of the northern Uduk, there could very plausibly have been a general reversion for practical purposes to the 'natural' line of descent through women; later rationalization and elaboration could well have produced the systematic matrilineally structured way of thinking which I have described for the northern Uduk.

I have spent some time giving an outline of the place of exchange marriage among the Koman peoples and among the southern Uduk in particular because the northern Uduk system of marriage and 'descent', although superficially different, is at heart based on the same principles as those underlying exchange marriage. The circumstantial evidence is very strong that 'the northern Uduk' before they arrived in their present homeland, possibly before they had been severely fragmented, and had subsequently assimilated many lost souls and ex-slaves, *did* practise a form of exchange like that of the Komo and Ganza, and though giving it up yet retained its logical and moral premisses. Past demographic and political conditions make it highly likely that this is what has happened.

MAYA'S STORY

I met an old lady, Maya, in a hamlet near Jebel Bisho in 1969 (not the same Maya as the Gurunya specialist mentioned in the previous chapter). Her story, not atypical, illustrates the conditions through which the modern society of the Komo and Uduk peoples has passed. Maya, who was probably about 70 years old, did not know the names of either of her parents. She did not even know the group, or even the people from which her father came. She knew, however, that her mother was from the Aru (that is, the Komo of Yabus Bridge, some of whom live on the Daga). Her mother took refuge with others on the summit of Jebel Bisho during the late nineteenth-century troubles, and was later captured by the 'Bunyan' raiders, who had beseiged the mountain. She was pregnant, and gave birth to Maya in captivity at 'Kujul's place' (probably at Bade, or some other centre in the domain of Assosa, nominally under the control of Khogali Hassan). Her mother managed to escape, and died soon after. A woman called 'Pencwa looked after Maya, and brought her away from Kujul's place. Some of her sisters, and her mother's brothers, remained there, but she has lost contact with them.

She then married a southern Uduk man of the Lake (whose father belonged to the Ganza 'clan' of Gashu) and gave birth to a number of children, some of whom died and one of whom, an adult man, is still living with her. Her first husband died, and she married a second. He was a Meban, who first came to the area as a boy, on a visit. He returned to his Meban home, but appears to have been an outcast of sorts, for there he was chased away by his brothers for bothering their wives. So he returned to the Bisho area and married Maya, without paying any bride-wealth, and later died. She still has one living son by him.

Although Maya was a Komo girl, her first marriage did not form part of an exchange, because she had no brothers, and had lost touch with the rest of her relatives. She was looked after by an Uduk woman; this situation is what is known as 'protection', and is the foundation of what may later become a recognized *abas* relationship. I believe Maya regards herself as Ḵamus or southern Uduk today, having been brought up by an Uduk woman, although her own mother was Komo and she doesn't know who her father was. She speaks Uduk and Ganza, but I believe she does not know Komo. The second marriage is very interesting in that the Meban husband, possibly very poor, was able to find a haven with an Uduk widow, although he was rejected by his own community. It is relevant to note that in the case of both marriages, one with an Uduk/Ganza man and one with a Meban, no reciprocation was made, and the children in both cases are classed as Uduk, and grew up with the mother. The Meban husband however left his mark behind, for he insisted that his eldest son, the one still surviving, should bear his own name, which is not the Uduk custom.

Maya's sons, having no sisters, were unable to make exchange marriages, and their children therefore 'belong' to their mothers.

This case illustrates how the fragmentation of families caused by political disturbance and the flight of refugees may result in the formation of 'matrifocal' groups, especially where marriage relations are fairly casual, and not reciprocated. In particular, the maintenance of a system of marriage by direct exchange of women becomes impossible when people lose contact with their relatives, and there are no stable communities. It is not straining the evidence too far to assume that the disturbance associated with the flight of the first Uduk settlers northwards to the Khors Tombak and Ahmar, perhaps two centuries ago, caused disruption of the ordered pattern of marriage exchanges similar to that caused by the late nineteenth-century troubles and recorded in Maya's story.

THE ORIGINS OF UDUK MATRILINY

It is by no means an uncommon way of thinking about 'kinship' to represent the continuity between mother and child as a natural link, and relationship through women as the basis of a natural community.[2] This appears to be the case with the patrilineal Didinga, for example, described by Andreas Kronenberg;[3] it is implied in the existence of matrilineally-recruited feuding groups among the patrilineal Murle;[4] and further afield, it seems to provide the fundamental principle of Tiv kinship.[5] In these examples, the principle of natural connection through a mother, her daughter and daughter's daughter is overlaid by those repeated transactions which take place over the women and their children or potential children; where bridewealth, as among the Didinga and Murle, or a sister as among the traditional Tiv, is exchanged for the fertility of a woman, the natural line of matrilineal connection is broken up, and 'patrilineal corporate groups' based on the property, rights and duties of those who have acquired the woman, are built up. It is possible, given this way of looking at kinship and descent,

[2] This idea is discussed in my essay 'Matrifocus on African women' (1978).
[3] See Kronenberg and Kronenberg, 1972.
[4] See Lewis, 1972, esp. pp. 107–8.
[5] See particularly East, 1939.

to represent patriliny as a system constructed through a series of contracts and transactions, for practical and political purposes overriding the natural linkage through women. But consider what typically happens when an individual transaction breaks down or is not fulfilled; if the bridewealth does not materialize, or if there is a divorce, the wife will be called back home, with her children perhaps; and these children will be linked through their mother to her descent group. Now it is possible to think in the abstract of a situation in which all transactions over the fertility of a woman are suspended, or made impossible for some reason. The latent principle of natural linkage through women may well be 'uncovered' and become the dominant principle of the kinship system. People will order and rationalize their relationships in matrilineal terms, in the absence of economic-political groups built up by those transactions which fragment the matriline.

I think it very likely that this is what has happened to the northern Uduk, and is happening to the southern Uduk. Given the Uduk attitude to transactions in general, it is clear that if the mutual substitution (*wan*) of one woman for another in marriage became impossible for practical reasons at some point in their history of movement, loss of women and disturbance, a transaction of the bridewealth type, being morally assimilated to the idea of *yol* (barter) would be ruled out. Given assumptions of the natural community of substance between mother and children, an implicit matrilineal principle already taken for granted would become an explicit jural principle in the creation of a new society.

The existence of a 'pocket' of matriliny on the ethnographic map is therefore not as odd as it may appear. If matriliny is thought of not as a thing, opposed as a system to patriliny, but as a principle, dormant in very many systems of thought about kinship, it may be brought to the surface by historical circumstances in one locality or another without requiring special explanation as an anomaly. Mary Douglas has suggested that matriliny is more flexible and less likely to be disposed of by history than had been previously thought; and the Uduk evidence confirms her general argument.[6] It offers an illustration of the circumstances in which a matrilineal system has

6 See Douglas, 1969.

probably originated: but perhaps the notion of 'origins' is not the most apt. The notion of 'survival', as with Uduk myth, is again more apt; through the circumstances of a history which has threatened the existence of the people, the matrilineal idea which was formerly a part of natural philosophy but of little practical or political relevance, came to be the means whereby, in theory and in practice, the people were able to survive political defeat, and, almost, social extermination. Their victory is echoed in such rituals as that of the Gurunya, where the natural fertility of women, and their central place in the village and the home, is celebrated.

I have already given an indication of the demographic and political condition of Uduk country in the late nineteenth century. Whatever may have been the state of their society in the earlier part of the last century, and it is very likely that the basic principles, in particular of matrilineality, were already well established, the factors which had caused their original differentiation from the other Koman peoples were intensified. Once again the people were made refugees, and in addition many were enslaved. There was a severe shortage of women, and of children.

Since the pacification of the region in 1904, the establishment of an administrative centre at Kurmuk in 1910, and the final inquiry which virtually eliminated slave trading on the Ethiopian border at Kosti in 1927,[7] the practical significance of the principle of matriliny, and of the groupings based upon it, has certainly increased. The imaginative and experiential relevance of socially close association through women, in peacetime, has also been intensified. I have explained in a previous chapter how settlements became far more dispersed, and more strictly 'matrilineal', with the establishment of *pax Britannica*, and how it is no longer necessary to go on living with your father until a late age because of the real possibility of having to fight at his side. With the increasing dispersal of smaller and smaller matrilineal hamlets, away from the hills which formerly were their protective and fatherly focus, marriage patterns have become more dispersed; former tendencies to endogamy within the hill communities, which helped to define the common paternal allegiances of children, have been loosened. At the

[7] See Arkell, 1928.

same time, relative peace has led to greater prosperity; more time has been spent on cultivation, and though large herds and flocks were lost during the disturbed periods of the past, during the present century, on the whole, people have been building them up again. In the period since the Second World War, they have also had the benefit of government and mission aid in the medical and agricultural fields. The population has been slowly but steadily expanding. With demographic and economic expansion, it has been in the main the local residential and co-operating community of the matrilineal hamlet which has been strengthened, in economic and political terms. Present conditions of peace and production, saving and spending, give greater practical structural importance to the matrilineally based group, whereas past conditions of insecurity and military readiness constituted the practical imperatives for the gathering of these small and defenceless groups around a common political and coterminously patrilateral focus, in the larger hill communities.

The establishment of law and order has paradoxically had another effect on the strengthening of ties within the matrilineal birth-group. This is again through the inhibition on violent action, even by a husband in response to adultery. The marriage tie is weaker, I believe, than formerly, because people can get away with adultery more easily than before; husbands are not so much to be feared, because they themselves are 'afraid of the government' and are unlikely to retaliate with violence. A weaker marriage tie, as I have described already, means stronger reliance by a brother and sister on each other. A man who can no longer exert much control over his marriage or an errant wife by the threat of force will find that he must rely increasingly on his sisters to provide beer and food for the cultivation of his fields. By implication, the ties between a man and his sister's children have also become stronger; and conversely, the authority of the father over his children has become more attenuated, and the relationship between them has taken on a more purely voluntary moral character.

Relations between demographic expansion, marriage, and matriliny work in several ways. From one interesting point of view, that of mixed marriages with other peoples around them, the Uduk, as a matrilineal society not requiring the payment of bridewealth at marriage, appear to act as a kind of ethnic sponge. Most mixed marriages involving Uduk appear to result in ethnic recruitment. The bridewealth-paying, 'patrilineal' groups with whom the Uduk occasionally intermarry, or have fertile liaisons, include the Berta, Cogo (a group probably of mixed Berta-Uduk origin anyway), Jum Jum, Meban, and scattered merchant families of northern Sudanese descent. Liaisons between the nomadic Arabs or Fellata, and the settled Uduk or their neighbours, are however very rare. In any mixed marriage, the affiliation of the children, and the right or obliga- tion to give them a home and look after them, arise from the circumstances of marriage payments. It is usually accepted on all sides that where bridewealth payments are made, the children should belong to the father; and where they are not, to the mother. Thus, for example, the children of an Uduk woman and a Meban father are said to be Uduk if no bridewealth was paid, but Meban if it was paid; and those of a Meban woman and Uduk man are Meban if no payment was made, but Uduk if it was. In theory, this looks a balanced situation; in practice, the net effect is a demographic gain to the Uduk people. This is because in very few cases is an Uduk man able to set up house with a Meban (or Berta or Jum Jum) woman, even a widow or divorcée, without being expected to pay bridewealth; and when this has been done the children are primarily 'his'. On the other hand, it is easy for outside men to set up house with Uduk women, if the women are willing; and no bridewealth is demanded. A few merchants do pay bridewealth for Uduk wives, and bring up their children as 'Bunyan'; but on the whole, when the union is this way round, the majority of children born remain with the Uduk woman, and are brought up as Uduk, especially when their father leaves, or their mother returns home to Udukland after living away with her foreign husband for a few years. Appendix 5 contains some detailed information on cases of this kind, and gives an undeniable picture of the demographic advantage to the Uduk of mixed unions. It was easier to find cases of mixed unions involving Uduk women than the rare cases involving Uduk men; the lowly position of the Uduk in the regional social hierarchy partly explains this. Most of those Uduk men who do manage to establish relationships with Berta or Meban women are of relatively high standing in the eyes of the outside world, such as sheikhs; and in most of these cases, bridewealth must be paid. On the other hand, access to Uduk women is much easier for foreign men, who may often regard them as temporary mistresses, rather than as wives, and of course they are not asked for bridewealth or other recompense by the woman's family, as they might be by peoples other than the Uduk. In both typical situations, the children grow up mainly with their Uduk parent, speak Uduk, and are classed as Uduk.

This material on the present-day processes of community expansion through marriage with outsiders echoes themes of traditional history and myth. The Uduk view of the past emphasizes the continuity and growth of the community through women, in times of peace; if an Uduk woman has children by an outsider, the community has naturally swelled; and if a man 'buys' a foreign woman, she and her children are assimilated just as many outsiders have been assimilated by richer, protecting birth-groups in the past. A man married to an Uduk woman 'for nothing', or a woman married 'for money' by an Uduk man, would not actually be called a *çiŋkina/*, but the analogy is not out of place. The *'kwanim pa* as a whole, as well as individual birth-groups (particularly the main Uduk birth-group, the Lake) and the territorial clusters, have expanded both through natural proliferation and through patronage over and absorption of outsiders; and these twin processes are matched today by the two modes of intermarriage with non-*'kwanim pa*.

In the beginning, say the northern Uduk today, the original village community of women was able to reproduce itself, to generate fresh life and grow, through bringing in the Gurunya, the male *çiŋkina/* creature of the bush. This theme is more than a fantasy, an arbitrary product of the cultural imagination. Among the northern Uduk, out of the vicissitudes of past migrations and encounters, a new society, dominantly matrilineal in thought and practice, has been formed from scattered fragments, from uprooted individuals and scraps of tradition. The Gurunya tale is emblematic. The elaborate cult of the Gurunya children, which makes each raw infant, bereaved at birth, into a whole person, is a collective 'work of art' fashioned from the actual memories and experience of the northern Uduk. In its own way it truly reflects and preserves that experience, and corresponds to the 'facts' of northern Uduk history as they can be put together by the academic investigator. Indeed this 'work of art' gives those facts their prime significance.

APPENDIX 1: NOTES ON THE UDUK LANGUAGE

The 'Uduk' language (*'twam pa*, speech of the homeland) is not mutually intelligible with any other language. Recognized by early observers as being a distinct language (Pirrie, see Waterston, 1908; Chataway, 1927; Evans-Pritchard, 1932), Uduk was grouped with Koma, Ganza, Mao, and Gumuz by Tucker and Bryan, which they suggested was perhaps an 'isolated language group' and to which they gave the name 'Koma'. Greenberg (1963) added the Gule language to this group, and used the term 'Koman' or sometimes 'Coman' to refer to this branch of his 'Nilo-Saharan' category. The structure of this grouping of languages is shown in the diagram, and suggests the historical distinctiveness of the Koman-speaking peoples:

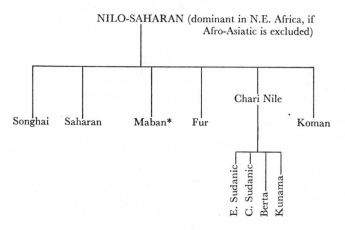

CHARACTERISTICS OF THE LANGUAGE

Robin Thelwall has pointed out to me that the Uduk language is of particular phonemic interest, since it combines the contrast of implosion/explosion at the same place of articulation, in two cases. The range of consonants in the language is unusually full and complete, though the vowel sounds are relatively few. This is in contrast to the Nilotic languages, for example.

All the consonantal phonemes are embodied in the system of orthography devised by the Sudan Interior Mission at Chali, and

* This is not the Nilotic Meban language referred to in this study.

used in the 1956 Dictionary. I have followed this system, which may be summarized in the following table:

	Labial	Inter-dental	Alveolar	Palato-alveolar	Palatal	Velar	Glottal
Voiceless	p	th	t		c	k	
Aspirated	p̱	ṯẖ	ṭ		c̱	ḵ	
Voiced	b	dh	d		j	g	
Ejective (explosive)	'p	'th	't		'c	'k	
Injective (implosive)	'b		'd				
Nasal	m		n		ny	ŋ	
Lateral			l				
Rolled			r				
Fricative			s	sh			h
Semi-vowel	w				y		

The glottal stop, occurring in the middles or ends of words only, is written /.

The vowels are written in the S.I.M. system i, e, a, o, u. Occasionally a letter is doubled, as in *uni iiyin* (they come); but this usage may imply emphasis, phonetic lengthening or heightened tone rather than a different vowel phoneme. However Dr Stevenson, who did not have the opportunity to consult native Uduk speakers but worked with information supplied by Mr. and Mrs. Forsberg, distinguishes ten vowels in his 'Grammar', as shown in the diagram.

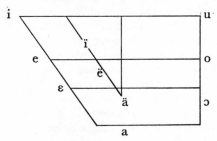

In the S.I.M. Dictionary, the five symbols used correspond to Stevenson's ten vowels as follows:

$$i - i, ï$$
$$e - e, \varepsilon, ë$$
$$a - a, ä$$
$$o - o, ɔ$$
$$u - u$$

The vowel system however awaits final clarification.

Tone is significant in the language; Stevenson writes (*ibid.*, p. 2). 'This is a fully fledged tone language, and intonation plays a large part lexically and morphologically.' Tone is not indicated in the S.I.M. orthography for connected texts (such as the New Testament), but in the Dictionary each entry is followed by a description of its pattern in terms of three tones, indicated thus: ., -, '.

Stevenson (*ibid.*, p. 1) suggests that Uduk has most of the characteristics of a 'Sudanic' language as defined by Westermann and Tucker. He notes, in evidence, that the etymological roots are largely monosyllabic; that syllables consist of vowel, consonant plus vowel, or consonant plus vowel plus consonant, and that 'the main character of the language is isolating, as particles are widely used to determine grammatical categories. A few prefixes are used, but there is no internal vowel change.' In his summary of the morphological characteristics of the language, he includes the following points: there is no grammatical gender, no case in nouns, and with a few exceptions (usually persons) no plural form of nouns. Nouns, verbs, and adjectives may often be formed from the same root, thus (my example):

from the root *'per* (red), itself an adjective, we may construct such forms as the following: *mom'per*—a red place, redness
'pera'per—very red, adj.
'pere'd—3rd person singular of verb, 'it reddens'.

Adjectives are often formed by reduplicating a stem, as in the example above. Ideophones are common, and make full use of the rich array of consonants in the language.

The sound of spoken Uduk is crisp, rhythmic, and musical, with its sharp monosyllables, precisely contrasted tones, implosives, and explosives. Speakers often employ emphatic exclamations, or long-drawn-out expressions of surprise or dismay. Conversation, and particularly the telling of stories or anecdotes, is much enjoyed. In the course of conversation, various styles are employed: for example, in an intimate group speaking rapidly and informally, many words may be elided and abbreviated, in the way that *is it not* becomes *isn't it* in English. This way of speaking is called *'bor 'twa/ e mis*, 'lifting the speech up'. It is not readily understood by those who are not native speakers. A special style is used in the abusive exchanges which take place between those who are licensed to 'joke'; *asor*, 'joking', is characterized by short, direct comments shorn of grammatical niceties; thus, *e ki 'per*! This could be translated 'Red eyes!' The normal statement 'Your eyes are red' might be *em pini tam 'per*. Storytelling employs yet another style, often using a historical narrative tense throughout. In addition to these spoken forms of the language, we may mention songs, and also the formal style used in the context of Church affairs in Chali, and the written style of the New Testament and other Biblical material. Most of the texts used in this book are spoken in the straightforward style.

Three dialects of Uduk are locally recognized, corresponding to the three main areas into which the Uduk are geographically divided. The two northern dialects, in Bellila on the Ahmar and the Chali area on the Tombak, are very close and there is scarcely any problem of mutual understanding. The difference is primarily that of accent. In Belatoma on the Khor Yabus, however, and further south towards Jebel Bisho, the dialect is markedly different. Many of the consonants are softened (for example, th becomes s, and dh becomes z), the vowels and tones sound less precise and sharp, and the language to an English ear has a flowing 'West Country' effect. There are substantial differences of vocabulary and word usage. A visitor from Chali, new to the southern dialect, has to enquire about the meaning of several words he hears, and others provoke discussion.

Except where stated otherwise, the dialect used in this study is that of the central (Chali) area.

Figures 1 and 2 suggest the range of languages with which the Uduk come in contact, and which some of them can speak. In addition, most Uduk speak a certain amount of colloquial Arabic, especially men, through contact with nomad Arabs, merchants, and police. Those who received education at the Chali S.I.M. station speak some English. People show great enjoyment in their command of other tongues; a couple of friends will often exchange witty remarks in Jum Jum, Meban, or Berta in the middle of a general Uduk conversation, to the confusion and delight of everyone else. People often teach each other foreign words, and my interest in the Uduk language was matched by the interest my friends showed in English.

I append two sample texts below, in the vernacular with a close interlinear translation. The first is an example of narrative style in the telling of a well-known tale, the free translation of which appears on pp. 68–9 above. The second is an example of Uduk style in explanation and exegesis, the type of text I have used extensively in the book as evidence for my account of Uduk opinion and belief. The free translation of this text appears on pp. 150–1, above.

1. The Birapinya Tree, as told by Tente. *Recorded in Waka'cesh, February 1966. Transcribed by Shadrach Peyko Dhunya and translated by him and W.J.*

Aris 'kwani iin 'peni monycesh mmosa barangu mun, dhali a'boma kamu/
Many people went from earth to-dance barangu there, and woman certain
nyang gu'bi shemen bway dhali a'di 'cok maa o'd. A'di ki woth nyara 'kup,
built hut beside path and she cooked food on-fire. She called-girls-back,
kana! nyara! iiyu rica garis, waa. Dhali nyara ki o a'di ki, egeh! ana
'You! Girls! Come grind okra, oh.' And girls said to-her, 'Eh! We
mina timini nyith washan e be. Kun tiya dok/e iiyini 'ko'd, a'di ki o ki,
shall to-others lose boyfriends.' Some others again came later, she said,
kana! nyara! iiyu rica garis, waa. Dhali nyara ki o a'di ki, egeh! ana
'You! Girls! Come grind okra, oh.' And girls said to-her, 'Eh! We
mina timini nyith washan e be. Dhali kun tiya dok/e iiyu be.
shall to-others lose boyfriends.' And some others again came.
A'di ki o uni ki, kana nyara iiyu rica garis, waa. Egeh! ana mina timini
She said to-them, 'You girls come grind okra, oh.' 'Eh! We shall to-others
nyith washan e be. Dhali jaŋ kamu/ bese/ din ma kam mmosus 'ko'd ti,
lose boyfriends. And one other at-last was by brother being-led later they-say,
dhali uni ki iiyu uni su/ besene/. Dhali a'di ki o ki jasi um gwansan
and they came they two at-last. And she said 'Just you those-people
iiyin 'ko'd um su/ san iiyu rica garis. Dhali uni ki ha gwo e mo tani
coming last you two there come grind okra. And they agreed-talk and-then
uni ii rica garis mo. Uni ki 'cok maa mo, maa ki is mo tani
they went to-grind okra. They cooked food, food became ready and-then
uni non maa mo. Uni ki shwa maa uni ki 'thur me'd mo tani uni ki ii mo.
they served food. They ate food they washed hands and-then they went.
A'bom ki o uni ki, iiyi san, dhalku/ ki ii 'koyu ki rash-rash.
Woman said to-them, 'Go then, don't go and-stay very-long.
Aha/ mina epa birapinya mo shunsan ba/. Uni cik gwo tani
I am-going to-burn Birapinya now.' They heard words and-then
sayu ari'cene/ tani la doku mo ka nyaŋ'ko'd. Dhali 'kwani bese/ saya
danced a little and-then early returned very-soon. And people still danced
barangu ti ki rash-rash-rash. Uni ki kapu sa mo tani iiyu besene/.
the barangu they-say a very-very-long-time. They were satisfied with-dancing and-then they came at-last.
Gamka birapinya epkina a'di mo. Dhali uni bese/ ki dot gwo ti ki,
They-found Birapinya burnt-by her. And they then asked questions it-is-said,

ayy! kana bway mane? Bway ti piyi'd mo ti tiyan tiya ti ki o gwo ti ki,
'*Oh! well our path is where?*' *Path they-said was-gone they-said some others then said,*

kana iikina mo 'te. Adhan bway ti di'd mo niin ti. Poshkina mo 'te
'*Let us go nevertheless.*' *Broad path they-said is there they-said.* '*Let us jump nevertheless*

isi dhan mo yin cabki kwany-kwany niin mana. Dhan ji gi turatur ti
to-there big place appearing very-very-open there.' *Big one who-was very-tall they-say*

ki la posh mo ntwa/a/ ma ya ya 'ce'd bwa mo ti ki ta'bur a'cesh.
then immediately jumped first went went broke in-middle they-say scattered on-ground.

Jaŋ kamu/ ti ki dok̲/e bathki a'di sho'k ya 'ce'd bwa a'cesh unis u/ ntwa/a/.
Another they-say again followed him in-footsteps went broke in-middle on-ground they two first.

Ari jamu jim kutakut ti ki mam dhana kamu/ jin turatur apo.
Small one who-was very-short they-say then carried big-one another who-was very-tall on-back.

Uni ki iiyu mo ti ki shuur! i'ko ka jishok ki thup! ŋ'ko ki e mo.
They came they-say shuur! *to-rest upright* thup! *to-remain alive.*

Jamu ki dok̲/e mama kamu/ ti uni ki iiyu ki shuur! thup! uni ki 'ko ki e mo.
One more then again carried another they-say they came shuur! thup! *they then remained alive.*

Dhali jamu ki yayo ŋ'ko'd poshku a'di 'de/ ya 'ce'dku bwa.
And one more then came after jumped-down he alone went broke apart.

Dhali tiyan tiya bese/ ki ushu 'koyu mo mun ti.
And some others then refused remained up-there they-say.

Dhali jamu o gwo ti ki, egeh! aha/ mina diku mo niiya. Dhali tiyan tiya
And another said they-say, 'No! I shall stay here!' And some others

ki cik̲ gwom piti tani uni 'koyu mo mis mun nyanye mis mun 'te/.
heard words his and-then they remained up there very-many up there just-so.

2. Comments on fatherhood, by William Danga. *Recorded in Wak̲a'cesh, June 1968. Transcribed by Shadrach Peyko Dhunya, translated by W.J.*

Dhali 'pen ma'dan, ibabam pini mini miiya nyori mun, /e mini mii,
And [if] from there, fathers yours will make hostilities there, you must,

/e mini mii, wak̲ki /e dini ibabam pini mun /e mini mii, /e mini mii
you must, whether you live-with fathers yours there you must, you must

wakki /e dini ibabam pini mun wakki /e dini ishwakim pini mun,
whether you live-with fathers yours or-whether you live-with mother's brothers yours there,
dhali anyor di'di mun, /e mini ya mun mmo/asi nyakki ibabam pini be.
and hostilities are there, you must go there to-fight together-with fathers yours.
Gom ibabam pini hil /e ki /e tana ara ŋa/. Ta'dam pini thip /e
For fathers yours look-after you while you are a small baby. Mother yours rears you
ki to ma babam pini. /E pi yim'batha'd. Ta'dam pini pi yim'batha'd
on things of father yours. You drink hot-water. Mother yours drinks hot-water
gom /e dhali 'ce'da ko. Eŋ gu'b pa babam pini be.
for you and to-fill breasts. In house at-home-of father yours.
/E ki piya ko besene/, 'peni to gi shwana a'di 'peni gu'b ma babam pini.
You then drink milk at-last, from things which ate she from house of father yours.
Babam pini ki thip /e, thip /e tagi /e ki ya ca mo besene/.
Father yours then rears you, rears you until you then go and-grow-up at-last.
/E mini misha shwakim pini mmoya shwa to mun ki jahanne/ yisa.
You will know mother's-brother yours to go and-eat things there immediately not.
/E mini ça'b e babam pini, wakka babam pini en /e ki sule/,
You will stay with father yours, and-if father yours loves you for long,
/e mini ca'b kani ya ta washan ki sule/, sule/, sule/,
you will stay like-that and-become young man [staying] on, and on, and on,
/e ki ya masha 'bom e uni kan be.
you then will-go marry a wife while-among them like that.
Wakki /e mini o ki ça'b e ibabam pini, /e ki ça'b e uni kani
If you wish to-stay with fathers yours, you can stay with them like that
ya ta washan mo. Masha 'bom /e ki nyaŋ gu'bi uni mahan. I ibabam pini mahan.
and-become young man. Marry a wife you then build hut with them there. With fathers yours there.
Tagi yil gi nna bwa o /e ki /e ŋapani ya paŋ 'kwanim pini besene/,
Until the-time when you feel that you want* to-go to-home of people yours at-last,
/e ki dhal /e ki ya ça'bi 'kwanim pini mun. Dhal /e ki ya bway
you then you go and-stay-with people yours there. And you then go on-path-to
pa ibabam pini tani, me'd yilkina/, uni 'cithki /e mi mo.
home-of fathers yours then, like a guest, they will cut-for you a goat.
Uni ki 'cithki /e mi, /e ki 'ka. Dhali wakki ibabam pini
They will cut-for you a goat, you will eat. And if fathers yours
bipa kamu/ cacaa, dhana rasim bip cacaayi, ŋapuni 'kosh mo, tani,
beast certain-one large, great male bull enormous, they want to-kill, then,

* literally, 'when your stomach (*bwa*) tells you that you want . . .'

nna uni 'kosh uni 'cena yisa. Uni ki ii tuli uçim buni is 'peni mun,
will they kill by-themselves not. They will go gather children theirs from there,
ihashi uçi. O ki dhal uçi iiyin. Uçi ki iiyu, uni ki 'kosh ka me'd buni
   yisa.
*send-for children. Saying let the children come. Children come, [but] they then
   kill with hand theirs not.*
Uni ki owa 'ciŋ kamu/ ki: /E a'di ti mini 'kosh bip jan.
They then say-to child a-certain: 'You are the one to kill bull this.'
Dhala 'ci bese/ ki jep bip ka thurmanyi 'ko'di mahan. Uçim buni gi
   dhotha uni be.
*And child then will chop bull with axe-on back-of-head here. Children theirs
   who were-borne-by them.*
. . . . . . Dhali uni ki 'kosh bip besene/ mon'thamo/ idhal 'ka besene/,
. . . . . . *And they will kill bull then in-morning and-then eat at-last,*
nyakki ibabam buni 'baar mo.
together-with fathers theirs all-of-them.

APPENDIX 2: POPULATION DATA

Table A1 is taken from the 1955/6 Census of the Sudan (the Census date for this area was 30 Dec. 1955) and lists the population total for the various Omodiyas of the Kurmuk District and the town of Kurmuk, and breaks the totals down into male and female categories:

Table A1

Omodiya	Total	Males	Females	Masculinity ratio
Regreig	7,495	3,880	3,615	107
Barun	4,975	2,661	2,314	115
Jum Jum	2,246	1,225	1,021	120
Keili	19,069	9,592	9,477	101
Ora	7,091	3,619	3,472	104
Koma	1,725	969	756	128
Uduk	8,300	4,477	3,823	117
Kurmuk Town	1,647	797	850	94
Total for Kurmuk area	52,548	27,220	25,328	107

Figure 2 (p. 9) shows the approximate location of these Omodiyas.

Some implications of the above table, and in particular the masculinity ratios, are discussed in Chapter 1.

Early reports on the area all point to a very sparse population west of the Berta Hills in the early part of the century, and several mention a scarcity of women (see Chapter 2, and James 1968).

According to the 1955/6 Census, the population of the Chali Omodiya was 8,300. This figure of course includes some non-Uduk living in the area; for example, a number of Meban villages are scattered among the Uduk villages along the Yabus, and a number of non-Uduk merchant families and craftsmen live in the Omodiya, especially in Chali. It excludes, on the other hand, a number of Uduk living outside; for example, a substantial number to the south, towards Jebel Bisho, are included in the Koma Omodiya.

In May 1968, with the help of assistants, who sometimes had the use of bicycles, a rough census was carried out for the Omodiya, which included a count of huts. At the same time an intensive census was made of a small population of 393 (of whom six were temporarily absent) who occupied 94 huts. There was therefore an average of 4.2 persons per hut. This figure was used to estimate the population of the Omodiya, though of course the sample area was very small and possibly not typical. However, 2184 huts were counted for the whole Omodiya, which gives a general population estimate of 9,200. The

extreme southern part of Uduk country, which lies anyway within
the Koma Omodiya, was not included in the survey; and I estimate
that if these and other Uduk speakers living outside the Omodiya
were included, the number would be in the region of 10,000. These
figures tally quite well with those of the Census; there appears to
have been a slight increase since 1956, but not a marked one.

The distribution of the population between the three main settlement areas is indicated by the hut survey; 19 per cent were recorded
in the Bellila area, on the Ahmar; 58 per cent in the central area, on
the Tombak; and 23 per cent in the Belatoma area, in the Yabus
valley. When speaking of the 'northern Uduk', I therefore refer to a
a population of at least 7,000 (1,700 on the Ahmar and 5,300 on the
Tombak); and in speaking of the 'southern Uduk' a population of
some 2,500–3,000, if allowance is made for those living outside the
Omodiya.

The material in Tables A2 and A3 which follow resulted from the
1968 surveys, as did the information for the settlement map (Figure
4, p. 26) and the table of birth-groups and their distribution by
region (Figure 7, pp. 179–80).

Table A2   Number of Huts and Hamlets per Sheikh (1968)

Area	Sheikh	Hamlets	Huts	Total Huts by Area
Chali	Yelo	9	84 ⎫	
	Muṭ	17	152* ⎭	312
Pam'Be	O'dime'd	41	243	243
Bigin	Gambi	5	26	26
Yilejada ⎫	Abdalla	4	33 ⎫	
and Wana E ⎭	Limpo	5	29 ⎭	62
Beni Mayu	Limpo	8	48 ⎫	
	Ḳa'bko	13	99 ⎭	147
Puduom	Utha	7	56	
Gwami	Gima	15	146 ⎫	
Borpa	Labib	11	143 ⎬	492
Gindi	Abdalla	16	147 ⎭	
Bellila	Zaid	29	168 ⎫	
	Gambi Said	7	50	
	'Bathko	6	40	
	Hathaṭ	8	36 ⎬	411
	Dhuna	10	47	
	Gambi	10	70 ⎭	
Belatoma	Wad-el-fil	57	248 ⎫	
	Puna	13	107 ⎬	491
	Ilo	11	49	
	Gilo	18	87 ⎭	
No. of Sheikhs: 19	*Total Huts for Omodiya:*			2,184

Some Sheikhs occur more than once in the table because their areas do not
correspond with the given territorial divisions.

* This includes 47 in the Market Village and 29 in the Church Village.

Appendices

Table A3.   Household Census, Pany Caran, Waka'cesh, and Kalagorko, May 1968

Hamlet Number	Huts Occupied	Huts Empty	Total Population	Males	Females	Male Household Heads	Female Household Heads
1	4	—	15	6	9	3	1
2	7	4	44	21	23	7	—
3	8	—	32	14	18	6	2
4	4	—	19	7	12	3	1
5	7	2	37	13	24	5	2
6	3	1	14	10	4	3	—
7	3	1	10	3	7	2	1
8	7	—	26	10	16	3	4
9	7	—	26	13	13	7	—
10	3	1	22	9	13	3	—
11	3	—	14	7	7	2	1
12	7	—	25	16	9	4	3
13	3	1	15	9	6	3	—
14	3	—	10	4	6	3	—
15	7	1	25	12	13	5	2
16	6	1*	26	10	16	4	2
17	5	—	25	10	15	5	—
18	2	—	2	1	1	1	1
TOTALS	89	12	387	175	212	69	20

Notes

1. The figure for male population excludes 6 absent labour migrants. If these are included, the sex ratio is approximately 0.85.
2. There is a discrepancy between the total number of huts recorded for these hamlets in the survey for Table A2, and those recorded by Abdel Ghaffar Mohammed for this Table. This is due to the dilapidated state of some of the empty huts, not all of which were counted for Tables A2 and A3. Taking the figure for the total huts of the sample area in the preceding survey (94) and using it to divide into the total population here recorded of 393, an average figure of about 4.2 persons per hut is obtained.
3. Multiplying the total number of huts recorded for the whole Omodiya in the preceding survey (2,184) by 4.2, an approximate estimate of the total population is obtained, of nearly 9,200.

* Occupied by W.J.

APPENDIX 3: GENEALOGY AND RESIDENCE IN A HAMLET OF WAK̲A'CESH (FOR MID-1966)

The hamlet is marked on the sketch-map in Figure 5, p. (29). The diagram illustrates the layout of the hamlet, and the letters identifying the huts correspond to the list of inhabitants which follows. The people in this hamlet fall into two groups, each clustered around one old lady. These ladies, Umpa and Dwarke, are regarded as grandmothers of those in the hamlet, and they are regarded as 'sisters'. However, as the genealogies show, they are not even first cousins, and the genealogical connection between them has been forgotten. Genealogical memories are short, and it is said that many relatives of the mothers of Umpa and Dwarke were lost at the time of trouble (at the end of the last century). But although the memory of relationship does not extend far into the past, links with others of the same local *wak̲* (birth-group), who share the same rights over cattle, rainstones etc., who have the same debt obligations and who share the same rule of exogamy and the same blood-friendships with other local birth-groups, are remembered. There are close relatives of this kind living scattered far over Uduk country, partly because this birth-group was broken up at the time of a smallpox scare in Chali in the late 1930s, and various members went their different ways (see the account in Chapter 6, above). Some are now in Bellila, some in the Yabus valley, and some in the village of Deim, in Bunyan country south of Kurmuk.

The genealogies, though obviously not showing every child born, do give a hint of the heavy loss of infant life. Some of the children who died did not even have names, others' names had been forgotten, and I did not like to pursue this sort of question with the parents themselves. The name 'Gurunya' occurs in characteristic situations.

Each genealogy represents the known descendants (not only in the female line) of a particular female forebear, the earliest whose name is remembered in her line. Each includes information derived from two or three informants. On the genealogies, those people resident in the hamlet are indicated by italics and a number of corresponding to the list of residents. The genealogies are arranged vertically to save space, the chronological sequence of siblings proceeding from the top and working downwards. A series of marriages is indicated by a sequence of = signs, in chronological order from the top. Solid black symbols precede the names of those who died before 1966, and open symbols for those who were living. The triangle stands for a male and the circle for a female, while squares indicate that the sex was not known by my informants. A question mark indicates that the name was unknown or not given.

The hamlet was first established in 1965, and in 1966, with 14 huts, was at its maximum size. In 1967 and 1968 it began to break up into smaller units as people moved off to rebuild on nearby sites.

Further material for five more hamlets may be found in my unpublished D.Phil. thesis (James, 1970).

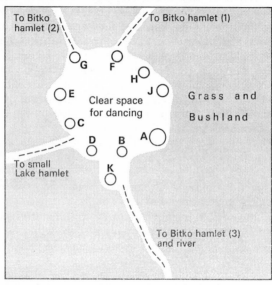

The main Lake hamlet of Waka'cesh, 1966

LIST OF HOUSEHOLD HEADS AND OTHER RESIDENTS

Hut Number	Household Head and Others Resident
A	1. Umpa (*old lady: see Genealogy I*).
	2. Her daughter
	3. Daughter's husband (*occasionally*)
	4.
	5. } Granddaughters of Umpa—daughters of A2
	6.
	7.

LIST OF HOUSEHOLD HEADS AND OTHER
RESIDENTS—*Continued*

Hut Number	*Household Head and Others Resident*
	8. Another granddaughter, by a different daughter of Umpa
	9. Grandson
B	1. Umpa's daughter's son
	2. His wife
C	1. Umpa's son
	2. His wife
D	1. Umpa's son's son
	2. His wife
E	1. Another wife of D1 (*temporarily absent*)
F	1. Dwarke (*old lady, 'sister' of Umpa: see Genealogy II*)
	2. Her daughter
	3.⎫ Granddaughters of Dwarke, daughters of F2
	4.⎭
	5. Son of another daughter
	6. Daughter of another daughter
G	1. Dwarke's sister's son
	2. His wife
	3.⎫
	4.⎪ Her daughters
	5.⎪
	6.⎭
H	1. Dwarke's son
	2. His wife
	3.⎫ Her daughters from a previous marriage
	4.⎭
J	1. Another wife of H1
	2. Son
	3. Daughter
K	1. Dwarke's son (*new wife due to arrive*)

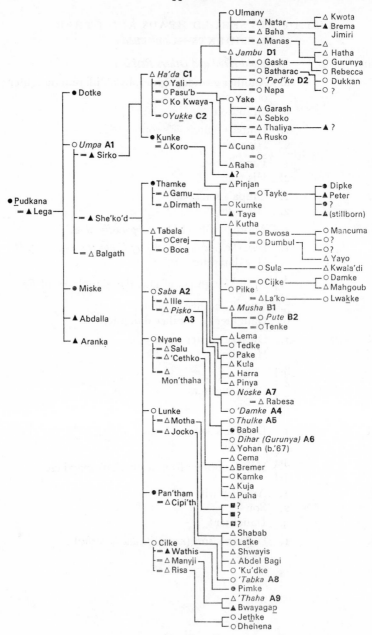

Genealogy I

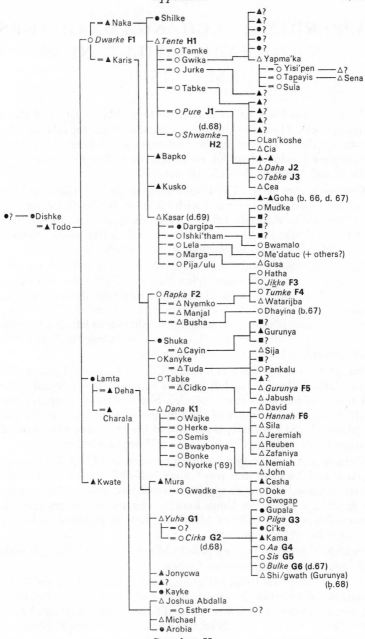

Genealogy II

APPENDIX 4: EXCHANGE MARRIAGES IN THE PABA HAMLET, NEAR JEBEL BISHO

Paba is a small hamlet, of only three huts (May 1969) and about eight people. Their genealogies, as shown, indicate the relationships between those involved in the exchanges listed below. A pair of marriages conducted as an exchange, or rather as 'revenge', is numbered A and B; thus 1A, 1B, 2A, 2B, etc.

Exchange 1. Two pairs of Uduk full siblings involved. Shwana took the initiative, and after one night with his bride, her brother came and took away Bikule. But she left him before giving birth to any children, and later Kodke left Shwana, *taking away all the three children* she had borne him (although, unfortunately, they all died later).

Exchange 2. Shwana and Bikule are involved here in an exchange with a Ganza 'brother and sister' (clan Parayo). I am not sure of their exact relationship. Shwana, I believe, again took the initiative, in marrying Bwangu'b (who had been previously married). Her brother came and took Bikule away, who shortly afterwards left him, without bearing any children. Bwangu'b remained for 'a long time', and then left Shwana, taking her children with her.

Attempted exchange 3. Shwana married Ukka, a Ganza girl (Anza clan from father). Two of her full brothers came to abduct Nyanke, the daughter of Shwana's sister (Bikule). She was taken away, but she refused to live with either of the brothers and returned home. The position of Ukka is clear; if she wishes she can leave Shwana and return home with her children, who will be regarded as Ganza.

Exchange 4. An exchange took place between two Uduk full siblings (Mosa and Nyanke) and two Ganza half-siblings (Bomagalla and Late), who were from one mother but different fathers (this suggests a matrifocal family on Uduk lines?). The two marriages are still successful, and the child of Mosa and Late is regarded as Uduk. Nyanke has yet to give birth.

Exchange 5. Between two sets of full siblings, one Uduk (though with 'Pekesh' father) and the other Ganza.

Exchange 6. Between Uduk full siblings (Wada and Kuttu), and 'half-siblings', 'fathered in the same village' (Anza, i.e. Ganza) but from different mothers, and different actual fathers (these two were Yekke and Belel). Yekke is already of ambiguous ancestry (see Exchange 5 above, of her parents).

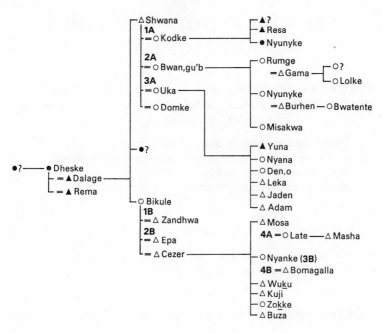

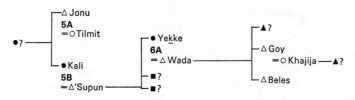

Paba hamlet: Genealogies (May 1969)

APPENDIX 5: NORTHERN UDUK MARRIAGE DATA

(a) Men in sample area in married state during period: 76
     Women in sample area in married state during period: 72
     Adult never-married men: 2
     Adult never-married women: —

         150

(b) No. of marriages recorded for the 76 men in sample: 103
     No. of marriages recorded for the 72 women in sample: 86

         189
     Less overlap where both spouses are in the sample: 31

         Total marriages recorded: 158

(c) *Stability of marriages*

	Valid, June 1969	Terminated by death during period	Terminated by breakdown during period	Don't know
No. of marriages in existence, Jan. 1966	111 66	7	35	3
No. of marriages established during period 1966 to June 1969	47 39	1	7	—
Totals:	158 105	8	42	3

Index of breakdown: $\left\{ \dfrac{\text{No. of weddings in period: } 47}{\text{No. of breakdowns in period: } 42} \right\} = 0.89$

More than five times the number of marriages terminated in breakdown, during the sample period, than terminated by the death of one
of the spouses.

(d) *Cumulative marital history (as of June 1969)*

	No. of times married							No. of wives men currently living with		
	1	2	3	4	5	6	7	0	1	2
Ever-married men in sample (74)*	24	22	12	9	1	5	1	10	56	8
Ever-married women in sample (71)*	32	20	15	3	1	–	–			

2. MIXED MARRIAGE DATA

By asking informants, in a fairly haphazard way, for details of any
marriages they knew of between Uduk and non-Uduk people, I
collected material on 37 cases.[1] Although the sample was not large or
necessarily representative, the patterns revealed were consistent, and
appeared to confirm my hypothesis that in the majority of cases of
mixed marriages, involving either Uduk men or with Uduk women,
the offspring would be classed as Uduk, and be brought up as Uduk
(see pp. 256–8).

Of the 37 marriages, 22 were between Uduk women and non-
Uduk men (8 'Bunyan', 7 Jum Jum, 4 Meban, 3 Cogo, 1 Mufwa
Burun, all of them from 'patrilineal' societies, normally paying bridewealth). In only 4 cases had bridewealth been paid (in one of these
cases it was only a roll of cloth). In 3 cases informants were not sure
whether bridewealth had been paid, and in the remaining 15 no
payment at all had been made. Of the 22 women, 8 were unmarried
girls, and 13 had been married before (informants were uncertain in
one case). The 4 cases in which bridewealth was paid included 2
girls, and 2 previously married women. In 6 cases, therefore, unmarried girls became the wives of outsiders without the payment of
bridewealth.

At the time of the enquiry (1969), children had been born to 3 of

---

* 1 man and 1 woman of the sample had died during the period, and for 1 man
I do not have information.
[1] I am not dealing with marriages to Komo or Ganza here, who do not pay
bridewealth but practise exchange marriage.

the marriages where bridewealth was paid, and in all 3 cases the children were classed as non-Uduk. There were 13 cases where children were born to unions in which no bridewealth had been paid, and in 11 of these the children were classified as Uduk, in 1 case siblings were split, some being regarded as Uduk and others not, and in 1 case, because the children were still living away with their father they were labelled as non-Uduk. Of the 3 cases where informants were not sure whether bridewealth was paid or not, the children were classed as Uduk in 2 cases, and doubt was expressed over the third.

There were 15 cases of marriage between Uduk men and non-Uduk women (the women were 4 'Bunyan'—all local Berta, 4 Meban, 4 Jum Jum, 1 Cogo, 1 Mufwa Burun, and 1 Surkum Burun). Bridewealth was paid in 11 cases (at least 7 were unmarried girls). The 4 cases in which it was not paid include 2 marriages to the same Jum Jum woman; she and the other 2 women in question had all been married previously.

Children were born in 8 cases of the 11 where bridewealth was paid. In 4 of these, the children were definitely Uduk, in 3 it was agreed that their position was ambiguous and one case I could not verify. Of the 2 cases where children were born to Uduk men who had not paid bridewealth, the children were Uduk in one case and non-Uduk in the other.

APPENDIX 6: UDUK RELATIONSHIPS TERMINOLOGY

There is a high proportion of self-reciprocal terms in the Uduk relationship (or 'kinship') terminology. Indeed the only relationships which may not be expressed, in one way or another, by a self-reciprocal term, are the husband–wife, mother–child and opposite sex sibling connections. Typical of other relationships named in the system, is for example, *iya*. This term is used by a man and his 'brother's children' in relation to each other, and by a third party of either in relation to the other. The most economical and precise definition of *iya* is not in terms of genealogically specified statuses but in terms of this relationship. It rests on the Uduk definitions of 'brother' (*akam*) and 'child' (*a'ci*). Once such key terms have been defined, in terms of genealogical positions, they may be used as 'bricks' to build up definitions of the rest. Thus the whole system may be defined in terms of its own first principles. The range of the word *akam* includes half-brothers and parallel cousins on both sides, and *a'ci* covers both male and female children, and therefore it would be tedious to define *iya* in terms of all the genealogical positions it could subsume, in relation to a speaker of each sex.[1] The meaning of the word is more conveniently conveyed by a sentence which could be a direct translation of an Uduk informant's explanation: 'The *akam* of a man and his *a'ci* are *iya*, and call each other *iya*.' The terms of reference in the list which follows are defined as far as possible in this manner.

Northern Uduk Kinship Terms of Reference
(In quotation marks, rough English translation)

No.	Term	Definition
1.	ASH	Wife.
2.	A'BOM	Woman, but may also be used for 'wife'.
3.	KATH ·	Husband.
4.	TA'DA	Mother.
5.	KUM	(his or her) mother; related to *kuman*, 'female'.
6.	DHAN TA'DA	Maternal or paternal grandmother, or grandmother's sister; literally 'great mother'.

[1] Another objection to definition in terms of genealogy is that this is not the exclusive manner in which the terms are applied by Uduk speakers; facts of residence, economic and political ties are equally important criteria.

Northern Uduk Kinship Terms of Reference—Continued
                (In quotation marks, rough English translation)

No.	Term	Definition
7.	DHAN KUM	Maternal or paternal grandmother, or grandmother's sister; literally 'great mother'. Same as No. 6.
8.	ARA TA'DA	mother's 'sister' (*'bwaham*), lit. 'little mother'.
9.	ARIN KUM	*ditto.*
10.	AKAM	Male sibling, half-sibling, or parallel cousin on either side, 'brother'. Self-reciprocal between males.
11.	'BWAHAM	Female sibling, half-sibling, or parallel cousin on either side. Self-reciprocal between females.
12.	BABA	Father (or mother's husband). Also DHAN BABA, grandfather on either side.
13.	COM	(His or her) father, Also DHAN COM, *ditto.*
14.	A'CI	Own child (or child of *'bwaham* for female speaker).
15.	YA/	Own son (or son of *'bwaham* for female speaker).
16.	'BWA/	Own daughter (or daughter of *'bwaham* for female speaker).
17.	DIṬI	Self-reciprocal between a woman and the child of her *akam*. 'Father's sister' and for female speakers 'brother's child' as well.
18.	SO'B	*ditto.*
19.	IYA	Self-reciprocal between a man and the child of his *akam*, or male *'kwaskam*. 'Father's brother' or 'Father's male cross-cousin', and for male speakers 'brother's child' or 'male cross-cousin's child' as well.
20.	SHWAKAM	*Akam* of mother or male *'kwaskam* of mother. 'Mother's brother' or 'mother's male cross-cousin'.
21.	NAM	Reciprocal of No. 20. For male speaker only, child of *'bwaham* or female *'kwaskam*. 'Sister's child' or 'female cross cousin's child'. *Nayid*, 'his *nam*'.
22.	TAṬA	Covers meanings of both No. 20 and No. 21. Self-reciprocal between man and

Northern Uduk Kinship Terms of Reference—Continued
(In quotation marks, rough English translation)

No.	Term	Definition
		child of *'bwaham* or female *'kwaskam*. Less often used.
23.	'KWASKAM	Self-reciprocal between the child of a man and those of his *'bwaham*; 'cross cousin'.
24.	MASE/	Self-reciprocal between a woman's husband or his *akam*, and her *akam* or *'bwaham*.
25.	YASHIM	Self-reciprocal between a man's wife and his *akam* and *'bwaham*.
26.	JIL	Self-reciprocal between two women who are married to men who are *ikam* ('brothers').
27.	MOK̲	Self-reciprocal between a man and a woman married to people who are to each other *akam* and *'bwaham* (i.e. 'siblings of opposite sex').
28.	MUGU	Self-reciprocal between two people married to spouses who are either *ikam*, *ibwaham* or *akam* and *'bwaham* to each other (i.e. 'siblings'). It includes Nos. 26 and 27.
29.	MAR	Self-reciprocal between a person and his or her spouse's *ta'da*, *baba*, *shwakam*, and in general all the spouse's relatives of the ascending generation. 'Mother-in-law', 'father-in-law', etc.

Notes

(a) *Terms of address*: Many of the terms above may be used for greeting and addressing people. Thus two 'brothers-in-law' might exclaim while snapping fingers, '*Mase/!*' '*Mase/!*' '*Masem pem!*' (My *mase/*). For *mar*, it would be impolite to say anything while greeting (in the special manner, see Chapter 5). *Baba* as a reference term is used only by a child of his father (or in general, any members of his father's birth-group), but as a term of address it is used reciprocally. Thus a man and his child, or any member of a child's father's birth-group and the child, may greet each other '*Baba!*' '*Baba!*' There are some terms which are normally used only as address in greeting, as follows:

1. Nyergon   Between cross-cousins
2. Monyer   *ditto*

3. Yelmadhin Between *ikam* ('brothers')
4. Madhin   *ditto*
5. Mudhu   *ditto*
6. Amwi   Between a *shwakam* and his *nam* ('mother's brother' and 'sister's son')

(b) *Plurals*: Nos. 2 and 14 have distinctive plural forms: *a'bom* becomes *up̱* (women or wives), and *a'ci* becomes *uçi* (children). Otherwise, all the terms of reference listed form the plural by the prefix 'i-'. If there is an initial short a, it disappears. Thus one speaks of *ikam* ('brothers'), *ishwakam* (mother's brothers), and *i/ash* ('wives').

(c) *Possessive forms*: With the exceptions of 2, 4, 6, 8, 12, and possibly a few others, the terms of reference may be modified so as to indicate personal possession. They have been listed in the third person (no distinction singular or plural) where a choice was open. Where possession is not indicated by an internal change, the possessive adjective follows the term.

(d) *Southern Uduk usage*: In the southern dialect (see Appendix 1) there is only one difference of kinship terminology, as far as I am aware, and that is the absence of No. 21 *nam* ('sister's child', etc). No. 20, *shwakam* ('mother's brother', etc.) is used as a self-reciprocal. This point is discussed in Chapter 5.

(e) *Blanket applications*: Some of the terms listed, although it is correct to say that their reference is *primarily* to an individual or individuals, on a genealogical model, may be applied *en bloc* to whole birth-groups or even clusters of closely allied birth-groups. Thus a person may speak of such an aggregation as *ibabam pem* ('my fathers'), and may speak of any individual of the whole group, even if a girl or woman or a man of the same generation, as *babam pem*, 'my father'. A female cross-cousin could thus be, at the same time but at a different level of classification, 'my cross-cousin' and 'my father'. Her child would be 'my *nam*' ('sister's son') and 'my father'. This usage would only be in contexts where the father's birth group was being thought of as a unit, and having given birth, as such, to oneself (see Chapter 4). The other terms applied in this blanket fashion to whole birth-groups are *idhan baba* (grandfathers; of which there are three categories, FF's birth-group, MF's birth-group and MBF's birth-group), and *imar pem* (my in-laws; of which there are two categories, my spouse's own birth-group and his or her father's birth-group).

The terms may be 'stretched' even further than this and a whole birth-group may be termed the 'children' of another; or a particular person may be said to be the 'father' of the whole population of a certain area (See Chapter 5). Such usage is conscious political imagery, based perhaps on selected genealogical connections.

BIBLIOGRAPHY

1. *Primary sources of information on the Uduk people and language*
(a) *Published material*

AHMAD, Abd-al Ghaffar Muhammad. 1968. 'Wajihen liwajih' (article on the Uduk in Arabic), *El Haya*, 19 July 1968, Khartoum.

BRYAN, M. A. 1945. 'A Linguistic No-Man's Land', *Africa*, xv, no. 4, 188–205.

CERULLI, E. 1956. *Peoples of South-West Ethiopia and its borderland*, Part iii of 'North-Eastern Africa' in the Ethnographic Survey of Africa, ed. D. Forde, London.

CORFIELD, F. D. 1938. 'The Koma', *Sudan Notes and Records*, xxi, no. 1, 122–65.

DAVIES, H. R. J. 1960. 'Some tribes of the Ethiopian borderland between the Blue Nile and Sobat Rivers', *Sudan Notes and Records*, xli, 21–34.

EVANS-PRITCHARD, E. E. 1932. 'Ethnological Observations in Dar Fung', *Sudan Notes and Records*, xv, no. 1, 1–61.

FORSBERG, M. 1958. *Land Beyond the Nile*, Harper, New York.

HILKE, H. and PLESTER, D. 1955. 'Forschungsreise in das Land der Präniloten im Südost-Sudan 1954–55', *Zeitschrift für Ethnologie*, lxxx, H. 2, 178–86.

JAMES, Wendy R. 1968. 'A Crisis in Uduk history', *Sudan Notes and Records*, xlix, 17–44.

—— 1969. 'The Uduk Gurunya Cult', *Proceedings of the University Social Sciences Conference*, Makerere, Uganda, 1968–9.

—— 1970a. 'Changing identity and social assimilation in the southern Funj', in *The Sudan in Africa*, ed. Y. F. Hasan, *Khartoum University Press*.

—— 1970b. 'Why the Uduk won't pay bridewealth', *Sudan Notes and Records*, li, 75–82.

—— 1971. 'Beer, morality and social relations among the Uduk', *Sudan Society*, v, 17–27.

—— 1972. 'The politics of rain-control among the Uduk', in *Essays in Sudan Ethnography, presented to Sir Edward Evans-Pritchard*, ed. I. Cunnison and W. James, Hurst, London.

—— 1975. 'Sister-exchange marriage', *Scientific American*, vol. 233, no. 6, 84–94.

—— 1977. 'The Funj Mystique: approaches to a problem of Sudan history', in *Text and Context: the social anthropology of tradition*, ed. R. K. Jain. ASA Essays in Social Anthropology, vol. 2. ISHI, Philadelphia.

286 *Bibliography*

—— 1978. 'Matrifocus on African Women', in *Defining Females: the nature of women in society*, ed. Shirley Ardener, Croom Helm, London.

—— 1978. 'Ephemeral names: the Uduk case', in *Aspects of Language in the Sudan*, ed. R. Thelwall, The New University of Ulster, Coleraine.

SELIGMAN, C. G. and B. Z. 1932. *Pagan Tribes of the Nilotic Sudan*, London.

Sudan Intelligence Report, no. 120, July 1904.

Sudan Interior Mission. 1963. *Mii ma K̲aniisa dhala Awarkan Gway* (Chali Church regulations and Hymn Book).

—— 1963. *Gwon this ki 'twam pa mo* (Uduk New Testament).

—— 1966. *Gway gi iDawuu'd* (Uduk Psalms).

TUCKER, A. N. and BRYAN, M. A. 1956. *The Non-Bantu Languages of North-Eastern Africa*, Part iii of the Handbook of African Languages, International African Institute, London.

—— 1966. *Linguistic Analyses: the Non-Bantu Languages of North-Eastern Africa*, International African Institute, London.

VALLANCE, D. J. 1908. 'Notes on the Ethnographical Specimens collected by Dr. A. Martier Pirrie', *Third Report of the Wellcome Research Laboratories*, 377–84.

WATERSTON, D. 1908. 'Report upon the Physical Characters of some of the Nilotic Negroid Tribes', *Third Report of the Wellcome Research Laboratories*, 325–76.

(b) *Unpublished material*

Anon. 1927. 'Reports on Eastern Frontier District, U.N. Province', Central Records Office, Khartoum, Dakhlia I, 112/17/102.

—— 1959. 'Hanbook [*sic*] Southern Fung District Blue Nile Province', August 1959 (duplicated, 41 pp.), Roseires (*copy now placed in Central Records Office*).

—— n.d. 'Notes on Uduk Customs' (typed, 9 pp.) Very similar to 'Customs', a Sudan Interior Mission manuscript, q.v.

CHATAWAY, J. D. P. 1927. 'Preliminary Notes on Uduk Tribe' (duplicated, 5 pp. and 3 pp. of vocabulary). Central Records, Dakhlia Office, I, 112/17/106.

JAMES, Wendy R. 1970. 'Principles of social organisation among the Uduk-speaking people of the southern Fung region, Republic of the Sudan', D. Phil. thesis, Oxford.

NICKERSON, G. S. 1906. 'Dar Fung and Burun Country' (typed, 20 pp.). Central Records Office, Dakhlia I, 112/17/102.

REIDHEAD, P. W. 1946. 'Report of linguistic survey among tribes Berta, Ingassana, Koma, Uduk, Jum Jum, Meban', Sudan Interior Mission (duplicated, 59 pp.)

STEVENSON, R. C. n.d. 'Notes towards a grammar of the Uduk language' (typed, 131 pp.).

Sudan Interior Mission 1956. 'Uduk Dictionary' (duplicated, 183 pp.). Reissued by the Sudan Research Unit of the University of Khartoum, under the names of M. Beam and E. Cridland, as their Sudan Language Monograph no. 4.

—— n.d. 'Uduk Grammar' (typed, 15 pp.). Unlike Stevenson's manuscript, these notes employ the orthography of the 1956 Dictionary.

—— n.d. Uduk Primers, I, II, III.

—— n.d. 'Customs' (typed, 8 pp. plus 5 pp. of stories in Uduk and English).

2. *Selected sources on the peoples of the Sudan-Ethiopian border*

AHMAD, Abd-al Ghaffar Muhammed. 1974. *Shaykhs and Followers: Political Struggle in the Rufa'a al-Hoi Nazirate in the Sudan*. Khartoum University Press.

ARKELL, A. J. 1928. 'A Note on the history of the country of the Berta lying East of Kurmuk within the Abyssinian Frontier—with special reference to the recent discovery of a considerable import of Berta slaves into the Sudan' (duplicated, 12 pp.), Central Records Office, Khartoum.

BENDER, M. L. 1975. *The Ethiopian Nilo-Saharans*, Artistic Press, Addis Ababa.

—— 1976. 'Nilo-Saharan Overview', in *The Non-Semitic Languages of Ethiopia*, ed. M. L. Bender, Michigan State University African Studies Center, East Lansing.

BENDER, M. L., BOWEN, J. D., COOPER, R. L. and FERGUSON, C. A. (eds.) 1976. *Language in Ethiopia*, O.U.P., London.

BRUCE, James. 1790. *Travels to discover the Source of the Nile, in the Years 1768–1773*, Edinburgh.

CAILLIAUD, F. 1826. *Voyage à Méroë*, Paris.

GREENBERG, J. H. 1963. 'The Languages of Africa', *International Journal of American Linguistics*, Part II, vol. 29, no. 1, The Hague.

GROTTANELLI, V. L. 1940. *I Mao*, Rome.

—— 1948. 'I Pre-Niloti. Un'arcaica provincia culturale in Africa', *Annali Lateranensi*, xii, 281–326.

—— 1966. 'The vanishing Pre-Nilotes revisited', *Bulletin of the Committee on Urgent Anthropological and Ethnological Research*, no. 8, Austria.

GWYNN, C. W. 1903. 'Report' in *Sudan Intelligence Report*, no. 106, May 1903, 1–2.

HARTMAN, R. 1863. *Reise des Freiherrn A. von Bearnim durch Nord-Ost Afrika in dem Jahren 1859 und 1860*, Berlin.

KRONENBERG, A. and KRONENBERG, W. 1672. 'The Bovine Idiom and formal logic', in *Essays in Sudan Ethnography, presented to Sir Edward Evans-Pritchard*, ed. I. Cunnison and W. James, Hurst, London.

LEJEAN, G. 1865. *Voyage aux deux Nils*, Paris.

LEWIS, B. A. 1972. *The Murle: red chiefs and black commoners*, Clarendon Press, Oxford.

ROBERTSON, J. 1974. *Transition in Africa*, Hurst, London.

SALT, H. 1814. *A Voyage to Abyssinia*, London.

SCHUVER, J. M. 1883a. 'Juan Maria Schuvers Karte vom Quellgebiet des Tumat, Jabus und Jal', *Petermanns Mitteilungen*, Band 29, 105–7, and map opposite p. 120.

—— 1883b. *Reisen im Oberen Nilgebiet*, Gotha.

STAUDER, J. 1971. *The Majangir: ecology and society of a Southwest Ethiopian people*, Cambridge University Press.

TRÉMEAUX, P. 1852. *Voyage au Soudan Orientale*, Paris.

TRIULZI, A. 1975. 'Trade, Islam and the Mahdia in Northwestern Wallagga, Ethiopia', *Journal of African History*, xvi, no. 1, 55–71.

TURTON, D. 1973. 'Referees and leaders: a study of social control among the Mursi of South-Western Ethiopia', Ph.D. thesis, London School of Economics and Political Science.

ZANNI, L. 1940. 'La tribu dei Gumus: note etnografiche', *La Nigrizia*, Verona.

3. *Other works cited*

BLOCH, M. 1971. 'The moral and tactical meaning of kinship terms', *Man*, N.S. vi, no. 1, 79–87.

BOHANNAN, L. and BOHANNAN, P. 1953. *The Tiv of Central Nigeria*, Part viii of 'Western Africa' in the Ethnographic Survey of Africa, ed. D. Forde, London.

BURTON, J. W. 1978. 'The fighting and the fishing spear: symbols and power among the Atuot of the southern Sudan', paper presented to the American Anthropological Association, Los Angeles meetings.

BUXTON, J. C. 1963. *Chiefs and Strangers: a study of political assimilation among the Mandari*, Clarendon Press, Oxford.

—— 1973. *Religion and Healing in Mandari*, Clarendon Press, Oxford.

DOUGLAS, Mary 1969. 'Is Matriliny Doomed?' in *Man in Africa*, ed. M. Douglas and P. Kaberry, London.

EAST, R. 1939. *Akiga's Story*, trans. and ed., R. East, O.U.P., London.

EVANS-PRITCHARD, E. E. 1935. 'The Nuer: Tribe and Clan', *Sudan Notes and Records*, xviii, no. 1.

—— 1940. *The Nuer*, Clarendon Press, Oxford.

—— 1956. *Nuer Religion*, Clarendon Press, Oxford.

FARIS, J. C. 1970. 'Non-kin social groups of the Southeastern Nuba', *Sudan Society*, v, 37–51.

HUFFMAN, R. 1931. *Nuer Customs and Folk-lore*, International African Institute, London.

LIENHARDT, R. G. 1961. *Divinity and Experience: the religion of the Dinka*, Clarendon Press, Oxford.

—— 1975. 'Getting your own back: themes in Nilotic myth', in *Studies in Social Anthropology: Essays in memory of Sir Edward Evans-Pritchard*, ed. J. H. M. Beattie and R. G. Lienhardt, Clarendon Press, Oxford.

MALINOWSKI, B. 1922. *The Argonauts of the Western Pacific*, Routledge and Kegan Paul, London.

MARX, Karl 1867. *Capital*, vol. i.

MAUSS, M. 1954. *The Gift*, trans. I. Cunnison (from the French original of 1925), Cohen and West, London.

SAHLINS, M. 1974. 'The Spirit of the Gift', in *Stone Age Economics*, Tavistock, London.

TURNER, V. W. 1967. *The Forest of Symbols*, Cornell University Press, New York.

—— 1969. *The Ritual Process: structure and anti-structure*, Routledge and Kegan Paul, London.

INDEX